Dad,

Some "light" read
for all your sp

love Karyn

SPYMASTER

SPYMASTER

WILLIAM J. WEST

WYNWOOD™ Press
New York, New York

Library of Congress Cataloging-in-Publication Data

West, W. J. (William J.)
   [Truth about Hollis]
   Spymaster : the betrayal of MI5 / William J. West.
      p.   cm.
   The Truth about Hollis, 1989.
   ISBN 0-922066-32-9 : $18.95
    1. Hollis, Roger Sir. 2. Great Britain. MI5—History.
   3. Intelligence officers—Great Britain—Biography. 4. Espionage—
   Great Britain—History—20th century. I. Title.
   UB271.G72H659 1990
   327.1'2'092—dc20
   [B]   89-48920
                                          CIP

Copyright © 1990 by William J. West
Published by WYNWOOD™ Press
New York, New York
Printed in the United States of America

For Rachel

Contents

Contents

Acknowledgements

I N a book such as this, relying on original research in public archives rather than the recollections of those involved who are now forbidden to speak even on matters of real historical significance under threat of imprisonment, a particular debt of gratitude is owed to the staff of the archives in which the work was done. In particular I would like to thank the staff at the American National Archives in Washington, DC, and at the FBI archives, also in Washington—the equivalent of MI5's archives, whose very whereabouts is a state secret in England—and at the Canadian National Archives in Ottawa, whose 24-hour access system was particularly helpful to a transatlantic visitor on a tight schedule.

In England I am grateful for the unfailing assistance of the staff at the Public Record Office at Kew whose computer-controlled keyboard document-calling system has made a researcher's task straightforward. I must also thank the staff at the BBC Written Archive Centre at Caversham, Reading, possibly one of the richest and most extensive sources for modern British history outside the Public Record Office itself; the staff at the Orwell Archive at University College London; and the Librarians at Exeter University Library and the Devon and Exeter Institution. I pay special thanks to Nicholas Spurrier for obtaining important political pamphlets not to be found in the great national collections.

I am grateful for interviews and help from Lord Mayhew, Lord Sherfield and Lord Houghton; from Rupert Allason MP (the author Nigel West) and John Hannam MP: and from Christopher Andrew, Mrs. I. D. Benzie-Morley, John Bulloch, the late Douglas Cleverdon, John Green, Harry Chapman Pincher, and not least staff of the British American Tobacco Company who were in China before the war, and also in England later. The book benefits from a number of quotations both from public sources, for which I am grateful to HMSO and the BBC, and books, for which I thank the authors and publishers whose names appear more fully in the bibliography. Finally and most important, I owe an inestimable debt to Colin Haycraft, my British editor and publisher, without whose lasting encouragement this book could not have been written, and to Alan Lang and my American publisher Bill Thompson, whose support and assistance have been invaluable.

In view of the great difficulty now attached to the writing of modern British history and the legal implications that can be found in even the most serious matters of current affairs this century, it is perhaps more than usually necessary to state that all the opinions in this book are my own and that I alone am responsible for the research and verification of the facts disclosed here.

Introduction

OVER the years American spymasters have harboured their suspicions about some of their British colleagues. As the procession of moles and known Communist sympathisers grew ever longer and the rank of those indicted rose with the passing of time, anything seemed possible. There were reassuring moments in the postwar years. J. Edgar Hoover, the spymaster's spymaster, once entertained Sir Roger Hollis, the head of the British equivalent of the FBI, MI5, and was so convinced by him that he gave him a treasured golf putter as a souvenir. But for once Hoover had been fooled. Had he known the facts about Hollis revealed here for the first time he would have insisted that Hollis was unsuited to hold any post in a western security organisation. Suspicions about even someone such as Hollis, in effect Hoover's opposite number, began to circulate in Britain during the sixties and these suspicions hardened over the next decade, particularly after the unmasking of Anthony Blunt. Who had been protecting him all those years? It then became known that a renegade MI5 officer living in Australia, Peter Wright, was writing a book that would prove the worst suspicions about Hollis. The undoubted facts he was to reveal were staggering enough.

Spycatcher was the result of Wright's labours, assisted by a television investigative journalist Paul Greengrass. The desperate attempts of the British government to get the book banned raised the highest expectations. They were not fulfilled. When the first edition of the book came off the presses in America, experts realised that Wright had failed to prove his case. Worse, his book was marred by sometimes ludicrous errors—those who knew Washington were amused by his description of the golden dome of the Capitol—and was presented as an autobiography rather than an indictment of Hollis.

The British authorities and Hollis's defenders soon came to regard the defeat in the courts in Australia as a success snatched from the jaws of defeat. Even Hollis's name remained virtually unknown in America despite the sale of millions of copies of the book. Best of all, Wright was seen to have been thoroughly discredited, a favourite bureaucrat's word, and reviews by learned British commentators soon began appearing in east coast literary journals not forgetting the golden dome on the Capitol. His book's success compensated him no doubt for the appallingly low pension rewarded him on retirement and served also as his reward for a courageous stand on the question of free speech. But he had failed to prove Hollis's guilt which was the one thing that had driven him on.

So little worried were the authorities in Britain that they did not even take steps to block importation of copies at the customs or through the post. Bulk shipments of *Spycatcher* flooded into the country at the very time that major newspapers were being obliged to follow the very letter of the law, and were being prosecuted when they broke injunctions which banned any mention of *Spycatcher*. The purpose of this action was not to stop the contents of the book becoming known but to act as a warning to others who might follow Wright's example. But in the minds of those masterminding these operations there must still have remained a nagging doubt that somewhere evidence damning Hollis might be found.

Spymaster is the first book to look at Hollis directly and put Wright's suspicions to the test. It provides evidence that has been lying undiscovered in open archives among the millions of files on the wartime and postwar periods available in Washington, Ottawa, and London and which the British authorities had hoped against hope did not exist.

The book makes a different case from *Spycatcher*'s but establishes, with cruel irony for Peter Wright, that he was right for the wrong reasons. Worse, a central figure in the case against Hollis was Claud Cockburn, a well-known Communist agent whom the committee investigating Hollis had actually raised with him. Hollis had sidestepped the questions by admitting that he knew Cockburn at university (Oxford at that time was not the usual spy's haven that Cambridge was) but that he had concealed the fact only so that he would not damage his chances of promotion. This was accepted. Had the lead been followed at the time, Hollis would have been subjected to further questioning which surely would have made his position and the ties linking him with Cockburn clear. Like Blunt, he too would have been stripped of his honours.

A generation has passed while the spies Britain failed to catch paraded slowly by. From Fuchs, who gave away the atom secrets, to Blunt, who had been allowed to remain a free man despite MI5's full knowledge of his guilt, the story has always been the same. Each failure, greeted by a flood of publicity, was followed by explanation and ritual reassurances that nothing like it could ever happen again. But behind the scenes even the highly secretive upper echelons of the British establishment realised that something was wrong and that a mole at their own protected level might exist. They began to doubt themselves. The response was to set up the committee that ended up grilling Hollis. (Imagine, if you will, Hoover being grilled for days on end by a committee of young hawks from the FBI and CIA all intent on proving that he was a Communist sympathiser, if nothing else. Yet that was what the British spymaster had been subjected to, so strong were the fears that the American suspicions might be justified.) Known as the Fluency Committee, from its code name, it was composed of officers from MI5 and MI6—the straight equivalent of an FBI–CIA committee—and for much of its existence had Peter Wright for chairman. It was only too understandable that he was the most hurt of all when Hollis cleared himself, even after being called out of retirement, when Wright too had retired, on the occasion when he ducked the first serious potential break in the case of the Cockburn question.

Wright was profoundly convinced not only of Hollis's guilt—and that he had been responsible for countless failed operations that had ruined Wright's own surveillance coups—but that he had left behind him potential for continuing disasters. Unfortunately Peter Wright was a hopeless choice for the essentially political task of determining loyalties and opinions of the group around Philby, Burgess and Blunt who were always political activists rather than spies in the vulgar sense.

It was a further irony that Wright owed his post as chairman of the committee to Hollis himself in an appointment made at a time when the committee was examining Hollis's deputy, then thought to be the most likely suspect for the elusive mole. Hollis had also assigned Wright the task of interrogating Anthony Blunt, which he did for hundreds of hours, literally, grappling with one of the most subtle intellects of his day. Blunt fooled Wright completely, and this can only have added to his sense of failure. When the opportunity came for him to leak information about the committee and its purpose he had ample motive for doing so and there was a certain inevitability in what followed. The intellectual games played by Blunt were as un-English as the passion for secrecy and the very existence of a political police which had only begun at the time of the Boer War. In the end they defeated themselves.

American readers who have gotten used to freedom of information legislation and the willingness of their leaders to accept any revelation and take the consequences would find the British system as it has developed this century hard to live with. Not only is the idea of a Freedom of Information Act fought tooth and nail by the authorities—there is nothing faintly equivalent to this in Britain—but there is in place an Official Secrets Act that makes it illegal to release the smallest scrap of information about any aspect of Government activity. Until recently it was a criminal offence to leak even details of the menu in a government staff canteen. A very junior clerk, Sarah Tisdall, was sentenced to six months' imprisonment for leaking a single sheet of photocopy of no great consequence only a few years before this book was written. It is obvious why Wright is obliged to live in exile in Australia and also why it has proved impossible for any other book based on insider information to be written. The duty of confidentiality, even about those canteen menus, lasts to the grave, and when an officer dies his effects are checked to see that no sensitive information remains.

There could be no Watergate in Britain. First the Official Secrets Act would prevent release of any information in the press—the investigative journalists in Britain bear no resemblance to those in America—and secondly any Watergate in Britain would almost certainly involve the civil servants who run the country rather than the politicians who control them. The disgrace of the *Spycatcher* affair in Australia was partly an error of judgement, but partly also the result of an establishment who would protect themselves without regard to embarrassment to their political masters. Those in America who hope for a British Watergate have already seen the most likely scenario in those days in a courtroom in Australia, carried out on the other side of the world, in someone else's back yard.

It may well be asked how *Spymaster* came to be written and where the information came from when no actual spy could be interviewed if the book was to be published in Britain, as it was. The answer is very close to that which led to the discovery of the vast cache of unknown writings of George Orwell in the BBC's archives recently: exhaustive search of material on public access but which has been ignored, usually because the amount of work involved was too vast without some key to begin the search. The recent FBI Library Awareness Program, aimed at preventing the KGB from getting technical data from open libraries, would have countered just the kind of search which the author has undertaken in such places as the BBC archives and the Public Record Office situated by the world-famous Kew Gardens in London.

The key to the search came partly from discoveries made about Guy Burgess in the BBC's archives which were published in *Truth Betrayed: Radio and Politics Between the Wars*. Research carried on even as the *Spycatcher* saga was being played out in the Australian courts and in America, and it became abundantly clear that neither MI5 nor the Peter Wright team had been through the BBC archives, or, more important, the Foreign Office archives in London.

What was discovered involved the wartime political activity of the Communists in Britain, including an attempted revolution in 1941 aimed at getting Britain out of the war, and this led on to matters going right up to the time Hollis was being interrogated. As the reader will learn, the most important discoveries about the Comintern agent Claud Cockburn began to make the names Cockburn and Hollis almost as important as Burgess and Maclean. It became obvious that a major vetting of MI5 files must have taken place for what has been discovered not to have been known by the MI5 team engaged on their molehunt twenty years ago; this is hardly surprising, for Hollis personally held all the important files and had a propensity for working unusually late hours.

Having pieced together information from long-neglected files, many containing actual MI5 reports, the question was how to present the new picture that emerged, and get the new evidence published with the rigours of the British Official Secrets Act to be faced.

Fortunately the obsessive secrecy which has developed in Britain this century is not the only tradition reflected in the law as it stands. The Public Records Act, which governs the release of information in the public archives, reflects the more liberal traditions of the Victorian and earlier ages. They ensure that there is an inviolable right to publish any document in the public domain released to the Public Record Office, whatever it contains. The same applies to British government papers which have been released in Washington and Ottawa. There is not the slightest doubt that the security authorities would have immediately banned the great mass of material published in this book were it not for the existence of the Public Records Acts. There have been determined attempts to interfere with the release of papers in America by means of having them rescheduled, although no case of a paper being so rescheduled has come to light in Britain in researching this book. That the material appeared in the first place must have been infuriating. There is a vetting procedure that is meant to prevent any MI5 or MI6 papers from ever reaching the Public Record Office, which is entrusted to retired officials employed as "weeders" to remove any such documents, in fact anything that might relate to security matters. Here the fortunate release of these papers was a classic case of too *much* secrecy. MI5 papers at the time had no indication of where they came from, simply a post box number. MI6 went further and had no heading at all, the papers seeming to be drafts or carbon copies. In each case the weeders failed to realise what the papers they were looking at were. There were in addition many papers released where the most astute weeder would have been unable to see reason for suppression. Their significance could only become plain with the passage of much time and the accumulation of other evidence, the stuff of history which makes the writing of it so vitally important.

It might seem puzzling that those involved in the first search for the moles, and later the investigative journalists, had not followed a similar route. There were two basic explanations. First the BBC's archives were inaccessible until the 1970s and it was widely believed that they had been weeded extensively, with sensitive papers held in what was called the Director General files. This was not the case and the records were almost entirely untouched although existing on a vast scale and without any detailed indexing of the kind found for Foreign Office papers. It was only in the eighties that researches of the kind that turned up the Orwell papers could take place, and then three years' full time work was needed. On the question of the Foreign Office papers the second explanation is more important as was explained to the author by a retired MI5 officer. The idea of the highly secret MI5, working under the aegis of the Home Secretary, needing to go along to the open files of the Foreign Office would have been unthinkable and the loss of departmental face too much to bear. They would naturally be assumed to have their own vital sources of information, and the Foreign Office was the department which had ultimate control of MI6—in many ways their rival organisation.

It is worth emphasising that the results obtained from archive research are far more reliable than those obtained from eye witnesses or participants writing forty or more years after the event. Memory across that kind of time span can be treacherous. Often key events are distorted in the light of feuds or subsequent change of *realpolitik*, and in one instance the actual person involved in a case for which the files had been discovered found the facts to be other than he remembered. He immediately took the evidence in favour of his own faded recollections, supplying background perspective of the kind which the bare facts could not. The discovery of the actual evidence in this way, as well as the elucidation of the facts, is a fundamental purpose of historical research that is often lost sight of in the modern world with its seemingly instantaneous dissemination of information. It is also a great part of its fascination.

Trying to find out the truth about someone, the writing of biography, is one of the most difficult of literary activities. In Roger Hollis's case any rounded picture of his personality is almost impossible for reasons that become clear. Far from being larger-than-life characters, such as J. Edgar Hoover, British spymasters are so anonymous that even their names were held to be state secrets in Hollis's time. At his death no one but his close family and fellow members of MI5 were meant to know what his role in life had been. The locations of the buildings in which he worked are still regarded as a state secret and none of them bear any identifying marks. What goes on in them is of course secret, but it is a secrecy that is so profound that it needs to be emphasised here for an American reader. Such happenings as the outcry over the FBI's Library Awareness Program would be absolutely impossible in Britain.

As Hollis worked for MI5 for the greater part of his life, this secrecy inevitably affected his private life. In the course of writing this book I have spoken with barely a dozen people who knew Hollis and were not part of the security services, and this in itself was an achievement. None would go on record as they had all become aware of what Hollis's job had been. However, the extent of the mystery surrounding the man can be seen from two examples. A colleague of his from before the war, who knew him and the first Lady Hollis socially, remarked, "I thought I knew Roger Hollis very well. My wife and I used to meet him and his wife socially right through the war years and after. But then something happened which made me realise that I didn't know him at all." The mysterious event alluded to occurred on his retirement at the time when Hollis divorced his wife; it must remain a mystery while those involved are still alive. Another colleague who worked with Hollis in liaison matters with another non-secret Government department was under the impression that Hollis was a Roman Catholic, as his elder brother had been, and was shocked to learn that this was not so and that he should discover it after so many years of close working contact on what he thought were personal terms.

Nothing resembling a biography could be written when Hollis's private life was clearly a complete mystery even to those who thought they knew him well. In addition, although family papers may exist they have been closed to researchers and have not been placed in any public archive. This is no doubt understandable as it must be an obvious corollary of the absolute secrecy of his job that Hollis would never become an historical figure of any kind. That he has is an accident of history for which none of his family could possibly have been prepared. A few fragments of letters written to his mother when he was in China have been published by Anthony Glees. It seems also that some were made available to Richard Deacon for his book *The Greatest Treason;* however, this book has been suppressed by its publishers for unrelated reasons. This would appear to be the full extent of personal papers that will ever be available to future historians.

Although the book is not intended as a biography, the focus is on Hollis throughout. The first three chapters do follow a strictly biographical form dealing with his life and family background up to the time he joined MI5. The following seven chapters deal with the world of spies and follow Hollis's life through the mirror of the agents and spies he was meant to be keeping track of as MI5's expert on Communist affairs. Some of these spies he worked with, others he knew; with perhaps the majority he shared one or more mutual friends. Sometimes we find his name appearing on a document that has leaked out and he then steps through the looking glass as a real person again. The last chapters deal with what has been called the "wilderness of mirrors," the chasing for moles after the event, and with the evolution of the entire spy book saga which has gone on for over a quarter of a century and is now assuming the appearance of a branch of modern political studies in its own right. The cases for and against Hollis are examined rigorously and then the new facts are woven together to present a picture of this complex man that moves the study of him and the whole case of political espionage to a new plane.

Publication of the book in Britain resulted in considerable controversy and in the unexpected emergence of new evidence which is discussed fully here. The publication of the book was not itself entirely without incident as might be expected of a book following hard on the heels of *Spycatcher* and offering new evidence. The writing of the book had been kept secret and the security on the project at the publisher's offices was so good that the authorities did not hear about it until news leaked in a gossip column in one of the main national newspapers a few weeks before the publication date. Within hours a letter was sent to the publisher by the Ministry of Defence, the equivalent of the Pentagon, asking that the book be submitted for vetting to establish if there had been any breach of the security regulations.

The department of the Ministry of Defence that deals with such matters is known as the Defence Press and Broadcasting Committee. The letter sent by the secretary of the committee candidly referred to the source of his information and sent a so-called D Notice, "D" standing for Defence, with formal advice of its purpose and the seriousness of the matter. No procedure of this kind exists in America where interference of freedom of speech in such a way would no doubt be greeted with cries of outrage if it became known. In Britain it is lived with, a relic of the war years that is still kept in operation, ostensibly as a contingency should some conflict break out in the future but actually serving very efficiently as both a check on all books going to press and a warning to authors and publishers of the dangers that lie in their path. The existence of this committee, of course, dates from earlier this century. Anything like it in Victorian England would have been seen as absolutely intolerable.

Within a short time it became clear that while the book contained a wealth of original MI5 papers, more indeed than *Spycatcher*, all had been obtained legally. Publication seemed likely. However, within days of actual publication an unattributable report made to a national newspaper pointed out that an MI5 officer *had* been named, unwittingly, in an inaccurate context. The only step possible was to withdraw the book, remove the two pages on which the name occurred, and replace these with two amended pages. This arduous exercise was carried out. The subtlety of the operation lay in the fact that few copies of the book were available at publication, even if outright suppression of the book was avoided. The text made available here to American readers is the correct one.

William West
Exeter, U.K.
7 November 1989

SPYMASTER

1
A Spymaster's Roots

S PIES and spymasters are, for Britain, a phenomenon of the twentieth century. To the Victorians the idea that any government would engage in full-scale surveillance of its subjects would have been unthinkable, something to be found in small states in middle Europe or further east. The intense liberal desire for personal freedom had seen the franchise extended to the majority of its citizens, and trade expanded all over the world. State interference of the kind now a commonplace would have been seen as an outrage. This tradition lives on in America, with its freedom of information acts, but has almost gone in Britain, despite recent political changes.

The fact that this secret state apparatus has sprung into being this century raises the question of how and where the spies and spymasters that ran it were recruited. It might be expected that the establishment would ensure that any post of great power was held firmly within its grasp, but even so the background of Director General of MI5 Sir Roger Hollis was surprising, perhaps the most unusual of any spymaster anywhere in the world. He was not drawn from the upper classes—a gentleman buccaneer of the kind found in fiction from John Buchan to Ian Fleming—but rather from the opposite end of the social spectrum, that of the established church.

Roger Hollis was born on 2 December 1905 in the cathedral town of Wells in Somerset, in the rural heartland of the West of England. At the time his father, the Rev. George Hollis, was Vice-Principal of Wells Theological College, having arrived there as chaplain in 1895. In 1898 George Hollis married Mary Margaret Church, daughter of C. M. Church, a canon of Wells. They had four sons, of whom Roger was the third. Roger's eldest brother, Arthur, became Bishop in Madras. The next, Christopher, who was converted to Catholicism at Oxford, became the well-known author, publisher and Conservative MP for Devizes. He left various accounts of life in the Hollis home at Wells, notably in his two volumes of autobiography. Not surprisingly the atmosphere was ecclesiastical. "My family connections were entirely clerical . . . I grew up not merely as a clergyman's son, but in a cleric-inhabited society, a sort of Trollopean world." It was a world that must have seemed even more Trollopean to his younger brother Roger. The youngest son, Marcus, was the most reclusive of the four, perhaps because he followed a similar calling to that of his brother Roger.

Early in Roger's life, in 1909, there was a sharp break in the family's untroubled existence within the calm ambience of Wells Cathedral when his father was appointed curate of the parish of Armley in Leeds. The contrast between the two worlds was great, and Christopher remarked on the austerity of life for a vicar in a large poor parish with four young children to bring up on a stipend of £400 a year, a sum which he augmented by occasional journalism for *The Guardian*. Nor were the harsher realities of Edwardian life absent from the parish, for it contained the Leeds hanging gaol, which the vicar had to attend.

The transformation from Wells to Leeds may have been a shock, but it was mercifully brief. In 1913 the family moved to their next parish, at Headingly, where Hollis senior was vicar through the war years. In 1919 he returned to Wells Theological College as Principal, becoming Bishop of Taunton, with his residence in Wells, where he remained until his death in 1944.

The brief stay in Leeds left its mark on the Hollis children, who began their educational career at Leeds Grammar School. The eldest son, Arthur, went from there to university, while Christopher moved in 1911 to Summerfields preparatory school before going to Eton. Roger seems to have begun there, but to have stayed only briefly, proceeding to Clifton College in Bristol. The general impact of Leeds on the children can be seen from the memory recounted by Christopher nearly half a century later. And there were echoes in the industrial life around them of struggles of earlier generations of Hollises. Although the family lived in an entirely clerical world, both Roger's paternal and maternal forebears had established the family fortunes through business. His paternal grandfather, Henry William Hollis, had been managing director of the Weardale Iron and Coal Company, and a Justice of the Peace; his maternal great-grandfather was John Dearman Church, a Lisbon merchant of Cork Quaker stock, whose son, C. M. Church, was born in Lisbon and spent much of his early life on the continent before ending up at Wells.

That the tone of family life in the Hollis household in Wells was ecclesiastical rather than in any degree political is clear from Christopher's unequivocal statement: "There was no deep interest in party politics in my family, and no member of it on either side who, so far as I am aware, had ever dreamed of playing any part in politics. But all my father's family had, I fancy, always been mildly conservative—though he himself after the war was to become mildly liberal and to second the nomination of the Liberal candidate at Wells in 1923." For a clergyman to second the nomination of a Liberal candidate before the war would have been indicative of strong political consciousness, particularly in a place such as Wells; but by 1923 the Labour party had come to the fore as the "left" opposition and the Rev. George Hollis's action would have indicated only a slight departure. The possible origin of this drift toward Liberalism can be found in his wife's early interest in politics, derived from her great-uncle R. W. Church, the famous Dean of St. Paul's and intimate friend of Gladstone.

The shift of political consensus in an unpolitical family is always difficult to follow. Indeed the art of politics in Britain is to chart such changes and act on them. Christopher was aware of this when he wrote his autobiography. He had to explain how he had become actively interested in political questions. *A fortiori* the same question faces those who suspect Roger Hollis of being that most profound of all political animals, a dedicated secret agent of a foreign power. Christopher Hollis analyses only his maternal family's political history but makes a convincing case for a slow move from one view of political personalities to another. His grandfather, the canon of Wells, had changed to Conservatism largely because he felt that Gladstone had betrayed General Gordon. This trend continued when a younger brother of the family, after whom Christopher was named, volunteered for service in the Boer War and was killed. The strong Liberal line at the time was close to that of the "pro-Boers," and a family who had experienced such a loss would certainly have been confirmed in a move toward Conservative views. Further, in later life Roger's mother used to recall with amusement how strongly pro-Liberal she had been. Christopher quotes her once as remembering saying when she visited a friend's house and was shocked to find in the hall a portrait of Disraeli: "I can't imagine how you can bear to sleep in a house that contains that man's picture." What brought the family back to Liberalism after the war is not clear, but, at the very least, it is obvious that the family was not a political hot-bed; there was no grounding here for an acute political mind of a far-left bent.

Roger and his elder brothers went through their school careers without difficulty. Clifton, which Roger attended, no doubt gave him a more interesting view of the world than his elder brothers had gained. The college's excellent name had been established under Percival, its first head, along the lines of Rugby where Percival had begun his career. But it soon acquired a character of its own. This was largely because it had been created for the children of citizens of Bristol, a long-established merchant city, and took day boys as well as boarders. The school was situated on the downs which throughout the nineteenth century had been a political meeting place similar to Hyde Park in London. During Roger's time fringe-left demonstrations abounded, including some by followers of Conrad Noel, Vicar of Thaxted, who had strong Communist sympathies and whose symbol was a cross with a hammer and sickle on it. The idea of a Communist vicar must have caused discussion among the Clifton boys. Noel certainly influenced many of Roger's generation, one of whom, Tom Driberg, he was to meet at Oxford and again on various occasions through the rest of his life.

The Hollis brothers all arrived at Oxford as promising undergraduates despite their different backgrounds. Arthur went to Trinity as a scholar, interrupting his life there with a period in the Army from 1918 to 1919 and going on to take a good degree. He returned to Oxford in 1926 to become for five years Chaplain and Lecturer in Theology at Hertford, Evelyn Waugh's old college. Christopher went as a Brackenbury scholar from Eton to Balliol, where he had a successful career, though with a social rather than an academic slant. He toured the world with the Oxford Union Debating Society, going from America to New Zealand and Australia and stopping off on the way back in Burma, where he looked up his old Eton friend Eric Blair, later the famous writer George Orwell but then a rather unconventional officer in the Indian Imperial Police.

Christopher's circle at the time is important for an understanding of the Oxford that Roger found when he came up, because it was to this group rather than to any friends of his eldest brother that he seems to have turned. A central figure was Christopher's lifelong friend Evelyn Waugh, who was also to convert later to Catholicism. Waugh's diary, published in 1976, provides an invaluable key to the generation which has been extensively chronicled both in literary memoirs and in fiction. Harold Acton was prominent. His position is described admirably by Michael Davie in the introduction to his edition of Waugh's diaries: "Harold Acton had been brought up in splendour at La Pietra, a villa overlooking Florence, and seemed to his Oxford contemporaries, by reason of his international interests and connections, to be years ahead of any other undergraduate in the University." One of Acton's main passions, of considerable interest in view of Roger Hollis's life after Oxford, was China. He obtained Chinese food when that was difficult and unusual, and even saw attractions in Chinese clothing. His interest led him, finally, to go to China, where he lived until the outbreak of war.

China featured in the background of a number of people at Oxford at the time, notably Waugh's cousin Claud Cockburn. Cockburn had been born in Peking, where his father, universally known as "Chinese Harry," had been a secretary at the British Legation. It is clear from Waugh's diary that Claud Cockburn, Christopher Hollis, Roger Hollis and Evelyn Waugh were constant drinking companions during Roger's time at Oxford.

Roger Hollis went up to Worcester College from Clifton with a Classical exhibition, but took what was then the somewhat unusual course of reading English rather than Greats. He plunged into the social whirl in which Christopher flourished and joined the circle of his brother's friends. There are two classic accounts in Waugh's diary of their drinking sessions. These were of a kind that generations of undergraduates must have known, though few would find record of it in diaries published within the lifetime of those involved. One Monday in December 1924 Roger Hollis was swept up in one of Waugh and Cockburn's sagas: "I had a dinner party of Claud, Elmley, Terence, Roger Hollis and a poor drunk called Macgregor. I arrived quite blind after a great number of cocktails at the George with Claud. Eventually . . . Claud, Roger Hollis and I went off on a pub-crawl which after sundry indecorous adventures ended up at the Hypocrites where another blind was going on." Unfortunately for Roger, Waugh's drinking sprees were not confined to Oxford, and there is a lurid account of one much closer to home. On a Tuesday in April 1926 Waugh turned up at Wells. His diary graphically conveys the results: "Rather an amusing afternoon at Wells. Roger Hollis and I lunched at the Swan and drank champagne and brandy mixed. After a time we were turned out. There was a market at Farrington Gurney. It was odd that we were not killed going there. After a time the man in that pub refused us drinks. I said I was Hobhouse of Castle Cary and that I would have him out of the pub in a month and he believed me and gave us heaps more drink."

The effect of all this on Hollis's family when news of it reached them, as it must have done immediately, may be imagined. It has been said that Hollis actually left home at about this time, saying that he could not live with the religious atmosphere there. This candid recollection of Evelyn Waugh's suggests that there may well have been another side to the break. However, it is not unheard of for a younger son of an eminently respectable family to go off the rails at university. Such happenings are commonplace, and the spirit of the time exaggerated the tendency for unconventional behaviour after the trauma of the most terrible war in history. But it is not the kind of behaviour that is associated with political revolt, particularly not with revolt based on complex socio-economic theories of the sort espoused by Marx and Lenin.

Indeed, in a world where Belloc and Chesterton were venerated, the course followed by Waugh and Christopher Hollis, the path to Rome, would have been seen as a more likely result of such lapses, if their moral being was once engaged. Any political consciousness would more likely be of a right-wing, or overtly fascist, colouring than the opposite. As a direct example, Christopher was received into the Catholic Church while still at Oxford by Monsignor A. S. Barnes. Barnes's cousin, whom Barnes had also received into the church, was James Strachey Barnes, one of the foremost English fascists, a personal friend of Mussolini's who chose to remain in Italy throughout the war. This of course was later, and there was never any hint of fascism in Christopher Hollis's circle; but equally it would be the last place to look for any kind of Communist tendency. Yet it is in this phase of Roger Hollis's life that we should seek the most obvious roots of a lifelong commitment to Communism, if the experience of the Cambridge Communists is any guide. Was there any Communist movement at all to be found in Oxford in the twenties, and was Roger Hollis in any way connected with it? From evidence which has recently come to light in Australia the answer would appear to be yes.

Communism in Oxford was never as strong as at the other ancient seat of learning, but it did exist. During the first war Rajani Palme Dutt, throughout his life one of the foremost members of the Communist Party of Great Britain, had been expelled from the university for his political activities. In the early twenties a small group of Communist party members were recruited. They were four in number and the leader was a Rhodes scholar from Australia, P. R. Stephensen. When MI5, who discovered the group at the time, reported the matter to the College authorities, there was a serious discussion as to whether Stephensen should be sent down. It was the correspondence on this which came to light in the Australian Archives, as a result, ironically, of the intense interest in such matters caused by the *Spycatcher* trial. The MI5 document there referred to four members; two of the others were friends of Roger Hollis's. One was Graham Greene, the other Claud Cockburn. Greene had candidly remarked that he joined in order to get a free ticket to Moscow for a holiday; Cockburn's involvement was far more serious, and his career as a Communist agent was to dog his friend Roger Hollis for the rest of his life, as we shall see. The other Oxford Communist whom Hollis knew at this time was Tom Driberg, recruited into the Party while still at Lancing where he was a contemporary, and fellow sacristan, of Evelyn Waugh. Maxwell Knight, whom we shall meet again, had arranged this quite extraordinary coup, urging Driberg to join the Brighton Communist Party, from whence he moved to the Oxford branch when he went up. It was no doubt the information he gave to Knight that established that Cockburn was a member of the Party, and also, no doubt, that Hollis was not, despite his friendship with Cockburn and Driberg.

Roger Hollis came down from Oxford in his second year without taking a degree. Today this would imply failure. No great career would be open in any top-grade Government or commercial organisation, let alone the chance of becoming the Director General of perhaps the most prestigious Government department of all. Among the Waugh set in the 1920s, however, going down without a degree was almost the thing to do, and it did not noticeably affect a person's chances in later life. As Christopher Hollis remarked: "I do not think I exaggerate when I say that the greater number of undergraduates who have won intellectual success in after-life— Evelyn Waugh, Alan Pryce-Jones, John Betjeman, Tony Bushell and others—all went down without degrees." Roger Hollis was in good company.

The explanation for the apparent contradiction between academic failure and later worldly success among so many was to be found, of course, in the fact that besides drinking and socialising Waugh and his friends were actively involved in literary activities and were also, many of them, from literary or publishing families. The literary salons in London and the intellectual magazines, unlike today's, were a genuine forum for intellectual thought and evolution, and they had their echo in Oxford. Harold Acton started a university magazine, *Oxford Broom;* Graham Greene edited *Oxford Outlook;* Waugh wrote for the more established *Isis* and *Cherwell;* Christopher Hollis himself edited *Cherwell* when it had a new owner and a brief access of funds; and there were many others in the same line. It was a natural progression for Waugh and the rest to go on to London and write, and their views on life were so powerful that they acquired considerable influence.

The more serious overtones to the thinking of Evelyn Waugh, Christopher Hollis, Greene, and the others can be seen in the circumstance of their conversion to Roman Catholicism, which in some ways was an echo of the resolution of the spiritual crisis of the Oxford Movement a century before. The absence of a specifically political dimension, the focus on literary and aesthetic concerns, no doubt accounts for the perhaps backward-looking response: only ten years later the slump and the emergence of German National Socialism under Adolf Hitler produced among a Cambridge generation a political response that looked consciously to the future. That the political response to the Cambridge movement still had a spiritual or moral basis and can also be seen as an echo of the conflicts of the nineteenth-century Oxford Movement despite the change in direction from right to left is shown by the fact that so many of the leaders, from Anthony Blunt downwards, were children of clergymen, or from particularly orthodox religious households. While their dedication to Communism could be seen at one level as the complete antithesis of the religious beliefs implicit in their background, it often also showed a deep-seated and fervently held belief in certain moral values which they felt to be lacking in the Church as they saw it in their own surroundings. While Hollis would no doubt have found the opinions of such people congenial in middle life, this was not a path he followed at Oxford where he was simply in reaction against his family. Rather he seems to have formed for himself an ambition which had within it echoes of many if not all of the interests of those about him: he would combine a journey to China with the journalistic activities of his friend Claud Cockburn by going there and working on a magazine. Through a family connection he even found a newspaper in Hong Kong that was willing to give him a start. This was one step ahead of the ambitions of the average Oxford littérateur who had gone down without a degree, and it suggests that Roger, unlike Christopher, had decided not to look backwards, go over to Rome and seek a literary, a-political life but to take his future into his own hands.

There seems little doubt that Cockburn's influence was strong here. Cockburn had become involved in journalistic work at Oxford, but it had been journalism of a political rather than a literary kind. His father, "Chinese Harry," had come out of retirement on his return from China and obtained a quasi-diplomatic position in Budapest. This was the world that Cockburn thrived in. Waugh described him in his autobiography on their first meeting: "I met a tall spectacled young man with the air of Budapest rather than Berkhamsted [Cockburn's school] . . . Claud was already captivated by the absurdities of Central European Affairs." His interests and forceful personality seem to have had a considerable hold over Roger Hollis, and when the three of them went out on their great alcoholic adventures through Oxford it seems to have been Cockburn's view of the world, with its political "middle European" aspects, coupled with stories of China and the opportunities it afforded that swayed him, rather than Evelyn Waugh's.

In sober moments, few though they may have been, Cockburn may have explained why he had joined the Communist party. Waugh's reference to Cockburn's having already been "captivated" by Central European affairs could well be a coded reference to his knowledge that Cockburn had joined the Party, and in later years Waugh habitually referred to Cockburn as his "Communist cousin." Speculation on the question when so few people are involved is perhaps unnecessary, and too redolent of the kind of thinking that has surrounded the Cambridge Communists; but, as we shall discover when we examine Cockburn's later activities and the close part played by Roger Hollis in them when he was with MI5, a close personal connection, with political overtones, was established.

2
China Days

CHINA has long exerted a spell over America. Between the wars the attraction was at its strongest, and the country was thronged with American visitors from wealthy tourists to businessmen and even missionaries. For the British, India and the fading splendours of the Raj were the equivalent sporting ground, with only the very rich going further east. Most were content to leave Hong Kong and China itself to diplomats on less favoured postings and the "box-wallahs" or traders who were in many cases there to compete directly with their American opposite numbers. BAT, the British American Tobacco Company, now a worldwide multinational which owns among other names Marshall Field and Saks Fifth Avenue and who were to employ Roger Hollis after he arrived in China, were a typical British China firm. Hollis would have heard of them at Oxford, where they regularly recruited graduate staff. Graham Greene, despite his Communist party membership, had actually taken up an offer of a post in China with BAT but turned it down after further thought.

Business and neo-colonialism were far from Hollis's mind when he conceived his ambition to go to China. This must have stemmed from Cockburn and his other Oxford friends who had either been born in China, such as Claud himself, or had become fascinated by the culture. Cockburn's stories, and those told by his father which earned him the nickname "Chinese Harry" in the first place, must have had a political tinge to them, and anyone setting out for a career in journalism there raised in this milieu must have had a good idea what he was letting himself in for. It was an unusual ambition for a man whose father was running a theological college.

Hollis's decision to go to China was not taken lightly and he persisted in his aim against family opposition. Their most effective ploy was to refuse finance for the journey. This would have been sufficient to deter most people of his background. The 1920s may have seen the final flourishing of the globe-trotting days of the sons of Empire, but to go abroad, especially to somewhere as remote as China, without the backing of an institution of some kind— whether the diplomatic service, a large company, or even for the religious, a missionary society—was a difficult undertaking. Once he arrived, without backing or a place, Hollis's social position would be as ambiguous as it would be today, unless he had ample private means, like his friend Harold Acton. Clearly he did not.

Undeterred, Hollis took a job with a bank in the city and set about saving the money he needed. In a year he had the funds required. Before setting off for China he went on a visit to America and Canada. New York was then at the height of the stock exchange boom that was to end with the crash of 1929. It is surprising that someone with Hollis's banking experience did not become involved in that world. Instead, like Cockburn who was also in New York at this time and saw the crash on the day it happened, he may have come away with a revulsion for the system he saw around him. Certainly Cockburn described himself as being changed from someone who was merely "pink" to a "red" of the brightest kind.

When Hollis returned to England he determined to set off for China immediately. His family had obtained for him his introduction to the newspaper in Hong Kong. It was not the career they would have wanted for him, perhaps, but it was what he was intent on doing. And there was always the possibility that he would follow in the footsteps of another famous Old Cliftonian, Sir Francis Younghusband, the journalist and explorer who had first travelled the inland route from China to India. This model for Hollis's ambition might, in fact, seem more convincing than the immediate example of Claud Cockburn, were it not for the fact that Hollis was so clearly in entire revolt against his background. Hollis no doubt drew consolation from the thought that when he set out for China his fellow students at Oxford would just have graduated and would be looking for similar positions in the London world, with less chance of success and narrower horizons. He had the satisfaction of being one step ahead and fulfilling an ambition which he had formed at Oxford through his own efforts. The fact that Cockburn had followed an exactly similar course, getting into journalism in Germany, and eventually on to *The Times*, suggests again the origin of his plan. Those who have suspected Hollis of being a Soviet agent seem to have been unaware of Cockburn's membership in the Communist Party at Oxford. If they had been, the exactly similar path followed by Cockburn and Hollis would have suggested irresistibly to them that both were acting under instruction, but it is not clear that the earlier Oxford group of Communists were under such close supervision by their spymasters as the later Cambridge circle.

In the popular accounts of Hollis's time in China and his reasons for going, all written as a result of the leaked knowledge of the Fluency Committee enquiry, there has been only one serious attempt to describe the China that Hollis would have found when he got there: Chapman Pincher's *Too Secret Too Long*. If the various leaked accounts of Hollis's interrogation by the Committee are accurate he must have had great difficulty in restraining himself at the ignorance, manifested later by Peter Wright in *Spycatcher*, of his time at Oxford, the general atmosphere there and the political realities of the inter-war period in China. There were many books in print in the 1960s which could have served as an introduction to intelligent discussion about what was the most complex political situation of all, which finally resulted in victory for the Chinese Communists under Mao Tse Tung. Some of them were written by a contemporary of Hollis's at Clifton, C. P. Fitzgerald, who had become so interested in China that he had spent most of his life there, finally leaving to become an academic authority on China in

Australia. His college friend Harold Acton had even written an amusing satirical novel on China, *Ponies and Peonies*, after he returned to England. Any of these, augmented by Hollis's own writing on China, which we shall examine in the next chapter, would have given his interrogators a key to the political reality of what was happening there and to why he became such a devoted admirer of China and such a passionate opponent of Japan. What is even more puzzling is that they do not appear to have consulted Foreign Office documents clearly listed in the Foreign Office's excellent indexes. These indexes contain many references to the firm for which Hollis worked when he was in China and, in later years, to position papers on the country by Guy Burgess, some of the most important of which, involving the creation of a split between America and Britain, we shall look at later. Burgess in fact had been interested in China all his life, and it is astonishing that no connection was made with Hollis's own interest at the time of his interrogation.

Harold Acton has remarked that his reasons for going to China were largely connected with the beauty of Chinese art and that he couldn't believe that Roger Hollis was interested in that. Indeed the China satirised by Acton in his novel is not the China to which Hollis attached himself; but it is worth looking at briefly because, for countless visitors at the time, it was the only visible face of expatriate China. It was the world of *The Last Emperor*, when treasures from the palaces of the deposed Manchu dynasty were pouring onto the market and the wealthy spent their time looking for costly jade, antique robes and jewelry, and the more knowledgeable sought out fragile porcelain from early dynasties. The main stopping place for anyone coming to Peking for the first time was the Grand Hotel de Peking which included an antique shop on the third floor, run by an American, Helen Burton, which was a mecca for serious collectors. The magnificent jewel-encrusted visitors' book has survived and provides a vivid picture, with photographs and illustrations as well as signatures, of her world. Occasional British visitors—Bernard Shaw and his wife, Osbert Sitwell—rub shoulders with innumerable Americans, from the Vanderbilts downwards. Her own circle included the etcher Thomas Sandforth who had a studio in Peking, the mystery writer Vincent Starrett, the film-star Anna May Wong, and many other painters and sculptors. It is difficult not to see specific parallels between Acton's satire and the world of Helen Burton—a world which, despite her acquaintance with Edgar Snow, had nothing whatever to do with politics.

Hollis arrived in Hong Kong in 1928 and started work as a journalist. However, he soon found more stable employment. This may be seen to parallel moves by all the successful "moles" to disguise their political allegiances by going into overtly "right-wing" or highly conventional prestigious occupations. Thus Philby and Cockburn both went on to *The Times*, Tom Driberg joined the *Daily Express*, and Burgess joined the Anglo-German fellowship before going to the BBC. In Hollis's case, however, there were undoubtedly more prosaic reasons. He was very short of funds, having underestimated the cost of his trip; he could easily have slipped into the bohemian expatriate world which Acton satirised— looking either towards the aesthete's paradise that Acton was creating for himself, or to the more worldly, and often lucrative, circle of private dealers in antiques, with occasional journalism to keep the wolf from the door if all else failed. Many lived just this life, but Hollis, with the memory of his lapses in Oxford an immediate caution, determined to climb back onto the rails. He landed a full-time job with the British American Tobacco Company, who were in business in China on a large scale, both in their own name and under the Chinese title The Chi Tung Tobacco Company. Hollis clearly came from a background that BAT would have recognized and, although he had no degree, he had at least made the journey to China, off his own bat, which was the very thing that put Graham Greene and others like him off.

BAT was one of the biggest British concerns in China. But the turmoil and upheaval of Chinese politics, which had remained unresolved since the overthrow of the last Imperial dynasty, were such that they had seriously discussed with the British Government the possibility of leaving China altogether. A decision had been taken against this drastic step a year before Hollis joined and they traded very profitably afterwards, but the situation might explain why they were prepared to take on someone like Hollis on a local basis as what they termed "non-covenanted" staff rather than through the usual formal recruitment systems originating in the United Kingdom.

BAT's difficulties were many. Foremost among them were financial difficulties. The currency was unstable and was to remain so until the brief period following the Leith-Ross mission in 1936. An additional complication was that China was on the silver not the gold standard, and American actions in the silver market had caused China great difficulties; even BAT had found itself involved in long-running legal battles with the American Government, according to papers in the Foreign Office archives. The next most serious difficulty, but more worrying on a day-to-day basis, was the continuing political upheaval. In 1929 there had been bitter clashes in north China between the Chinese and Soviet forces, and the Chinese Eastern Railway, owned and run by Russia, was attacked. This railway ran through Manchuria and connected Vladivostock with the Trans-Siberian Railway, on which Hollis was later to travel on his brief visit home to England on his four-yearly leave. In 1931 the Japanese invaded Manchuria and set up the puppet state of Manchukuo under the deposed Chinese Emperor Pu Yi.

Japan's arrival on the Chinese mainland transformed the trading position, and BAT was threatened with the loss of a considerable part of its trade in Manchukuo to cheaper Japanese produce and Japan's natural tendency to monopolise her trade wherever she could. Hollis, in a letter to his family, said: "As for the Japanese, they'll move us all out of North China unless something is done to stop them." Nevertheless BAT carried on trading, even expanding, acquiring land at Mukden in Manchukuo, where it already had a factory, this time to set up a printing works. No doubt this was an attempt at diversification, and at reducing its dependency on what were effectively Japanese local suppliers. BAT's Mukden operations were to cause it a great deal of trouble, and these difficulties which were political, involving the Comintern, may have been a reason, in addition to illness, why Hollis and some of his colleagues left China in mid-1936.

Besides external problems with Russia and Japan there was always the internal problem of the civil war, or wars. A situation of great complexity was liable to lead to suspension of trading activity, or even the kidnapping of employees, who could be held to ransom. The central conflict was between the Chinese Government and the Communist Party, which even then was under the leadership of Mao Tse Tung. At the end of Hollis's time in China Chiang Kai Shek made an agreement with the Communists in his struggle against the Japanese, and this made things even more difficult for BAT, which had for long been conscious of the dangers of Bolshevism. As early as 1930, Archibald Rose had submitted a paper to the Foreign Office on behalf of the company entitled *The Menace of the Rise and Spread of Communism during the Civil War*. His foreboding had special application to BAT, particularly in Mukden, as we shall see.

Not all firms took a jaundiced view of Japan's activity in Manchukuo, or subscribed to the popular, largely left-inspired, opinion that Japan was organising a reign of terror. After the establishment of Manchukuo there had been an immediate transformation of the economic situation. Railways expanded at twice the rate they did in China itself. An authority on Manchuria, F. C. Jones, wrote: ". . . the Japanese built up in Manchuria an industrial potential far ahead of anything which existed elsewhere in Eastern Asia excluding Japan and the USSR." As Hollis himself was later to remark in London: ". . . capital and capital goods will be needed in quantities far beyond the capacity of Japan alone, and increased purchasing power will create a demand for high grade goods which only foreign manufacturers can supply." Delegations of British businessmen visited Manchukuo, and many sought a way out of Britain's difficulties in the Far East by re-establishing the good relations which had existed with Japan earlier in the century when she had been Britain's valued ally. Foremost among those supporting these moves was the then Chancellor of the Exchequer, Neville Chamberlain. It was to cause Chamberlain some difficulty at home, as one astute observer has remarked:

Chamberlain argued that a friendly arrangement with Japan could provide the solution of commercial difficulties and, in the friendlier atmosphere created, Britain and Japan might arrive at some understanding over naval matters . . . This approach would have ignored China's national feeling and was likely to have political repercussions at home and abroad which Chamberlain chose to ignore or perhaps was prepared to risk.

The repercussions referred to took the form in Britain of vigorous protest at Japan's actions. Students and others were encouraged by Communist front organisations to walk the streets with placards urging the public to boycott Japanese goods and so on. The central purpose of these moves was to prevent at all costs a powerful Japan appearing on Soviet Russia's far-eastern border, but this was carefully concealed beneath a cloak of fighting "fascism," supposedly the driving intellectual force in Japan, as well as Italy, Germany and latterly Spain.

It is clear from the few of Hollis's letters to his family published that Hollis took a strongly anti-Japanese line. In his later years in China this would also have implied a pro-Communist line. However annoyed BAT might have been about their difficulties in Manchukuo, that would not have been a road they would have travelled. They had particular reason to be annoyed with the Communist Party at this time, for reasons alluded to before, which we shall look at now more closely.

The particular difficulty experienced by BAT and all other British trading houses in China was that they themselves were the main target for Communist infiltration. The Chinese Communist Party had realised early on that Chinese working for British companies could travel widely and freely and were immune to supervision by any local gendarmerie, as the police were called. They could always claim, if they were stopped for any reason, that they were on company business, and they knew that foreign companies in China were protected. The authorities, of whatever complexion— Chinese, Japanese or Manchurian—were aware of this and kept a careful watch for an opportunity to confirm their suspicions. Even the British diplomatic service was not immune to this kind of supervision; in 1931 an employee at the British consulate at Chefoo was accused of having Communist connections.

Early in 1936 BAT was given a hint that something was amiss when the authorities denounced H. V. Tiencken, the head of BAT in Manchukuo, as President of the Manchurian Communist party. The charge was dismissed as absurd, particularly as only a few weeks before an Irish Presbyterian missionary had been accused of holding the same post. However, in April 1936 the authorities moved again, this time without warning, to arrest fourteen BAT employees on the grounds of working for the Comintern. These included BAT's principal sales agent in Mukden and his general manager. The Directors of BAT assumed immediately, as did the British authorities, that this was simply brigandry of a kind well known in China, particularly as a considerable sum of money had also been taken and the manager had apparently been obliged to write out a cheque for $14,000 soon after his arrest. However, when they complained formally, the chief of the Mukden gendarmerie immediately appeared and gave full assurances that the charges were genuine, that the prisoners would not be ill-treated, as all too often happened, and that all money seized would be returned as soon as the case was closed. BAT would then be informed of the result of the investigations.

Arrests of this kind presented acute difficulties for local diplomats, as they still do today. While the relatives of those detained and their employers understandably want immediate action, they have to consider the possibility that there may be something in the charge, that the civil authorities may have acted correctly, and that any precipitate action could rebound on innocent third parties. The British Consul-General in Peking, P. D. Butler, wrote to the Foreign Office giving the background to the arrests: "It is possible, though not established, that the arrests may be connected with that of a Jewish photographer named Josephus [sic] who was accused early in April of acting as a spy for the former Soviet Consul-General. Forty-eight hours after being taken into custody he died, allegedly by his own hand." Another colleague wrote: "The local Japanese authorities appear to be genuinely convinced that many employees of foreign—particularly British—institutions have been involved in communistic activities. When the suppression of communism is in question the average Japanese policeman is not a sane person and I am afraid that, however much we may protest, 'third degree' methods will still be used." Yet another minuted: "It is not difficult to believe that at least some genuine Soviet espionage does go on," a classic example of diplomatic understatement.

One of the methods by which the authorities can influence matters in such cases is to leak a story to the press, and that is what was done in this instance. An article appeared in *The Times* on 9 May 1936 under the highly misleading headline ANTI-BRITISH PURGE IN MANCHURIA, with the sub-heading EMPLOYEES ARRESTED AND TORTURED but with no mention of the Comintern or the reason for the arrests—it was an anti-Comintern purge not an anti-British one. The author of the piece was described simply as "A correspondent in Manchukuo" but papers in the Foreign Office files reveal that this was in fact the author and journalist Peter Fleming (brother of Ian Fleming, the creator of James Bond). The actual letter confirming the arrangement from the man on the spot is preserved. It also points, incidentally, to the sort of work Hollis was involved in for BAT:

> Before these new incidents had started I had, on the suggestion of the News Department [where Guy Burgess was later to work], furnished Mr. Peter Fleming of *The Times* with material for an article on the arrests of last autumn. He has sent me for approval the draft of his proposed articles. In view of these new arrests it is a matter for consideration whether some mention of them should not be included in the article. He would of course have to obtain the approval of BAT.

The actual article is included in the file establishing the authorship and the circumstances.

It is doubtful whether they would also have known of the highly misleading headline, which presumably a sub-editor thought would make the item more alluring. It is very probable that the BAT official who was in liaison with the press on such matters was Hollis, as it is certain from letters to his family that he had had such dealings with Fleming, some of which were not entirely satisfactory. He wrote home suggesting to his family that they look at an article in *The Times* for 14 December 1935, clearly under the impression that he would be given credit for what was his writing. In fact there was only a general credit, as in the BAT story, and, according to Chapman Pincher, exhaustive search in *The Times* archives shows that they knew nothing of Hollis's work—Peter Fleming was "their man in China." Hollis may have become aware of what was happening, and this would account for an uncharacteristically barbed remark in another letter he wrote at the time:

> I wonder if I am writing to be, in general, so truthful. Practically all other people, as far as I can see, lie blatantly as soon as they get around the nearest corner. It doesn't seem to do much harm and, in the case of people who have a real gift for it, like Peter Fleming, is exceedingly amusing.

Chapman Pincher concludes that Hollis was acting out a "Walter Mittyish" view of himself when he wrote to his parents about his journalism, but we can now see that this is mistaken and that not only did Hollis probably write articles—he was to write a particularly lengthy and formal one for a learned society when he returned to Britain, as we shall see—but his work for BAT involved him in this direct collaboration with journalists. The only description of what Hollis actually did for BAT during his eight years till now has been that he worked for the advertising department. This job seems to have been much closer to what we would call public relations, and would explain why his work on a newspaper in Hong Kong might have been a qualification. Pincher later asked the rhetorical question "Why did the Comintern need to recruit Roger Hollis, a young tobacco company employee?", going on to answer it himself: "There is now, in fact, a proper answer to that question. According to a major work on Sorge produced in 1984 by the East German writer Julius Mader, BAT was helping to finance Chiang Kai Shek's military costs and the Sorge Ring needed to penetrate it."

In fact, as we have seen, the Comintern had no need for agents in BAT because they already had a considerable number. The book he quoted serves two purposes as disinformation: it conceals the fact that the Communists were operating on such a massive scale in China and also slanders BAT, a capitalist firm *par excellence*. The attempt to suggest that BAT would have funded Chiang Kai Shek is clumsy, since it would only, in any event, fit a narrow timescale, the brief period before Chiang Kai Shek and Mao Tse Tung joined forces to fight the Japanese. In fact BAT officials in China at the time are adamant that no such funding took place. A possible reason for approaching Hollis was that he was a European, whereas most if not all of the men arrested were Chinese, despite their senior positions. Possibly an approach made to Hollis at this time turned into an actual recruitment, but there is no evidence and it is more probable that at this stage Hollis simply reacted against what he saw happening to people he knew on a daily working basis by giving them his loyalty without becoming directly involved.

The case against the senior sales official at Mukden ended later in the year when he was found guilty and summarily executed. The cheque obtained from him was shown to have been offered voluntarily, being the amount he said he had received from his Comintern contacts. Far from its being extorted, the authorities had not even cashed the cheque, and they returned it when the case was over and it was no longer needed as evidence. All the money which belonged to BAT or was held on their account was also returned in full. The relevant file in the PRO contains no further comment. The implication appears to be that the verdict, if not the punishment, may have been justified.

The other aspects of Communist life in China at the time which Pincher mentions and which are of interest for the possible inferences that can be drawn about Hollis's life there concern the American author and journalist Agnes Smedley, and an army officer, Tony Stables, traced by the Fluency Committee team, who shared a flat with Hollis early on in his time in China in 1931.

Agnes Smedley arrived in China in May 1929 shortly after Hollis. She immediately adopted a high profile in the expatriate community, writing articles and doing liaison work for a number of organisations directed against the British presence in India. A year after she arrived she had assumed such importance that the authorities raided her home and seized all her papers. No Comintern papers seem to have been found. Instead there was a large quantity of periodicals and pamphlets, many of which she had edited, put out by the Shanghai Branch of the India Youth League. She was nominally earning a living as the China correspondent of the *Frankfurter Zeitung*, and anyone on the fringe of the journalistic world, as Hollis unquestionably was, would soon have heard of her. After the raid she became an even more prominent figure and worked in a bookshop in Shanghai much frequented by Europeans and expatriates generally known as "The Zeitgeist Bookstore." This was a general bookshop which also specialised in left-wing literature from all over the world. It would no doubt have been the shop that carried the mimeographed news-sheet produced by Claud Cockburn in the thirties, *The Week*, which he proudly said was distributed in China. To spend time trying to deny that Hollis knew her, especially as he is said to have candidly agreed during interrogation later that he did, would seem to be misplaced effort. The fact that he admitted it suggests that he probably met her through the bookstore or some innocuous social contact. Had there been anything more sinister at that stage, the Shanghai police, which had many English officers in its ranks, would have found out about it, particularly as Smedley had been raided already and was an obvious focus for left-wing sympathisers. It is more likely that Hollis simply took notice of what was happening in that world and discussed it with people like Peter Fleming from a journalist's standpoint. His own experience of the Comintern, of its activity in BAT and of how the authorities dealt with it, occurred at the very end of his time in China and may have brought home to him the significance of the fringe world which Smedley and another left expatriate, Arthur Ewert, whom he appears to have known casually, only talked of.

Hollis's link with Ewert, mentioned both by Pincher and in *Spycatcher*, is particularly interesting as it refers to his life in 1931, before the Communist activity had gathered strength. Moreover it shows the close links between the life style Hollis adopted when he first came to China and the life style he had in England, typical of expatriates newly arrived in the country. Chapman Pincher's account is fuller and more accurate than the one in *Spycatcher* which, curiously, has been shaped to prove the *simpliste* case of a straightforward recruitment by Ewort, an active Communist agent. It concerns the Army officer, who was found later with considerable difficulty, who shared a flat with Hollis in Shanghai:

> [The interrogating officer] learned that most of Hollis's friends whom the Army Officer [Tony Stables] had been able to list had been diplomats and businessmen with some of whom he played golf. The army man expressed concern about one of them called Ewert and whom he described as an "international socialist" . . . He said he found the relationship difficult to understand because Hollis's politics appeared to be conservative.

The immediate resumption of his enthusiasm for golf almost makes one wonder whether he brought his clubs with him from England. Certainly Hollis also kept up the social life which he must have known would appeal to his parents, and he duly wrote home about occasions which would seem as easily recognisable as a game of golf to the people reading them:

> Yesterday I went on a picnic with the very charming wife of the British consul at Darien, the wife of one of our Directors who has a son at Clifton, a pleasant local couple and a couple of wealthy but leisurely globe-trotters. There is a pleasant English couple staying at my hotel . . . he is a schoolmaster whom I knew from earlier days in Hong Kong . . .

There are a number of reasons why Hollis should be meeting someone like Ewert at the same time as enjoying picnics and rounds of golf with friendly local worthies, the most obvious being the same reason that he met Peter Fleming: an extension of his interest in journalism. Ewert for his part might well have been curious to know why a BAT man was interested in journalists. Knowing that the Comintern had infiltrated BAT he might have suspected that Hollis was trying to pump *him* to get information on this subject for BAT.

As the years passed and the political situation developed there can be no doubt, if only from his own writing, that Hollis's views moved steadily to the left, and he would have been unlikely to break off contacts with people such as Ewert and Smedley, and Ruth Kuczynski, the GRU (Soviet military organization) agent runner code-named "Sonia" who was also in China and much involved with Ewert and his circle. At the same time, as will be made clear, the shift to the left was general, and any close friendship he might develop would not necessarily be conspiratorial. In any case it is particularly difficult to follow the allegiance of even dedicated Communists in China at this time.

After the troubles in 1929 between Russia and China had been patched up Stalin adopted a policy of collaboration with the Chinese against the common enemy Japan. This was at a time when those same Chinese authorities were engaged in a bitter struggle against Mao Tse Tung. Many exiled white Russians actually became Soviet citizens at this time in order to make their position easier than that of stateless persons. There was an understanding that they would not return to Russia. They were known as "radishes"—because they were red outside but white within. There were also "beefsteaks": those who appeared colourless or innocuous on the outside but were in fact red through and through. Thus one might find oneself talking to an expatriate who apparently hated his native Russia and yet was a Soviet citizen. Even such a case as that was simple compared with many, and it was this kind of situation that sent visiting correspondents rushing for help to an "old China hand" as soon as they arrived to enable them to write their stories with some hope of getting it right. Hollis no doubt aspired to be such a guide and certainly assisted Fleming. But as time went on even a permanent resident could begin to loose bearings and find that he had drifted beyond the point at which he would normally have changed course. A classic example, as we shall see shortly, was Archibald Clark Kerr, later Lord Inverchapel.

In 1934 Hollis came home on leave. Rather than go by the normal routes, by which he came out and finally returned, he decided to go through Russia on the Trans-Siberian railway. Much has been read into this. But the journey was one of the great journeys of the world, as it still is, and BAT employees frequently made it out of sheer adventure. Many people even now go to Russia only because they are making that historic journey. Hollis's defenders have pointed out that he hated Russia and said so in his letters. One indeed is a classic example of abuse, and a departure from his normal tone:

> . . . the next morning we arrived in Moscow . . . Lenin's tomb looked rather like a high-class public lavatory without dignity or artistic merit. Our guide was most enthusiastic as was to be expected but I have never seen anything which depressed me so unutterably as Moscow. It was like driving through a drab slum of three and a half million people, every-one ill-dressed in the most deplorable ready-mades . . .

The unmistakable period snobbery in the phrase "deplorable ready-mades," combined with the sacrilegious reference to Lenin's tomb, would indeed suggest that Hollis's grand-parents' capitalist instincts were sound and well, especially as he also mentioned the "unspeakable" sight of rows of empty shop windows. However Chapman Pincher has correctly pointed out that many devoted admirers of the "socialist experiment in Russia," as it was referred to among the faithful, were shocked by what they saw in Moscow. More significantly, as has been explained, such views could perfectly well have been held by someone who was a keen supporter of Mao Tse Tung and the Chinese Communists and hated what he saw in Moscow because he hated the European civilisation of which it was by then a debased example.

When Hollis returned to China in 1934 he was probably already suffering from the illness that was to cause him to leave BAT and his promising career in China and return to England. Early in 1935 he wrote:

> Rather an unpleasant experience . . . I woke up on Monday with an attack of bleeding like the one I had after the West of England golf championship . . . I am going to be X-rayed as soon as we can arrange it, and I'll let you know the worst.

"The worst" proved not so bad and with immediate care at a Canadian missionary hospital he made an almost complete recovery although he had one relapse in England during the war. He wrote home with a favourable report from his doctor:

> I shall, of course, have to be very careful for another year or two, because apparently one can never absolutely get rid of the bug once it is there, but I'm living a perfectly normal life except that I avoid late nights and violent exercise.

He would most of all have to avoid the kind of strenuous life lived by any European in the Far East.

Change was clearly in the air. He would also have found the political climate altering. Things were moving more rapidly towards the situation in which Chiang Kai Shek was to ally himself, after some mild persuasion, to Mao Tse Tung in a common front against Japan. Agnes Smedley, far from being prosecuted, was allowed to do radio broadcasts, aided by an enthusiastic young New Zealand Rhodes scholar of far-left opinions who was visiting China with his father, an Anglican clergyman. There was at the same time a marked tendency for businessmen and the large firms such as BAT to move towards the Japanese view of things and for the diplomats to move the other way. The Ambassador who succeeded Alexander Cadogan, Archibald Clark Kerr, found himself thrown cheek-by-jowl with his Soviet opposite number when the Japanese attacks on China proper were under way. His attachment to Russia became so strong that he was appointed Ambassador in Moscow in 1942 when bridges needed urgently to be built after the disastrous tour of Stafford Cripps. John Costello has painted a portrait of Clark Kerr which shows that even someone in his position, holding the views he did, was not necessarily thought of as a spy or as someone holding unacceptably odd opinions:

> The amiable pipe-smoking Ambassador never made any secret of his sympathy for the Soviet Union. He was given to lecturing his Foreign Office colleagues on his favourite topic and they tolerated his "steady passion for the Soviet Union," re-

garding it . . . as just another harmless eccentricity in a veteran diplomat. Yet even if Inverchapel was not a "spy" in the strict sense of the word, the evidence suggests that the Foreign Office blundered in its failure to appreciate that . . . his favourable views of Russia made him a major security risk.

These events occurred of course after Hollis had returned to Britain, but they show that an attachment to China at that time could readily produce even in a veteran diplomat a profound reorientation in loyalties when once the Chinese and Russian Communists had mended their fences, as they have intermittently ever since. After the war Clark Kerr was appointed British Ambassador in Washington. There his pro-Soviet views and eccentric personal behaviour finally brought about his recall. Hollis came from the same melting pot although a businessman rather than a diplomat, and without Clark Kerr's eccentricities.

The situation for a BAT employee was difficult. Japanese demands in Manchukuo strengthened, and BAT found that when they next wished to build a cigarette factory they had to re-register the company as a Manchurian company in a way which would involve its loosing the benefits associated with its cherished extra-territorial rights. At first they refused, but after consultation with the Foreign Office they went ahead. Once the decision had been made the Japanese response was so favourable that they soon found themselves agreeing, for example, to use green tobacco grown in Manchukuo. When it was pointed out that hardly any tobacco was grown in Manchukuo the Japanese replied that they would be planting great areas with BAT's valued advice. BAT obligingly provided two of their best experts in the field, who advised on the suitability of land and estimated the number of families that would be needed to work it. BAT do not seem to have been perturbed when they learned that the farmers would in fact be Japanese immigrants and pursued their normal policy of cooperating fully with the local government in power.

For someone who had grown as attached to China as Hollis had this presented a real problem. But the difficulty was compounded when the position on Communist infiltration was dealt with. In the light of the acknowledged Comintern infiltration at Mukden, BAT agreed to Japanese suggestions that it should employ secret agents of their choosing to infiltrate the workforce to give them the earliest possible warning of any Communist trouble. Unfortunately there is no record that Hollis made his feeling plain on the matter, but he was not alone in his sympathy with the Chinese, as the view of another expatriate manager, conveyed to the Foreign Office by the British Consul-General at Harbin, M. E. Denning, made clear:

> Mr. Gilliam, the American Manager of the BAT Co. here has been told that as a result of the arrests in Mukden it was believed that certain communist elements existed in his factory. It was therefore suggested that the company should employ an agent, to be appointed by the police, who would make the necessary investigations. Mr. Gilliam, who privately has never been in favour of the step now irrevocably taken by BAT [of reorganizing as a Manchurian Company] told the police that he must consider the matter. But he quoted the incident to me as an instance of the helpless position to which his company had been reduced as a result of abandoning its extra-territorial rights.

A Marxist would have seen this as a classic example of the expropriater expropriated, and indeed that seems to be how Hollis saw it, judging from the talk he gave on the wars in China after his return. Although, as we have seen, there are signs that he might well not have taken the pro-Japanese company line, they would be no more than indications at first easily balanced in his companions' eyes by his "conservative" enthusiasm for golf and middle-class social life. But then over the next few years he moved into a position which was without doubt that of a "red" supporter of Mao Tse Tung and the Chinese Government rather than the business empire of his estwhile employers, or Japan, or indeed America, BAT's great rival in business in China. That Hollis was obliged to return home to Britain because of illness has obscured the fact that he was, in any case, rapidly moving to a point at which he would have been at loggerheads over policy with his employers. Had he remained in China working for BAT there is no doubt that he would also have found himself working with the Japanese secret police whom BAT agreed to take on under cover of being their workers, and he would not have been alone in having violent objections to this. The Comintern activity that Hollis was acutely aware of at the time is the first example of political reality being forgotten or suppressed that made Hollis's position incomprehensible to the spycatchers that came later. Neither Wright nor Pincher attacking Hollis, nor those defending him, knew anything of it, although Pincher's journalist's intuition brought him closer to the truth than many.

Any doubt about Hollis's position was clarified by his talk, which both his attackers and defenders have unaccountably ignored. It took the form of a full-scale public lecture to a meeting of the Royal Central Asian Society for later publication in their journal (see Appendix 1) and was given after he had left BAT but before he joined MI5, a time which has come to be known from *Spycatcher* as the "missing two years."

3
A Spycatcher Is Appointed

THE legendary ability for people in Britain from the right background to fall on their feet is proved once again in Hollis's case
when seeming disaster was turned into a brilliant new career.
From a man turning thirty invalided out of a moderately ambitious
commercial career, he became first a spycatcher soon to be considered an expert on the most sensitive area, Communism. And this
in turn was to lead him to one of the most secret and powerful jobs
in the British establishment, the head of the security service itself.
It is interesting to notice that his brothers' careers were also flourishing and all were being shepherded along by the head of the
family whose own career was moving steadily forward by more
conventional processes to the dignity of his Bishopric.

However, even with this kind of backing, and there is nothing
quite the equivalent in America or Russia of having a Bishop for a
father, the early stage along the path did not prove easy. It took
what seemed an age before the right words were spoken and a
niche found for Hollis, but in reality the period from summer 1936
when Hollis returned from China to early 1938 when he was recruited into MI5—the "missing two years"—is in fact barely eighteen months in a full and busy life. The importance placed on this
period, which was a difficult one, a hiatus caused by illness, and a

particularly sticky illness at that, has stemmed entirely from the spycatchers' close examination of his past in an effort to find time during which he could have been recruited as a Russian agent. It was thought almost certain by the now notorious Fluency Committee that his enrolment in what Kim Philby called an "elite force" had taken place in China, which was, as we have seen, riddled with agents of every kind. But the publication in 1982 by Anthony Glees of the restricted selection of previously unknown letters from Hollis to his parents covering the entire period of his time in China, some of which we have quoted, seemed effectively to have defused this charge. Attention was therefore switched to the "two missing years." The specific charge was relayed to the world for the first time in detail in July 1984 over the appropriately modern medium of television by the chairman of the Fluency Committee, Peter Wright:

> Sir Roger dealt convincingly with questions about his career—
> except for a two year period immediately before joining MI5.
> We were of the opinion that he was hiding something. He
> seemed unprepared to tell us what went on. He avoided tell-
> ing us exactly who he was meeting at the time, what he was
> doing.

The most obvious reason for Hollis's reticence about this difficult time must be dealt with first. This is that his illness, tuberculosis, was not one which was normally discussed: like cancer today, it was often fatal, and cure was uncertain if immediate action was not taken. Together with malaria, it was one of the main hazards faced by Europeans working in the Far East. George Orwell caught it in Burma. Unfortunately for him he was not working for a firm like BAT, who took the closest interest in their employees' health and welfare. Orwell's illness went undetected, or was identified only at a late stage, and little or nothing was done to treat it. As a result Orwell died when he was only 49, having written his masterpiece, *Nineteen Eighty-Four*, virtually on his death bed. Hollis was given immediate treatment in China at a Canadian missionary hospital and later in Switzerland, but he was lucky. In the circumstances it is surprising that he kept as level a temper with his interrogators while they probed this area of his life as he appears to have done. Hollis took a light view of his illness and at one point compared his plight to that of De Quincey: "De Quincey found solace in opium, but I need something more than dreams to live on. It is curious that both De Quincey and I should have left Worcester without a degree." And there is a clear implication here, as far as would be permitted in a letter written home, that he had tried De Quincey's opium as well.

Although both the detractors and the defenders of Hollis have looked at the period in some detail, major points have been overlooked, including the fact, already noticed, that Hollis gave an extensive account of his view of events in China based on his detailed knowledge. And once again there has been a singular lack of contemporary perspective which could have been gained by examining straightforward evidence in diaries and elsewhere.

When Hollis returned from China he took up the normal round of life with his family in Wells, the earlier break with his family forgotten. There is always a period of cultural shock for people returning home from long periods away in a totally different environment. Hollis was certainly due for extensive leave, even discounting a period of recuperation. He quickly looked up his brother Christopher and they took the first opportunity to see Evelyn Waugh. Waugh described the visit on 16 September 1936 with typically understated brilliance: "Hollis's and Christopher's brother Roger came to dinner. Agreeable and dull evening." In view of Hollis's traumatic experiences in China we can safely assume that Waugh had not drawn him out and that Hollis was already exhibiting that extreme reserve for which he was known in later life. Waugh had himself just returned from his second visit to Abyssinia and was finishing his travel book *Waugh in Abyssinia*. He had also been reading for review Peter Fleming's *News from Tartary*, an account of Fleming's journey overland from China to Kashmir following the example of Younghusband. From Waugh's brief entry in his diary there is no sign that he made any connection between Hollis's appearance and the book he had just been reviewing.

For his part Hollis must have found Waugh greatly changed from the man he had known as a drinking companion in Oxford. Waugh had become a notable figure in the literary world and on the fringe of upper-class Catholic life, and his views on political questions would have reflected this. The drift of Hollis's thought on the China question would have made any idea of supporting Franco in the Spanish civil war an impossibility; yet that would have been Waugh's inclination in view of the documented atrocities against the Catholic Church in Spain committed by the Communists.

In November 1936 Hollis went up to London to discuss his career with BAT. He had already decided to decline any further appointment unless, presumably, they made him an extraordinary offer, for he had made an appointment for that same afternoon with Peter Fleming at his office in *The Times* hoping to establish a journalistic connection once again. With hindsight he might have realised that this was not the sort of connection that Fleming would want to encourage. The mystique embodied in the title of Fleming's best-selling *One's Company* would not have stood well with the constant reminder that he owed line after line of his reports printed in *The Times* to Hollis's amateur efforts. The only result of the interview was a commission for a single article, which does not seem to have appeared, and a promise that Fleming would try to get him books to review for the *Times Literary Supplement*.

The rebuff appears to have been so personal that, when he discovered that his old university friend Roger Fulford was also with *The Times*, he went back for another try. Unfortunately he had no better luck. As I established in *Truth Betrayed*, Roger Fulford was a member of the broadcasting and literary circle which had Guy Burgess, Anthony Blunt and Harold Nicolson as its leading lights. Burgess's powers of patronage at the BBC were particularly valued and he had brought a number of travellers to the microphone to give accounts of their journeys in far-off places. If Hollis had met Fulford socially it might have been thought that he would soon have been drawn into this group, and a broadcast of his experiences in China would have been expected: not only would the China question have been topical, but Burgess's own rebuff by *The Times* would have created some sympathy. However, Hollis would probably not have fitted entirely into the peculiarly exclusive world of

Burgess and Blunt at this time. Unlike them and the others in the circle, Hollis was unmarried simply because it was unusual for businessmen working permanently abroad in remote places to get married until they were well established. In fact he was shortly to become engaged to a local girl, the daughter of a west-country solicitor, and their marriage at Wells Cathedral took place in the middle of the so-called "missing two years."

Some time early in January 1937 Hollis realised that he was getting nowhere with his hoped-for career in journalism. He approached BAT again and they found him temporary employment with the Ardath Tobacco Company. This was in the accounts department, though he was described as an assistant manager. It was not an important post, but he went ahead and became formally engaged to Eve Swayne in February on the strength of it. He did not, of course, stop looking for a more worthwhile career for himself, and Glees, using family papers, has recorded that he made a number of approaches to companies, and also wrote to the Oxford Appointments Board during the year.

Some time before his marriage, the date is not clear, he went to Switzerland for a further cure, which appears to have been satisfactory. Although there were occasional breaks in his later career attributed to his earlier illness he went on to lead a full life. The molehunters have tried to find significance also in this visit, since there were many known agents in Switzerland at the time, including the GRU's "Sonia" Kuczynski. But a more likely explanation is the very natural one that Hollis, knowing he was about to get married, approached BAT on the question and they naturally agreed to set his health to rights as far as was then possible.

An intrinsic weakness in Hollis's attempts to find employment, obvious now, was that he was still preoccupied with affairs in China, and his knowledge extended far beyond what an ordinary businessman would have acquired. None of the jobs he was looking at reflected this specialist knowledge. The only obvious calling for someone in his position would have been journalism, but he seems not to have wanted anything less than a desk at *The Times*. At some point, again it is not clear when, Hollis was invited to deliver the lecture we have mentioned to the Royal Central Asian Society, an opportunity he seized eagerly, choosing as his subject "The Conflict in China" on 20 October 1937. The talk, printed here in Appendix 1, is interesting as showing both the depth of Hollis's knowledge, which he had obviously been adding to continuously as events developed, and his acute understanding of the political significance of events there.

After a joking allusion to his father's calling as Bishop of Taunton ("I shall not attempt to make any *ex cathedra* pronouncements . . .") he drew attention to the astonishing fact that Chiang Kai Shek and the Chinese Government had reached some sort of "working agreement with the Red Armies." After adding that this had "inspired a firmer attitude towards Japan," he made no further reference to the Red Army, even though its presence and activity were crucial to any understanding of what was occurring. He appeared to take the line that they were simply now part of the Chinese Government forces fighting against Japan. This omission seems also to have struck the audience. So much so that one member of the society asked if the Red Army to which Hollis referred was actually the same Red Army that had completed the so-called Long March, made famous since by Edgar Snow and other commentators. Hollis replied succinctly: "It is the same Red Army and they are now in the Government fold. It is difficult to find out what promises General Chiang Kai Shek had to make to get their adherence [he had been kidnapped by Communist forces and had been obliged to come to an agreement] and also his own liberty . . ."

The general tone of his remarks was entirely against Japan. Though he stopped short of outright abuse he did make a savage allusion to Japan's possible use of gas warfare before withdrawing it with the remark: "I mean this quite impartially: the Chinese have no more humanitarian instincts than the Japanese in warfare, but the Japanese have the equipment and the Chinese have not." In one place he makes remarks which were not only against the Japanese but smacked almost of Russian propaganda:

> Ever since the seizure of Manchuria Japan has been strengthening her defences along the Soviet border. From Korea

around to Chahar these defences are highly organised and equipped with wireless stations, landing grounds and adequate garrisons. West of this they have established a series of military missions and depots running along the Russian border as far as Chinese Turkestan . . .

Certainly it is difficult to see how he can have known this from his own observation. His final words made his pro-Chinese position absolutely plain:

The temptation to look into the future is one which few can resist and I confess to a belief that Japan is digging her own grave in the present war. China, even in the humiliation of a defeat by the neighbour she despises, has learned that the Japanese are not invincible, and Japan's bombs have sown the seeds of a new patriotism . . . Japan cannot suppress a nation-wide determination in so vast a country. China will bide her time, but when the time comes she will return to the leadership of Asia. The world will be the better for so mighty an ally in the cause of peace.

But it also suggested strongly his political views, for the slogan-call for the "cause of peace" was then the current Communist line and absolutely unmistakable. Indeed the preliminary approach made to possible future agents was nearly always expressed in terms of an opportunity for them to help fight for "the cause of peace." Burgess's attempts at recruiting his friends were always couched in these terms, at least according to Goronwy Rees's account, and this is confirmed by Philby's admission to Flora Solomon that he was engaged on dangerous work "for the cause of peace."

BAT were experiencing good trading conditions in Manchukuo at this time along with other British companies, particularly insurance companies, whose business was better than it had been for many years. Had news of the talk got back to BAT it would have been awkward for him, but it seems that Hollis may in fact have been no longer working for BAT. He gave up his job with Ardath in October giving as the reason: "He just could not bear it." It would perhaps be of a piece with Hollis's (reticent) character if he had resigned, knowing that the talk which he felt bound to give would make his position impossible. The talk also provides indirect evidence that he was not an agent at this time, except perhaps the most obvious "agent of influence." The audience would have been influential, and would have come away with the clear impression that his sympathies were emphatically pro-Chinese with a "blind-spot" on the "red" question with the fairly obvious inference to be drawn that this blind-spot might be a more positive sympathy.

Kim Philby giving the same talk at the time would have adopted a strongly pro-Japanese line. An overtly Communist speaker such as D. N. Pritt, the Communist lawyer and *de facto* leader of the movement in Britain, or Claud Cockburn would have described the role of the Red Army as greater than it actually was and would not have missed the opportunity to bring in a reference to the similar struggles going on in Spain. Hollis was simply giving an account of what was happening as it was known to him, with clear, simple indications of where his own sympathies lay. The only propagandist element was his reference to the Japanese build-up on the Soviet border, which he cannot have known about from his work in BAT as contemporaries at BAT are sure that none of his duties would, or could, have taken him along the border that he describes.

If Hollis had been hoping for some introduction from the talk leading to a career, or simply employment of any kind, he was disappointed. In the ensuing months he and his wife were obliged to give up their flat in London and move in with his parents. They travelled on the continent on a minor business assignment, but it was only for the briefest of periods and they were back in Wells for Christmas.

The "missing two years" came to an end when Hollis was recruited to MI5, some time not later than 13 March 1938. The precise details of the recruitment have remained uncertain, and this is hardly surprising. Even the BBC have ensured that personal files are closed for seventy years after the death of the employees concerned, not only for legal reasons, but because recruitment into what were in their day the most lucrative and prestigious appointments was often based on unavowable personal connections. In Hollis's case it has even been suggested that he owed his recruitment to a masonic influence. He is supposed to have joined a lodge in Shanghai. Then, through his father, a connection has been suggested with Sir Vernon Kell, the veteran Director General of MI5, who is also said to have been a mason. Today the very idea that freemasonry would be permitted to exist in an organisation acutely conscious of the need for "positive vetting" of anyone having binding loyalties to any outside organisation would be absurd. In addition, the wider spread of university education and the general fading of late-Victorian superstition and Edwardian snobbery would reduce to non-existent proportions the number of recruits who would see "the masons" as anything more than a harmless joke. In Hollis's day masonry was still taken seriously in some quarters, and Peter Wright records in *Spycatcher* his father's conviction that his son would never get on in MI5 unless he "joined." In Hollis's case the fact that his family denied that he was ever in any lodge seems to settle the matter.

A more plausible reason for Sir Vernon Kell's interest in Hollis as a potential recruit was that he also had spent part of his early days in China where he had been an intelligence officer at the time of the Boxer Rebellion. Hollis's experiences would have interested him greatly not least because he too had suffered a breakdown in his health while in China, which had affected his career.

On the question of Hollis's background, a colleague of his has been quoted as saying, anonymously under the present state of the law in England:

> If he learned that Hollis's father was a bishop, that would almost make Hollis home and dry for a job. Not that I am suggesting that Hollis wasn't a sound choice, but simply that Kell tended to think on those lines.

This leaves aside the delicate question of whether Kell actually knew Hollis's father. Kell was a deeply religious man and had many contacts at all levels in the established church, while not looking any too favourably on Roman Catholics. But this is to pry too closely into the establishment's secrets: the family have drawn a veil over this side of things simply remarking that an original introduction was obtained through Hollis's wife's family. No doubt this was so, but once made the initial enquiries into Hollis's application would have revealed his favourable pedigree. Later we will look at the appointment as it must have seemed from Hollis's point of view, and those of his family and friends with whom he could have discussed the new career he was about to take up.

After his recruitment into MI5 any strict biographical treatment of Hollis becomes impossible. But, just as a biographer can find out a good deal about his subject from the books he read and what he said about them, so we can follow Hollis in his MI5 career by looking at the spies he was meant to be investigating. While their activities were secret, MI5 had to deal with other Government departments, especially the Foreign Office, and, with the influx of German refugees from Nazi persecution, any of whom might be Communists, it was highly likely that MI5 reports would appear in open FO files for the war years. A search of relevant files has confirmed this. As the weeders who examine files before they go to the Public Record Office either had no general instruction to remove MI5 letters or simply failed to recognize them, it is possible to gain a good understanding of what Hollis was doing as he worked his way through the world of spies.

4
The Red Menace –
MI5's Best Man

THE fear of secret Communist activity, the red menace, of the kind that produced McCarthyism has also appeared in Britain and with almost as strong an effect. Winston Churchill himself, in the early twenties, filled the Albert Hall with a "kick out the reds" campaign which he must have looked back on with wry amusement during the war. But these periods have usually alternated with others when the red menace seemed less important. Hollis joined MI5 at such a time. A few years earlier Anthony Eden, British Foreign Secretary, had given the speech that welcomed Russia into the League of Nations. Then the Spanish civil war and the popular front movements had swung a mass of intellectuals from the older universities over to a left view of the world, many becoming Communists themselves. This was the environment which created Burgess, Blunt, and the others.

Like the FBI in America, Britain's MI5 wanted recruits with a knowledge of Communism, and Hollis's experiences, which it seems he did discuss with his future employers if only in a misleading way, would have been welcome. The fact that he came from an older generation, and did not talk of Spain and the International Brigade as other young recruits with a knowledge of Communism were inclined to do, was an even better recommendation.

He could be seen as a budding expert in a difficult area who knew the field but had not himself been contaminated in any way. This line of reasoning perhaps explains what would at the time have been an unusual choice for MI5, however good Hollis's introduction was.

A reader brought up on nothing but today's spy books, factual or fictional, with their seemingly endless allegations about infiltration of the security services, might be forgiven for thinking that MI5 in the middle years of the century was so infiltrated that it could almost be seen as a Communist cell in itself. The perception of this organisation, once so secret that an ordinary citizen would never even have heard of it, was somewhat different at the time, as an intriguing remark made by Kingsley Martin, editor of the *New Statesman*, shows:

> It happened that I was able to meet at a friend's house one of the top people in MI5. From the beginning he was ready to listen to the argument that the communists would in the long run be allied in the war while the fascists were a potential fifth column. He told me that he had the utmost difficulty in persuading his staff that the fascists were the people to watch and sometimes arrest and he constantly had to correct idiotic, trivial persecution of the left.

We may wonder who the very insecure senior MI5 officer was who so obviously enjoyed pulling Kingsley Martin's leg (no very difficult thing to do). But it can be seen that the normal image of MI5 was of an organisation of the right, perhaps of the far right, no doubt thronged with ex-Indian policemen who saw Communists behind every lamp-post. There is no denying that there had indeed been a preponderance of ex-India men and views in the earlier MI5 and MI6, but the recruitment of Hollis as an expert on Communism shows that things were no longer what they had been. With the war the influx of recruits to both branches of the secret service took delight in decrying these people whose perception of the world was somehow linked to that expected of a "pukka sahib."

In fact, as we noticed in the early activities of Agnes Smedley in

China, as she organised material for Indian Communist front organisations, India was one of the Comintern's most important targets, and from before the war right up to present-day Afghanistan the Indian Communist party itself has been by far the most loyal to Moscow of any Communist party outside Russia. The international endeavours of the Comintern aimed at India included the activities of exiled Indians living in America, some of whom took part in clandestine broadcasts to India from San Francisco, causing the Indian authorities considerable annoyance. As a result far from being old fogeys sipping tea and reminiscing about their earlier pig-sticking days, the ex-Indian policemen in MI5 and MI6 were great experts on International Communism in all its facets. The atmosphere in which Blunt, Guy Liddell, Hollis, Burgess and the others flourished marked a change very much for the worse and was an important reason why the "moles," as they came to be called, prospered. It has often been said that after Russia entered the war in 1941 it was understandably difficult to distinguish people who were supporting a gallant ally from spies. But the infiltration, or leftward slant, of MI5 began earlier. Kingsley Martin's story, besides revealing the prevailing image of MI5 as ultra-right, also suggests that there may well have been a senior figure who was responsible for this left inclination that proved so damaging.

It has been alleged, notably by Chapman Pincher, that Hollis held such a central position at the time that he personally prevented action being taken against known Communists. This seems unlikely in the early stages of the war, at least when MI5's duties were plainly set out for them in terms of making recommendations for the detention of suspect aliens under the Emergency Powers regulations. There were a number of people whom the Communist Party would have liked protected, if possible, but who were detained, such as Hans Kahle, whom we shall meet later, and the Kuczynskis, who were all open Communists. But there were also people like zu Putlitz and Klaus Fuchs who were not known officially as Communists and whose detention Hollis might perhaps have been thought able to prevent. In reality there is little he could have done, because the recommendations for detention were so numerous and his staff were working so intensely that he could not have disagreed with their recommendations without drawing attention to himself.

Mention of those who were not officially known as Communists raises a question that will be seen as vital to an understanding of exactly what it was that Hollis *was* able to do. Although some were "officially" not known to be Communists—that is, did not appear on MI5 lists of those with known affiliations—Hollis had a ready cross-check to hand that would enable him to realise their true allegiances immediately. This was his file on Cockburn. It is worth noting some of the names that Hollis would have known about if his file on Cockburn was even tolerably complete. First in importance at the time was zu Putlitz, a German diplomat who had been spying for the British and done valuable service before escaping in 1940, just in time, from Belgium, coming to England with the help of Klop Ustinov (father of the actor Peter Ustinov). Zu Putlitz was a close friend of Burgess's and also of Blunt's to whom he owed a great deal and whom indeed he specifically thanked in his autobiography published after the war in East Germany. Much has been written of Putlitz by Glees and others. What has not been pointed out is that his oldest English friend was Claud Cockburn, who had met him first in 1926 in Germany, then in 1929 in America and then again in Britain. Secondly, there was a long-term friend of Cockburn's who had often travelled with him on journalistic assignments in Europe, Sefton Delmer. Delmer wrote an autobiography in two volumes which describes in detail his view of the world and the part he played in arranging black radio propaganda from Britain during the war. We shall be examining it in a later chapter; but it is worth notice here that it has been argued that Delmer was in fact a Communist agent. His close connection with Cockburn lasted at least until the sixties when both took a strong interest in a weekly publication, written much in the spirit of *The Week*, called *Private Eye*.

Among the Germans who would have appeared in Cockburn's file the most important was perhaps Hans Kahle. Cockburn first met Kahle in Spain where he was commanding a detachment of German volunteers in the International Brigade. He met him again when he escaped to England after the failure of the Communist campaign in Spain, and may have been the person who introduced him to the prominent scientist J. B. S. Haldane and his wife Charlotte. The Haldanes acted as his sponsors and protectors as far as they could until he was detained under the Emergency Powers Act and deported to Canada, where he became friendly with Klaus Fuchs. On his return Cockburn and Haldane welcomed Kahle back and saw him installed as the official military correspondent of the *Daily Worker*.

Cockburn was also a close friend of the Kuczynski family, being particularly close to Jürgen Kuczynski who was instrumental in putting Klaus Fuchs in contact with the GRU network, led by his sister "Sonia," which ran him as a spy when he was in England. We shall see more of this group and their activities shortly, but it is worth repeating here that Sonia had been in China at the same time as Hollis; if they ever met there, it would be interesting to know how soon it was before they discovered their mutual friend. Indeed if Cockburn was in contact with Sonia in China he might have arranged an introduction from around the world, courtesy of the Comintern. Such speculations, however, at this stage belong to the wilderness of mirrors. What is clear is that Cockburn's file, which as we shall see definitely recorded his membership in the Comintern, could well also have shown his link with Sonia Kuczynski and certainly would have mentioned his friendships with the other more publicly distinguished members, notably the father Professor Robert Kuczynski who was privileged to have a campaign started for his release when he was detained under 18B led by none other than D. N. Pritt.

Perhaps the most important person in this group connected through their friendship with Cockburn, if not also through their membership of the Communist Party and secret activity as GRU agents, was Peter Smollett. In his biography of Philby, *Philby: The Life and Views of a KGB Masterspy*, Philip Knightley describes Philby unequivocally as "the most successful penetration agent ever." Without disputing the title, anyone looking closely at the achievements of Peter Smollett, known before his naturalisation as H. P. Smolka, would have to concede that here at least was a worthy competitor for it.

Born in Vienna in 1912, Smolka became a journalist in the Central European mould on which Cockburn, Philby and the others modelled themselves. He first came to England as correspondent of the *Neue Freie Presse* of Vienna, later switching to the *Prager Presse*. In the summer of 1936 he went to Siberia at the invitation of the Soviet Government after meeting Professor O. Y. Schmidt, Chairman of the North Sea Route Administration that dealt with Siberia, at the Soviet Embassy in London. Later he amusingly recounted how he had first called in error at the house next door to the Soviet Embassy, then the London home of the Rothschilds, and had been directed to the correct address by their butler. Siberia then meant labour camps and the hard truths of real life in Russia under the Stalinist regime which was growing ever more oppressive, at least as far as the propaganda war was concerned. Smollett saw Siberia as it appeared to the Russians, a wild frontier where great strides were being made in exploration and scientific research, of all of which they were clearly proud.

On his return Smollett had no difficulty placing his articles in *The Times*, unlike the unfortunate Hollis. Smollett had great success. His articles appeared regularly and were later published in expanded form as a book, *Forty Thousand Against the Arctic: Russia's Polar Empire*. Precisely how he got his introductions is not clear, although Sir Harry Brittain seems to have been of considerable help. That the contacts existed at the highest level is obvious from his next major venture, in 1938: the setting up of a press agency in Europe. Rex Leeper at the Foreign Office press department, which we have already come across in reference to Peter Fleming, seems to have known him well, judging by the letters sent to him about the project. On 16 November he wrote to Leeper, "I have pleasure in informing you that I have now joined the Exchange Telegraph Company to be in charge of the newly organised foreign Department," signing himself "Smolka-Smollet," a hybrid name he briefly adopted on his naturalisation, which occurred at this time. His next letter, on 23 November, was more to the point, confirming that he was setting out to visit Prague, Warsaw, Budapest, Bucharest, Belgrade and Berne to establish contact on behalf of the

new Exchange Telegraph foreign agency. He then made an astonishingly bold request:

> I would be much obliged if you would kindly inform his Maj-
> esty's representatives in the capitals concerned of my forth-
> coming visit. I would appreciate an opportunity of discussing
> with them the local press situation and particularly the ques-
> tion of how straight news from this country stands in relation
> to the tainted propaganda there put out by other official and
> semi-official agencies.

Leeper obligingly sent out a Foreign Office telegram, repeated to
all the relevant departments, giving Smollett, as he was now
known, *carte blanche:* "The author who is well known to this Department has achieved a considerable reputation as a writer in International affairs . . ." Smollett had ended his letter with a
personal plea: "I should be most grateful to you for securing a good
entrée for me with the British Diplomatic Missions . . ." and
Leeper could not have done more for the young man, still only 26
years of age. It was a coup which even Philby would have been
proud of and, since he was apparently involved in Smollett's various news agency ventures, Philby no doubt admired him greatly for
it. The idea of a Soviet agent going around the capitals of Europe
with full accreditation from the British authorities puts the struggles of MI6 and Dansey's vaunted secret section X at the same time
in a salutary perspective. If there was any doubt about the British
commitment to Smollett it was soon to be put to the test, for he and
his wife were among those who took refuge in the British legation
in Prague after Hitler entered the city in 1939. The story of their
escape, in company with Otto Strasser and other anti-Nazi leaders,
has still to be told. Most remained in Europe but the Smolletts
went straight back to London where they resumed their highly
successful career. Smollett was destined for one of the most influential positions of all, the Soviet Desk at the wartime Ministry of
Information, a post obtained for him through the personal introduction of the Minister, Brendan Bracken himself.

Collectively these people represent a group of agents, not previously identified, who succeeded as well as the agents who have so preoccupied the molehunters and spy authors until now. Smollett's own position was one of such eminence that it might be suggested that he could have acted as an umbrella sheltering the others, and this umbrella could be yet another reason why the other spies were not seen as such by MI5 at the time or later. However, Hollis must have fully understood who these people were and their allegiances. Their most public face was that seen, as might be expected, at the evening receptions held by Maisky, the Russian Ambassador. Colleagues of Burgess's at the BBC recall vividly that these were the most important social functions he attended and he never missed one. The simplest check by MI5 officers or Special Branch on those entering and leaving would have given the identities of all the people in Cockburn's circle, had it not been readily available from the phone taps and bugs in the Soviet Embassy and the *Daily Worker* offices.

While it is a fact the only one of the group who either knew or had contact with Cockburn and was not detained was zu Putlitz, this was not because of anything that Hollis was able to do. Information that has recently come to light in the Canadian National Archives has provided an exact account of how zu Putlitz was got out of Britain through the personal intervention of "C," the head of MI6, with Lord Vansittart. In May 1940 Vansittart approached the Canadian authorities in London about the finding of possible places of safety for certain Germans in Canada. Zu Putlitz was one. Otto Strasser, then in Lisbon and a particular concern of "C"'s, seemingly because of light he might be able to throw on the failed attempt on Hitler's life in the Bürgerbräu bomb plot, was another. In a report from Washington on zu Putlitz the Canadian official responsible, W. C. Hankinson, gave a full account of the background:

> In May 1940 I was approached by Lord Vansittart and zu Putlitz himself with a suggestion that Putlitz should be allowed to proceed to Canada, since the time approached when all able-bodied Germans would be subject to general internment . . . I did not pass this suggestion on to Ottawa since he

had no friends there, instead I proposed to Vansittart that he
should make arrangements for zu Putlitz to go to a West Indian
Isle and this was carried out . . .

It is clear from this that all Vansittart's attempts to have a special
case made out for zu Putlitz, despite his services for MI6 as an
agent, were of no avail, and he would have been detained if he had
not gone to the West Indies. Clearly Hollis in MI5 could make no
case for any of the Germans he might have wanted to protect, such
as zu Putlitz, when nothing could be done even at this much higher
level.

That Hollis could not help zu Putlitz and the others does not
mean either that he would have been without value simply as an
agent. He was in a position to report to any controller he might
have had just how closely MI5 was able to follow Communist
activity in the trade union movement, where they were doing everything they could to impede the war effort, especially during the
Battle of Britain when aircraft factories were plagued with strikes
and disruptions of all kinds. In March 1940, for example, MI5 came
into possession of some minutes of an unofficial shop stewards'
movement and their "Manifesto of the Provisional Committee of
the Aircraft and Engineering Shop Stewards National Council."
The political line being followed was that the war was an imperi-
alist war and that every step should be taken to bring about peace.
The background policy was that of "revolutionary defeatism" ad-
vocated by Lenin in 1917.

Only rarely does action appear to have been taken against the
individuals responsible. What happened in one case, that of a shop
steward called William Mason, suggests why. Mason had been
found by his workmates sticking up a poster demanding immediate
peace. They had taken him into custody while the police were
called, who then decided to hold him for his own protection until
it was established whether he was guilty of an offence under the
Emergency Powers regulations. It appeared that he was, and Mason was sent to London from his workplace in the Midlands. He
had gone a long way through the process that would have led to his
permanent detention under 18B when his case was taken up by the

Communist Party whose man he was. In a matter of days pamphlets appeared demanding Mason's release, with graphic accounts of his long service to the cause of the working man and world peace generally. Allegations of harsh treatment hovered in the background. Mason was released. We have noted that similar campaigns were run by Pritt against the detention of the Kuczynskis; but there the case was easier to understand, for those concerned were after all refugees from the Nazis. It is clear that Hollis in MI5 could have done little to affect matters one way or the other, though he could have played down the extent of the movements. This would have been less and less easy, as we shall see, when the Communist Party went ahead with more positive campaigning through a major front organisation calling for a "people's peace," a natural extension of the "cause of peace" slogan used by Hollis in 1937.

The political tone changed with Hitler's conquest of the greater part of Europe in May 1940. MI5's veteran leader Kell was sacked, and a new security authority was set up called the Security Executive, which sat with Lord Swinton as its chairman, and was consequently often referred to as the Swinton Committee. MI5 had a seat on this committee later occupied by Hollis, but MI5's line, which was in fact perceived as favourable towards the left by the committee, was not always followed. In particular the Executive took a very objective view of the Communist Party. In this they were at odds both with MI5's line as followed by Hollis and the senior officer who spoke to Kingsley Martin, and with the Government's more open policy towards the Party and Russia which was being followed in the hope of splitting Russia from Germany. R. A. Butler had set the scene with a statement in the House of Commons in July 1940:

> The Policy of H. M. Government has been and remains to improve and strengthen the relations between this country and the USSR. Success in this policy has appeared more likely since March of this year when the USSR made a friendly approach to H. M. Government and proposed the resumption of trade negotiations . . . H. M. Government at once responded to this approach from the Soviet Government and it

is to be hoped that the discussions which H. M. Ambassador in Moscow is at present engaged in may finally remove any danger which may have been apprehended that the Soviet Government would work either economically or militarily against Britain in the interests of Germany.

The Security Executive were of course aware of this policy, but they were also aware that any action of the Soviet Union could be taken as an attempt to lull Britain into a false sense of security for the benefit of their ally, Germany. They were particularly aware that, though Butler had mentioned Russia's possible economic and military roles, nothing was said about political warfare. One of their earliest actions was to commission a report on the activity of the Communist Party in the trade unions, and MI5 duly sent in all they had on the shop stewards' committees. No doubt they pointed out, as they always did, that the evidence they had could not be produced in a court of law, and the public outcry which had been engendered when Mason was detained showed that chaos and perhaps a general breakdown of public order would result from wider action. Detention of the leading officers of Sir Oswald Mosley's British Union Party, countrywide, had resulted in the detention of 1800 men, with no steps taken to ensure that their families would be looked after. There would be many times that number if the trade union extremists and CPGB members were detained.

The Security Executive were obliged to accept the validity of these propositions. However, on one question they took a strong line, and that was over the two publications put out by the Communist Party of Great Britain, the *Daily Worker* and *The Week*, which was supposedly run by Cockburn as an independent news sheet. The *Daily Worker* was by far the worse offender. Never once did it give even the slightest support to the war effort. Anyone who read it at the time who was not a regular reader would have been astounded that it was not suppressed, or at the very least prosecuted for sedition. The Security Executive took this view themselves and repeatedly asked MI5 for information which would enable them to prosecute the proprietors, who included J. B. S. Haldane and the "Red Dean," Hewlett Johnson. But the officer in MI5 responsible for the *Worker* persistently said that he could provide no evidence that would stand up in court, thus blocking any action. When the paper was finally suppressed, in circumstances which will be described in the next chapter, the officer concerned was actually named. He was Roger Hollis.

The possibility of there being any misunderstanding about Hollis's actions here—that he was acting under a general policy directive, for example, or that his superiors might have been the guilty party—is removed by an incident which took place in 1940 over a particularly offensive *Daily Worker* editorial.

The Security Executive sent a strong request to Brigadier Harker, who was then running MI5, requesting *immediate* action and the production of substantial evidence that would clinch the case, since the article concerned was blatantly seditious. Harker in reply gave details of why he could not be of any assistance and why nothing was being done:

> I have not discussed with the Police or the Director the possibility of such prosecution [of the *Daily Worker* for sedition] but the attached file relating to the case of Claud Cockburn (840,119) is an illustration of the difficulties. It seems to me from that file that the police have very little information of a kind which could be produced in court as *evidence* about the secret machinations of the communist party.

The first thing to be noticed here is that in mentioning the Cockburn file Harker provides us with contemporary documentary evidence that Hollis was dealing with Cockburn's file at the time, since it was he who was dealing with the *Daily Worker* and must have submitted Cockburn's file to Harker. This is important, because until now all writers on the question have had to rely on statements from Peter Wright and others that it was so. There is as yet no contemporary evidence that Hollis kept the file in his own safe throughout the war years, as Wright and the other Fluency Committee members maintain and has not been disputed, although such evidence could easily come to light as research in the Public Record Office proceeds. It is quite sufficient, for the general case

76

against Hollis, to know that it was in fact he who dealt with Cockburn's file and with the *Daily Worker* and its sister news sheet *The Week*, and that it was he and he alone who was preventing action being taken against them. At the same time he was protecting Cockburn. The only obvious explanation for Harker's view was that Hollis was using Cockburn as an agent or that his information was being obtained from someone close to him, or by some illegal means such as a phone tap, but this is unlikely.

Although we do not have the Cockburn file itself, and if it still exists it will almost certainly have been weeded, we do have an abstract of its entry for Cockburn prepared by Hollis as part of a general history of the CPGB. The Security Executive requested this and then copied it to Washington in exchange for a similar history of the Communist Party in America. It has been released in the National Archives in Washington. It was prepared in late 1940 after the difficulty over prosecution of the *Daily Worker* and should therefore be a good guide to how Cockburn was seen by Hollis and how Hollis wanted him to be seen by the Security Executive:

> *Claud Cockburn* is pre-eminent among those staff members [who assisted the editor William Rust] and serves as diplomatic correspondent of the *Daily Worker* under the alias Frank Pitcairn. An Oxford graduate Cockburn was for a time Foreign Correspondent of *The Times* in the United States but later developed conscientious objections to working for a capitalist newspaper and resigned. He is a journalist of outstanding ability with a wide range of well placed contacts, and in addition to serving with the *Daily Worker* he publishes his own venture *The Week*, a confidential news-letter written in such a way as to conceal its affinity with the Communist Party. *The Week* is intended primarily to propagandise better educated circles than those reached by the usual communist literature. Cockburn follows the usual straight communist international line in Foreign Affairs, and with his experience has proved useful as an occasional representative on the Western European Bureau of the Comintern.

There is no trace here of anything other than a favourable verdict on Cockburn, with more than a hint that Hollis admired what his old university friend stood for. It is by far the most flattering entry in the report. If this genuinely represented Hollis's view it is hardly surprising that no action was taken and that the Communist Party grew confident enough to move their campaign from the factory floor and the columns of the *Daily Worker* and initiate a full-scale national movement with strong revolutionary overtones, appealing for a People's Government and a People's Peace.

5
January 1941 –
Britain's Failed
Revolution

A MERICA in the twentieth century has mercifully escaped two of the most serious threats that can confront a country—invasion from without, and violent revolution from within. In 1940 and early 1941 Britain faced both of these dangers in real earnest. Although the threat of invasion in 1940, the Battle of Britain, and the blitz that followed it have been written about extensively, the other danger, a shameful episode at a time when the majority of the nation were united under Churchill as they had never been before, has been entirely ignored. Predictably the revolution failed, but that it should have even started or, once begun, have been allowed to continue for months requires close investigation.

The Communist Party were at the centre of the attempt but since they were under close observation by MI5, in theory the movement should never have been possible. The main purpose of a political intelligence officer charged with overseeing Communist affairs in Britain, even when she was fighting a war against fascism, would be to see that no active revolutionary movement got under way. When Stalin's Russia, which had always been in the vanguard of the fight against fascism, signed the Nazi-Soviet pact in August 1939 and effectively made common cause with the

German Nazi Government, supervision of the Communists in Britain should have been all the more vital. Hollis, as the officer concerned, was fully aware of this, as he had already seen the liaison established between Russia and Chiang Kai Shek in China, a model, albeit of lesser significance, for the Nazi-Soviet pact. If a similar revolutionary movement were to be successfully established in Britain the European War, not then a world war, would clearly come to an end, with Germany and Russia the two main powers and Britain an island on the periphery with allegiance to Russia.

The astonishing chain of events which took place in Britain exactly along these lines culminated in a would-be revolutionary assembly which took place in London. Delegates representing over a million people were intent on bringing about a revolutionary change with a "People's Government" and a "People's Peace" passing motions which they hoped would start a movement parallel with that which had taken place in Russia in 1917. The movement was coordinated between Moscow and Berlin. Moscow dealt with propaganda on the ground, using as its principal organ the *Daily Worker*, with its political leader-writer Frank Pitcairn (that is, Claud Cockburn) steering the campaign's rhetoric, while Berlin produced related propaganda over the air which exactly complemented what was appearing in the *Daily Worker*, with appeals to the British to stop fighting and make a People's Peace.

In describing the movement that came to be known as the "People's Convention" it should be said from the outset that there were always people, such as George Orwell, who saw that it was nothing more than a cynical attempt fostered directly by Moscow in collaboration with Berlin to get Britain out of the war which, after Dunkirk, was effectively over. This view was held by many in the Labour and trade union movement and was expressed most vigorously in print in the left-wing paper *Tribune*, notably by Orwell and especially John Strachey who had lately split with his Communist colleagues and was able to describe in detail exactly what the policy of revolutionary defeatism meant and what the real purposes of the Communist Party were in launching the nominally independent

Convention movement. Orwell was never forgiven by the Communist Party or their sympathisers; it was at this time that rumours that he was working for the security services, recently confirmed by American sources, began to circulate. There is little doubt that the banning of *Animal Farm* by the Ministry of Information in 1944 was a by-product of this bitter struggle in 1940 seen in the columns of *Tribune* and the *Daily Worker*.

Although the rest of the press largely ignored the Convention movement, perhaps as a result of the censor's stops, Hollis and MI5 would have been quite sure that they were not alone in perceiving what was happening. With the natural divisions in British society other members of the Security Executive may well not have been aware of exactly how strong the movement was becoming until they saw posters on the streets. They would then have asked MI5—that is Hollis—what was going on. We cannot know the extent to which Hollis played down the significance of the movement, but the difficulty he made over the *Daily Worker* suggests that he would not have exaggerated what Cockburn and his colleagues were doing while preventing at all costs any move against their papers.

The first sign that the Communist Party of Great Britain intended to respond to Germany's victory in Europe and Britain's evacuation from Dunkirk by a major political campaign calling for a People's Peace came in an official Party statement published in the *Daily Worker* on 22 June 1940. Six days later William Gallagher, the Communist MP, expressed the opinion in the House of Commons that "the time has come for a complete reorganisation of the Government in the form of a People's Government." Then, on 7 July, at meetings at Holborn Town Hall and the Conway Hall, a committee with the slightly awkward title of "The People's Vigilance Committee" was set up to pursue aims almost identical with those of the Communist Party, though it was not officially stated that it was run by the Party. Its manifesto, *A Call to the People*, was written by D. N. Pritt who, as we have seen, was in the forefront of the movement to get key German Communist detainees freed. The appeal was cunningly worded to imply falsely that the com-

mittee had the support of the Labour Party in a tactic used right up
to the days of Harold Wilson:

> To those who are not socialists or members of the Labour
> Party the appeal is equally urgent. The old order is passing,
> after it has worked incalculable evil in this twentieth century,
> hitherto so tragic and murderous, yet possessing in its capacity
> for material progress as infinite promise of a freer and happier
> life for all. Let all men and women of all classes give their
> thought to the future, rally to this policy, and find their way
> out of tragedy into peace and prosperity.

There then followed a succinct summary of the statement issued in
the manifesto which was identical with the Communist manifesto
issued a few days previously: The Men of Munich must go; We
must be friends with the USSR; Our democratic rights and our
trade union conditions and practices must be restored and maintained; Our standard of living must be defended, and profiteering
must be stopped; We must have a People's Government and a
People's Peace.

A more demoralising programme in a country at war could not be
imagined. Yet much of it appeared to be echoed in Butler's speech,
already quoted, which was widely reported in the press at the time.
No doubt Hollis, responsible for monitoring Communist activity,
was duly recording all these facts and identifying the Communist
Party members, such as the chairman Harry Adams and the vice-
chairman W. J. R. Squance, who were running the organisation
under D. N. Pritt. If he was monitoring Cockburn's activity, or
using him as a source, he would have rapidly built up a picture of
the entire operation. If he did not know through these sources of
the involvement of Berlin in the programme, the MI5 officers who
censored the BBC's monitoring units' output in their daily *Summary of World Broadcasts* would soon have pointed out broadcasts
appealing for a People's Peace that exactly echoed the calls put out
in London, many on "black" stations such as "Workers Challenge"
purporting to be in England. Even Attlee was aware of the broadcasts and complained about them in a public speech.

A fierce correspondence ensued between him and D. N. Pritt which was published as part of a bitter pamphlet war, with the title *Another Lie Nailed: The Pritt-Attlee Letters*. This revealed that Pritt had been in communication with the enemy—both with supposedly "underground" Communists in Germany, whose letters he freely quoted, and with the German authorities, who denied that there had been any mention of the People's Convention in the German *press* within Germany—correctly, since the propaganda had been confined to their English-language radio stations, black and white. It is quite clear, as we shall see, that for six months nothing was done about the movement by the authorities, who let it run its course, no doubt lulled by Hollis's anodyne reports and his blocking of action against the *Daily Worker*, the campaign's mouthpiece.

With the wartime Party truce in operation, the conflict that rapidly developed around the People's Convention movement, as it was soon renamed, took on a much wider significance; it was the only movement which totally opposed the war at a time when Britain was at her lowest point. It is essential for an understanding of the background to Hollis's work in monitoring the Communist Party that we should examine the campaign in some detail. Many of the figures involved, such as Alan Nunn May, are to be found mentioned in the molehunters' analyses of Hollis's failings. The need for some account of these events is all the greater because they have been almost entirely neglected, although they rank among the most remarkable in modern British political history.

After Britain and Russia became allies, the whole episode became embarrassing to all sides: to the Communists because they had clearly been acting with Berlin to bring the war to a rapid end, to the right because any idea that a revolutionary movement could exist in modern Britain in whatever guise was anathema. None of the books on Hollis or the Soviet moles mentions the People's Convention movement at all, even though its supervision must have been the most important job that Hollis had at this time. That the Fluency Committee grilled Hollis about why he had not said that he knew Cockburn but did not even mention the movement suggests that MI5's files had been so thoroughly weeded by then that even they did not know what had happened in 1940 and 1941.

The first campaign seized on by the People's Convention was the question of bombing and the need for adequate shelters. Far from strengthening public morale under the severest trials it had ever experienced, the movement sought to break morale at every point. The advent of heavy bombing on London had long been anticipated by the Government; back in 1936 the Cabinet had believed that Mussolini would attempt a "mad dog" attack on London with his bomber squadrons, which had recently flown across the Atlantic to America. Yet no real thought had been given to such obvious expedients as the use of the tube tunnels as shelters. Immediately after the first raids Londoners took the law into their own hands and occupied key stations. The first was Elephant and Castle, followed by Chalk Farm, in what was described as the biggest working-class demonstration the capital had ever seen.

The Communist Party, in collaboration with the People's Convention organisers, set up so-called "deep shelter committees" using J. B. S. Haldane, a pioneer of concern on Air Raid Precaution, as spokesman, with Nunn May a main supporter. Haldane is now known to have been used as a GRU agent right through the war. When this was revealed in *Spycatcher* many of his family and friends denied that this was possible; his activities shown here reveal his political views beyond doubt. Genuine shelter committees which had sprung into existence were taken over by the Communists in what were sometimes violent struggles. Claud Cockburn unhesitatingly followed the Party line with malicious allegations to inflame public protest, remarking in *The Week:* "The deep shelter committees have been broken up by gangsters hired for the purpose, with complaints to the Police proving of no avail . . ." He proceeded to report at length a rumour that a child had been crushed to death in a stampede for one of the shelters, claiming that the authorities had deliberately hushed up this and similar deaths. When it was pointed out that no child had been reported missing, he replied:

> Since there are no coroner's inquests on air-raid casualties and since scores of children unattended from many areas of London run wild in and around the shelter in question, like the

"homeless children" of the Russian revolution, this evidence, or lack of it, is less strong than it would have been in peace time.

Every article that Cockburn wrote at this time was preoccupied with the possibility of immediate revolution on the streets of the capital. They were the worst kind of sedition at a time when the morale of the British people was being tested as never before. Cockburn has been seen in later years as a "character" whose eccentricities were to be tolerated. The reality was that his activities at this time rank among the most offensive in the history of British journalism and he did not scruple even to run disguised pro-Nazi propaganda at the behest of his Soviet masters in the Comintern. A particularly unsavoury example occurred in 1940 over the Polish question. The Vatican had delivered to the British Government by secret means the first detailed dossier of Nazi atrocities in Poland; this had been published both as a book and as innumerable details in British propaganda stories. In order to counteract this, Cockburn published a story that the Vatican was secretly negotiating with Hitler to establish a new closer concordat.

The story was widely believed and was yet another instance of the Communist Party playing the anti-Catholic card which, as they had early learned, was invaluable in dealing with certain sections of the English establishment. This kind of exploitation of social prejudices was one that required the most detailed knowledge of what people thought and did, and explains the thirst for "gossip" which has puzzled many observers of the activity of Communist agents. Hollis, reading all this as he updated Cockburn's file, if he was doing his job, must have been taken back to the very similar activities of the Communists in China. There was a particular parallel in their infiltration of the student movements in China which he had remarked on then in letters to his parents. It was repeated in Britain in 1940. The situation in Cambridge, for example, the home of the so-called "ring of five spies," was particularly interesting both in showing how the People's Convention worked and the point at which the University authorities were forced into action. After initial pamphleteering and word-of-mouth propaganda a meeting was arranged for a large body of undergraduates to be held at the Dorothy Café, much frequented by left-wing students. It was to be addressed by D. N. Pritt. But two hours before he was due to speak the owner was forced to tell the student organisers that he could not allow it to go ahead.

A protest demonstration went to the Proctors, who had apparently been responsible, and made vigorous protest. In giving their reasons for not allowing the meeting to proceed, they pointed out the dangers of a disturbance and said that their primary concern was "that they were unwilling to allow members of the University to lay themselves open to prosecution under the defence regulations." This phrase strongly suggests the intervention of the security services, through the Special Branch no doubt, for such a specific reason could not have been given in those words unless in fact they had been informed that direct demonstration against the war and for peace at the meeting would be taken as an infringement of the Emergency Powers regulations.

Soon after the main Convention meeting in London, in January 1941, a meeting was organised by the Cambridge Undergraduate Council at the Guildhall on the topic "The Freedom of Speech in War." Prominent among the speakers, and one of the principal organisers, was Raymond Williams, at that time secretary of the Union Society, who revealed that the authorities had gone beyond banning the Dorothy Café meeting by suggesting that it would be in "good taste" if the Union Society ceased its world-famous debates for the duration of hostilities.

Overt action of the kind which appears to have been taken by the security authorities here is interesting in showing that they were fully aware of what was going on, no doubt informed by Hollis and his colleagues. It could be said that, while prepared to let a genuine political movement run its course in the public arena, they could not be seen to allow any continental or Chinese-style student disturbances to develop, particularly as many of those involved would shortly become officers in the armed forces.

Another central plank in a genuine revolutionary movement was, of course, strong support for industrial workers and a strong base in all factory committees and union movements. It was here that

Tribune and other Labour papers took their firmest stand. At first their policy was to ignore the Convention movement, but correspondence began to come in from workers. This letter from a Durham miner is perhaps typical:

> I see you are declining to make further comment on the Communist controlled "People's Convention." Perhaps you are justified in London but in several other places people are being fooled by it and I wish you would print the circular which the Durham Miners Association has sent out which puts the matter quite plainly.

The most characteristic complaint was that individual union members, often senior officials, would put themselves forward as delegates to the Convention when their unions were unaware of it or disapproved of it. The organising secretary of the Convention, who in real terms ran it, Arthur Horner, President of the South Wales Miners Federation, was the most obvious example. *Tribune* pointed out that the Union had not backed the Convention and had actually voted against involvement. The *Daily Worker* took the other view, and clearly thought that revolution was indeed about to break out. *The Week* echoed this in Cockburn's best style:

> The first sporadic opposition in the factories has also gained enormously both in strength and cohesion and is expressing itself in support of the now famous five point programme of the People's Convention. The character of the support ranging from shop-stewards of virtually every important aircraft factory to leading artists and musicians leaves no doubt of the breadth and depth of the opposition [to the war] that has gathered and is gathering. It is clear from the character of the press attacks and other attacks upon the People's Convention Movement that the industrialists are above all alarmed at the strength of the "drive" developing on the wages issue . . . it is essential from the viewpoint of the industrialists to interfere drastically with . . . some form of compulsion in industry.

There are signs here of a leak, for industrial conscription was indeed being considered at this time and seems to have been one of the positive steps taken by the Government to deal with the possibility of industrial unrest, if not revolution, of whose strength in the absence of normal political processes they only had anecdotal evidence.

We have mentioned the German radio broadcasts in English supposedly being put out by stations operating illegally in Britain. It has been suggested that few people listened to these stations, the main one being "Workers Challenge." But evidence that they were listened to, and that their line was very close to that of the People's Convention, has been found in accounts by one of the few radio reporters to mention these broadcasts, Fred Harold in *Tribune*. The myth of the BBC's unbroken record of broadcasting with undiminished strength throughout the blitz cut no ice with him:

> I tried to get the BBC 9 o'clock News in London last night. It was almost impossible to get or hear when got, in fact I gave it up. But on the Medium waveband no less than FIVE Nazi or Nazi-controlled radio stations were coming in at full strength all the time.

He also gave a clear idea of how close the radio stations were to each other in content, with hints on how to tell one from the other:

> Now that Goebbels runs his "Workers Challenge" radio station it is exceedingly difficult to separate one propaganda from another. They borrow each other's phrases without hesitation. I have found only two litmus tests which are still valid. The Fascist will bring in spite against the jew sooner or later whereas the Communist will not. The Communist will speak of Russia and Stalin with a sort of religious reverence which can immediately be recognised and separated from the sort of uneasy evasiveness with which the fascist deals with the subject.

With such determined propaganda it is hardly surprising that the organisers of the People's Convention, and even more their naïver followers, thought that they really were taking part in the build-up to what would be a turning point in British history.

The Convention when it finally happened was a complete anticlimax. No revolution broke out and the authorities took only relatively few steps, which effectively guarded against all possible dangers. Celebrities on the platform beside D. N. Pritt and the other leaders included Beatrix Lehmann and J. B. S. Haldane. Also present were the future Prime Minister of India, Mrs. Gandhi, and Krishna Menon. (The presence of the last two cannot necessarily be taken to represent any commitment to the Communist cause.) For the most part the audience appear uninspired and more curious than militant. They look like the sort of people who, if there had been no party truce, would probably have attended any fringe party political meeting.

The bland reality did not prevent Claud Cockburn from describing the meeting in terms which were almost certainly the cause of the closing down of the *Daily Worker* and his own paper. A study of the photograph taken at the Convention does not reveal a single soldier in uniform. This did not deter Cockburn's ringing account of events following on the Convention:

> What is the biggest event this week? You may have your own notions about it, but I think this. I think that the biggest event this week is the fact that in 56 different barracks and camps of the Army men are gathering together to listen to their delegates—their soldiers' delegates—reporting to them on the proceedings at the People's Convention, and at the same time those soldiers were meeting . . . scores, hundreds of thousands of workers not in uniform were doing the same thing or preparing to do it in all the great factories of the mighty warmachine of Britain.

A classic example, no doubt, of wishful thinking, but quite sufficient for the Security Executive finally to lose patience at such obvious incitement and to arrange for the paper to be suppressed within twenty-four hours. The file on the decision to suppress the paper shows without doubt that Hollis was the MI5 officer dealing with the case. The Security Executive made their report to the war cabinet, which on the same day issued the relevant instructions:

> The War Cabinet, having decided that the *Daily Worker* [and *The Week*] should be suppressed the Secretary of State [Herbert Morrison] made an order under Emergency Powers Regulation 2D. The procedure had previously been discussed with Mr. Canning, Mr. Hollis of MI5, Mr. Innes of the Lord Advocates Department and the relevant orders and notices were drafted.

It is natural to ask, in view of Hollis's undisclosed friendship with Cockburn, whether he attempted to warn him beforehand in any way. There is in fact direct evidence that there was some prior warning, described by Patricia Cockburn in *The Years of The Week*. After explaining that the issue of *The Week* which was banned had been mild compared with the normal issues, and that it had been concerned with affairs in the United States, Ireland and Chile, she continues:

> Rather absurdly as things turned out, the editor [her husband, Claud Cockburn] had allowed himself to be persuaded by friends in high places that a couple of innocuous issues of the paper would save it. In reality the decision to suppress it had been taken a considerable time before. The issue of 15 January was seized by the Police before it could appear and was banned.

In fact, as we have seen, the decision to suppress the paper was taken within twenty-four hours, in the face of opposition from Hollis at MI5 who was still, no doubt, putting forward Cockburn's file as a reason why no action could be taken. If there is any truth in the suggestion that the Cockburns had been warned by "friends" in high places that action might be taken against them, it is difficult to see who it could possibly have been other than Hollis himself. If Hollis kept the Cockburn file under lock and key it was not available to others in MI5. They, in any case, would not have been following the affair in detail, which would have been essential if a timely warning was to be delivered. Hollis must have realised that there was a risk that the *Daily Worker* would be suppressed. This could not be avoided if the Convention meeting had anything like a success. But he may have hoped to get a stay of execution on *The Week*, which was particularly valuable as a propaganda weapon aimed at the literati and upper-middle classes, whose naïvety was such that they failed to notice the Communist policies behind its flippant tone. In any event Hollis's failure to disclose his friendship with Cockburn at this serious juncture is most damaging for his case.

Anyone looking at photographs of the People's Convention can see that the meeting was by any proper "revolutionary" standards a failure unless it was going to be a particularly quiet "English" revolution. Despite Cockburn's boasting about soldiers going back to their barracks in the "1917" spirit there was nothing resembling this to be seen. The closure of the *Daily Worker* and *The Week* and the general clamp-down that this initiated was sufficient to quell whatever life there was in the movement, despite the fact that the various sub-committees of the Convention continued in action. Nor was any member of the Communist Party or any other person detained under the Emergency Powers regulations. This was particularly noticeable over the suppression of the *Daily Worker*, since the only other paper to be suppressed in the war, the British Union paper *Action*, had seen its staff detained wholesale, including ordinary employees of the printers who had no connection whatever with the paper's political controllers. The most drastic action taken overall seems to have been Bevin's introduction of industrial conscription. Whether this could be directly attributed to a need to cope with the success of the Convention movement among the organised workers through the shop stewards' movement is open to question. Although Arthur Horner and his comrades were well known, their activities were also well understood. The British Labour movement generally had come to know the methods of Communist infiltration only too well. But even if there was no link it would have served as a timely reminder to those attracted to the idea of a People's Peace that the country was in fact at war and was going to remain at war until victory was achieved.

The most amusing post-script to the whole affair was provided by Cockburn himself:

> With no papers to work for I felt as if I had been suddenly castrated. I worked irritably and ineffectively as a sort of Public Relations and Press Officer for the congeries of loud-mouthed committees called the People's Convention. I detest committees, conferences and public speaking, and since the People's Convention involved a non-stop experience of all three I used sometimes to wonder at that period whether I had died without noticing it and was in hell for my sins.

What had undoubtedly died was any possible concern for the truth on Cockburn's part, for despite his close involvement in every stage of the movement, right down to his article in the final issue of the *Daily Worker*, he makes no mention of his role in the affair other than a comic account of the actual suppression.

When the Official Report of the Convention came to be published, an anti-climax if ever there was one, there was an amusing echo of Hollis's earlier experiences in China, for one of the messages of support read out at the Convention was from Mao Tse Tung:

> The great Chinese People have experienced three and a half years of heroic war of liberation and will continue with ever more solidarity fighting and crushing Japanese Imperialism and its lackeys for a new democratic country. Hoping for a strengthening of international militant solidarity between the British and Chinese peoples.

The statement had been cabled from Chunking and must therefore have gone through the censorship, when it would have been reported to Hollis in the usual way. No doubt he would have agreed with every word. Although its militant note would not have chimed in with the Convention's appeal for a People's Peace, it shows how close the Chinese Communist line was to that which was to be established when Britain and Russia joined forces after the German invasion of Russia, and to Hollis's publicly expressed line before the war. Appropriately the Convention movement was wound up the morning after the invasion.

There has been considerable discussion about Stalin's apparent ignoring of Churchill's warnings that Hitler was about to invade Russia. Churchill had his information from intercepted German communications and, in view of the subsequent debacle, it has seemed entirely plausible to believe that Stalin stubbornly refused to listen to him until the very last moment. In fact matters were not as simple as that. Files in the Public Record Office establish that D. N. Pritt, still leader of the People's Convention movement, was closely involved in moves by Stalin to avert what was only too plainly about to break upon him.

Butler's speech, quoted earlier, pointed the way to stronger trade between Britain and Russia, and that approach developed in the months following. But there were stumbling blocks. Principal among them was the position of the Baltic states and Turkey. Stafford Cripps in Moscow had failed completely to come to terms with Stalin on these and other matters and was cordially hated there. Stalin knew that things had rapidly gone to the bad between himself and Germany from the beginning of 1941, although it is not clear whether his failure to deliver the promised revolution in Britain had any direct connection with this. He had been obliged to build up his troop concentrations on the German border, and the Germans had built up theirs. In a final desperate move he tried to deal directly with Churchill in London, using as an indirect route D. N. Pritt, who in turn approached Anthony Eden through Sir Walter Monckton. Russia frequently resorted to unofficial approaches of this kind rather than more formal diplomatic moves, and the use of such channels did not stop with the death of Stalin. A seeming attempt to use John Profumo, the ill-fated Minister of War in Macmillan's government at the time of the Berlin and Cuban missile crises, was to cause an acute crisis of a different kind as will be seen at the conclusion here.

The detailed points Pritt made, embodying in precise diplomatic terms the exact situation vis-à-vis the three parties, were an attempt to use every possible argument to show that, whereas Britain, and Churchill, were convinced that a German invasion of

Russia was unavoidable, Russia did not think so. Indeed Stalin was convinced that, if only Britain and Russia could come to terms in the matter of the Baltic states, a question of disputed gold and shipping, and over Turkey, a question of warm water access for Russia with other "minor" details, a formal treaty between the two countries could be entered into and Germany would then *not* invade Russia.

Eden circulated Pritt's letter to Butler, who remarked on several errors in it, and to the senior Foreign Office official, Orme Sargent, who agreed that it should be ignored. The approach came to nothing, and within weeks the invasion of Russia was a reality. The People's Convention was wound up and the Communists who had previously been sabotaging the war effort whenever possible immediately executed a complete *volte face* and threw their full weight into the fray. "The Revolution that Never Was" was consigned to history.

6
Our Soviet Comrades – Britain at War

WHEN the Nazi-Soviet pact was signed in August 1939 the members of the British Communist Party had to do some hard thinking in order to arrive at a justifiable position. When Germany invaded Russia on 22 June 1941 the British public as a whole had to come to terms with a similar shock: Russia was now an ally.

Winston Churchill took a *realpolitik* view, saying that he would make a favourable reference to the devil himself if he were to aid Britain and the allies in their struggle against Germany. His immediate broadcast to the nation provided the leadership without which a new public consciousness of the situation would have taken many months to establish. But in the weeks immediately following the invasion determined efforts still had to be made to change the public's mind. This was done mainly through the media, which then meant the BBC and the press. Both worked in collaboration with the Ministry of Information (MOI), taking advice on policy from the Russian department there which, as we have mentioned, was run by Peter Smollett.

The BBC was to some extent autonomous, but it had a producer working for it who was an expert on Russia, a close colleague of Smollett's and a personal friend—the ubiquitous Guy Burgess. It is no exaggeration to say that the image of Russia which was placed in the public mind in Britain following Churchill's broadcast was largely the work of Smollett and Burgess, both of whom, we now know, were Soviet agents, and their colleagues. One cannot but admire the Soviet spymasters for having two of their men in such crucial posts at the very moment they were needed. At the same time the British equivalents of these spymasters would clearly have had great difficulty in believing that the two men were not simply doing a job, and that their Soviet sympathies were not merely what the politics of the hour demanded of them. If Hollis had announced that he suspected Burgess or Smollett of having Communist loyalties, he would have found little sympathy for his denunciation, for wasn't it quite obvious that these were the views they *would* have— shared indeed with Churchill himself, his faithful henchman Brendan Bracken and a growing proportion of the British public?

The very idea of a penetration agent, now a commonplace, was then new and original. Further, by this time Hollis was working with colleagues in MI5, notably with Anthony Blunt, Guy Liddell and Roger Fulford, who were close friends of Burgess's. He candidly admitted seeing much of Blunt socially during the war and would thus also have met Burgess, at the flat which they shared. As has been suggested, he may well have come across the circle before the war when he looked up Fulford, subsequently recruiting him into MI5. But this is not to say that Hollis was necessarily guilty by this association. There is a considerable difference between sympathising with a political viewpoint, acting as an agent of influence, as Hollis could be seen to have acted over the *Daily Worker* affair, and actually crossing a street to hand over documents and information to an agent of a foreign power, however close an ally.

In projecting an image of Russia in the public mind Smollett adopted a variety of tactics. In public, and in dealings with the Foreign Office, he could take a position mildly critical of Russia, or at least one that strained to be objective. But within the corridors of the Ministry of Information he was totally committed to the Russian cause and international Communism. His memoranda, some of which have survived in the Public Record Office, show that he worked either directly in collaboration with the Soviet Ambassador Maisky or through Maisky's press attaché.

A good example of the system at work can be seen on the occasion of the 24th Anniversary of the USSR. A Political Warfare Executive directive was sent to all newspapers and the BBC saying that the event was to be treated as a Russian news item, and in that sense only, with no actual celebratory coverage. News of the directive appears to have reached the Soviet Embassy, who telephoned Smollett and sent round their press attaché to discover what he intended doing by way of publicity for the anniversary which was "the National Holiday of the USSR." Smollett's first line of attack was on his old stamping ground, *The Times*, where he called up an editorial, despite the PWE directive. As he minuted:

> I arranged with Carr of *The Times* [E. H. Carr], unofficially, that there would be a first leader in *The Times* which will be very friendly and possibly a turnover [a feature discussion other than an editorial].

His next problem was with the BBC who had received the PWE directive through the policy liaison official Ivone Kirkpatrick (a staunch anti-Communist who was to head Lord Mayhew's Information and Research Department—IRD—after the war). They naturally followed this line. Smollett suggested to a colleague at the BBC that they might consider a programme of music, with a complimentary programme "in view of the very obvious step taken by Maisky which was no doubt intended as a definite hint that they would welcome something," but they declined. He was a little at a loss on how to proceed next, when the Foreign Office phoned him to ask what was being done in the press and on the BBC. Smollett seized the opportunity and said that the BBC were only planning a news item, under instruction from Kirkpatrick, but without mentioning that this was due to a PWE directive. He then suggested the musical programme which he had agreed with Maisky's attaché and asked directly whether the Foreign Office saw any objection.

In due course the Foreign Office let their wishes be known to Kirkpatrick, and the programme went ahead, on condition however

that the Internationale should not be played! No doubt the PWE
were annoyed to find their directive circumvented. If they pressed
a direct enquiry it would have foundered on the MOI's Russian
Department, which Brendan Bracken defended against all criticism, as he did all his staff throughout his time as Minister. As
examples of a brilliant agent of influence at work it is difficult to
choose between the ability to order an editorial from *The Times*,
which Smollett did here and at other crucial times, such as the
controversial occasion when the British took action against the
Communists in Greece, and the ability to run circles round the
PWE. No doubt Philby acted with such dexterity on many occasions, but the actual evidence is never likely to come to light.

Smollett's need to struggle against the PWE and Kirkpatrick
shows that not everyone fell in immediately with the pro-Soviet
line. Among those who did not was the Security Executive, as we
have seen. In October 1941 they issued a fresh study on the CPGB
in the form of a "considered answer" to the question "How far
should the Communist Party's professed support of National Unity
and the National Effort be accepted at its face value?" The report
itself is still classified, but to judge from the reactions of an American official in London, A. J. Drexel Biddle Jr., its tone was plainly
critical. It is also clear that the report was not prepared by MI5, i.e.
by Hollis as the Communist affairs officer, but by "a high ranking
British Authority who serves in the confidential capacity of liaison
in matters of security between the British and Allied Governments
[excluding Soviet Russia of course]." It is interesting that MI5,
with their seat on the Security Executive, were no longer the only
compilers of such reports, though it is not clear whether their
change in status at the creation of the Security Executive was as a
result partly of a collective drift towards the left in their ranks
which made them no longer an obvious choice for such work.
Certainly many of their officers were actual penetration agents, as
has become notorious, and this may well have been associated with
some such drift within the organisation continuing after the creation of the Security Executive. Later revelations have established
that the one MI5 officer who unquestionably held right-wing views
was Maxwell Knight. At about this time Knight prepared a paper,

The Comintern Is Not Dead, which was submitted to Hollis, who rejected it with the observation that it was "too theoretical." All other papers Knight sent that in any way reflected on the generally established line on the Communist Party had to go to Hollis's desk, and got no further, according to Knight's secretary Joan Miller, in her autobiography, *One Girl's War,* which is still banned in the United Kingdom. Whether Knight's opinion which he sent to Churchill's security man at No. 10, Major Morton, reached the compiler of the Security Executive report will probably never be known, but the report does establish that Knight was not entirely on his own in being suspicious of the Communists, while also making clear that Hollis, as the MI5 expert on Communist affairs, was certainly not pressing any anti-Communist line himself, rather suppressing the reports of those who were and protecting Cockburn and his associates.

Smollett surmounted his difficulties in the next few years by creating a public image of Russia which was as far as possible from the pre-war "Stalinist purges" view. Play was made with the religious revival being experienced in Russia, a phenomenon the authorities there apparently viewed with favour. The best example of his work is perhaps the following circular put out in February 1943:

Arguments to Counter the Ideological Fear of "Bolshevism"

(1) We [This was an official MOI paper for the BBC and all newspapers and newsreels] should show that all the horrors associated by German propaganda with the Bolshevik Bogey— destruction of culture, break-up of family life, forced labour, prison camps, seizure of property, destruction of religion, elimination of freedom, etc.—have in fact been perpetrated by the Nazis themselves in Occupied Europe. In short the so-called "Red Terror" is merely a reflection in the Nazi propaganda mirror of the reality of the Nazi Terror.

(2) We should build up a positive picture of Russia which implicitly refutes the Nazi picture of the Bolshevik Bogey, stressing such points as:

(a) The patriotic feelings increasingly displayed by the Russian people and encouraged by Soviet leaders during the war, with appeals to past Russian national glories, etc.

(b) The great contributions made by Soviet Russia (in contrast to Nazi Germany) to science, learning and culture, and the continuity which they show with Russian cultural and scientific tradition from the past.

(c) The development of small savings and personal property and individual initiative in the USSR, as showing that the "small man" thrives in Russia. By contast the small man has been completely betrayed by Hitler, who, having climbed to power on his shoulders, now proceeds to liquidate him.

(d) The creditworthiness of the USSR as contrasted with the Germans in international business transactions.

(e) The increasingly tolerant attitude of the Soviet authorities towards religion. (Note: this argument must be used with great discretion and supported with evidence that is likely to command respect. It should be accompanied by reasoned explanations of the changed attitude of the Soviet Government towards religion, viz: their increasing confidence in the stability of the regime and the loyalty of the Churches in Russia; and even then it should only be used in addressing people already sympathetic to the USSR on other grounds. For the rest it is best to try to remove the question from the sphere of religious controversy altogether; or to take the line—adopted by certain Portuguese and Spanish bishops—that in respect of religion Soviet policy is certainly no worse than that of the Nazis, and that while the Soviet attitude to the Churches has been improving, that of the Nazis has steadily deteriorated. At the same time we should expose the hypocrisy of the Nazis' propaganda line on this point, and their inability to convince— e.g. their own bishops, who did not rally to the anti-Bolshevik crusade.)

(f) In building up this positive picture of the USSR, we should encourage all *specialist* interest in Russian achievements, e.g. by interesting military audiences in Russian military techniques or doctors in Russian medical services, etc.

(3) We should point to the major change of direction which has

taken place in Soviet policy under Stalin. While the Trotskyist policy was to bolster up the security of a weak USSR by means of subversive movements in other countries controlled by the Comintern, Stalin's policy has been and continues to be one of maintaining a strong Russia maintaining friendly diplomatic relations with other governments—a policy which has been justified and confirmed by the events of the past two years. If Stalin maintains the Comintern in being, it is merely as a second line of defence which will be proved superfluous to the extent that he can rely on the co-operation of Britain and the USA.

We should quote evidence to show that parallel with this development in Soviet policy there has been a change in the type of personnel in power in the USSR. The ideologues and doctrinaire international revolutionary [of which Smollett was the epitome!] have increasingly been replaced by people of the managerial and technical type, both military and civil, who are interested in getting practical results.

(4) Bearing in mind that in many countries fear of Bolshevism arises, particularly among the ruling classes, as a reflection of their fear of internal disaffection owing to inadequate social conditions, or to the atmosphere of unrest and disorder following on the cessation of hostilities, we should stress:

(a) That countries with a progressive social policy at home have nothing to fear from Bolshevism. The best antidote to internal "Bolshevism" is an internal policy designed to provide decent standards of living and security.

(b) That Britain and the USA, with the other United Nations, intend to restore and maintain military security, law and order, and economic stability both in Europe and the world, and are preparing plans to that end.

(5) We should point out that, even supposing the USSR wanted to extend its influence throughout Europe, it will not, in the immediate post-war period, have the physical resources to exert undue influence. The food, consumer goods, etc. which Europe will so urgently need when hostilities cease can

come only from the West and not from Russia, which will itself be a deficit area.

This last point is interesting in showing that the allegations that Stalin had a blueprint for dominating as much of Europe after the war as he could was already being countered by propaganda within Britain. A practical example of how the Communist Party actually behaved was shortly to be found in an incident in Algiers in which, as we shall see, both Hollis at MI5 and Cockburn were to be directly involved.

Smollett did not have to wage his war against the BBC entirely from the outside. Burgess had already built up an important position for himself and a high reputation for his knowledge of Russian affairs. When the German invasion came he was immediately called upon for his opinions on the kind of talks the BBC should be putting out if they were to give the right impression of Russia and create a sympathetic picture of her within the shortest possible time. His recommendations did indeed show wide knowledge:

Draft Suggestions for Talks on Russia

The suggestions which follow are put down hastily, as the problem is urgent.

I have had several informal conversations with John Strachey and Professor Bernal [J. D. Bernal] and one or two people at the MOI and the Foreign Office, but what follows is not intended to be in any sense a worked-out scheme:

(1) Literature: Not much to be said here. We should all probably agree on what must be done from the Russian classics. The suggestion has arisen that *War and Peace,* if intelligently handled, could be both an illustration of great Russian literature and topical, the crossing of Beresina, Kudenov, Borodin, the burning of Moscow, etc., all the instances about which the public is reading in the press.

There is also the famous hunting scene which is probably the most beautiful description of old Russia and which was Lenin's favourite passage in Tolstoy, and one which he is said to have been reading, and to have referred to, during the hunt that took place on the day of his death.

Modern literature: The obvious name here is Zoschenko. This man's satires are well known over here. They have the advantages of painting a picture of contemporary Soviet Russia, of being humorous, of not being Bolshevist propaganda, and of being the sort of thing that could not be published by the Nazi régime in Germany. There are also young Soviet writers, such as Nicholai Tikhonov and Ilya Ehrenburg who are translated.

(2) Science: Professor Bernal will advise, but he is on Government work and is not often available in London. He has suggested J. G. Crowther (who has spoken for us—badly, but who is in touch and would know who to go to). Haldane, if the ban is lifted, would obviously be an excellent man. Bernal says that he would be prepared, if asked, to arrange a very friendly approach for me to Haldane, who he says, is now more difficult than ever.

(3) Culture: There is possibly something to be done both in history and the arts. Dr. Klingender and Dr. Blunt are possible speakers on Art—neither are Communists [This statement is vitally important as we shall see]. Christopher Hill (a Fellow of All Souls) is a Communist but is also probably the best authority in England on Russian historical studies. Ballet and Music are probably easily covered.

On wider topics for 9.20 talks audience, the problems are greater. Three themes are suggested as being of interest and contemporary importance and capable of being covered without any too great tendentiousness.

(i) A concept of economic planning: The Soviet Union were the pioneers in economic planning, which is now a fairly "safe" subject, or at least one which is frequently talked about in our programmes. It is suggested that Barbara Wootton, whose book on Planning has a high reputation generally in academic circles might be used as a speaker here. I don't know what her broadcasting is like. On town and civic planning Sir Ernest Simon is an authority, both in general and on the work done by the Russians.

(ii) The Soviet Union treated as a federation of States. It is

suggested that though the political and economic independence of the nationalities of the Soviet Union is purely fictional, there is nevertheless here a topic of general importance
and interest, and one in which the Soviet Union has done
some interesting experiments.

It seems probable that the Turkomans, the Uzbeks, have
had—at any rate among the youth—an impression of national
life and vitality, at least on the cultural side. There is probably
material in the work that has been done in producing written
languages and fostering contemporary culture of the Aborigi-
nal people in Central Asia, Trans-Caucasia, etc.

John Lehmann has written a certain amount of interesting
stuff on Trans-Caucasia for the *Geographical Magazine* and
should be safe on this topic. Ella Myatt and C[ontroller]
H[ome] [i.e. Sir Richard Maconachie] would probably have
something to say on Central Asia. There must be others.

(iii) Carefully handled there should be room for an objective
talk on the foreign policy of the Soviet Union. Its peasant and
agrarian policy which, though tendentious for other countries,
can probably safely be tackled for the home audience here.

Burgess's identification of Hill as a Communist at this time, first
noticed in *Truth Betrayed*, has answered many questions. The key
point is that, as MI5 had to vet all those who appeared at the
microphone for their political reliability, Burgess, in recommend-
ing people for talks which any producer might put out, had to give
their political status accurately after consulting MI5. If he had not
done so—if, for example, he had concealed the fact that Blunt was
a Communist when MI5 knew he was—the first producer to use
him would have run foul of MI5 immediately. We can be sure
therefore that MI5 *did* know that Hill was a Communist then, and
that they did *not* know that Blunt was.

What is also clear from Burgess's recommendations here is that
he was quite open about his affiliations: nearly all his chosen speakers were Communist Party members or of the far left. The matter
was not immediately obvious to the public because outsiders did
not know how talks were arranged, and Burgess's speakers would

be spread through the entire output of the BBC on all its channels home and overseas. But complaints were registered, usually by Conservative backbench MPs and, the charge having being made, it fell to Burgess's Talks Director George Barnes to produce an answer. This he did, writing to the Controller of Home Programmes, Sir Richard Maconachie, on 17 June 1942:

> The allegation that our broadcasts are biased towards the left, if repeated will fester. As it is based upon a misunderstanding of the nature of the Corporation's work I suggest that the following points be made in reply [he then rehearsed the facts before making his crucial argument]. Since ideas for programmes originate with producers, their political views, if any [sic!], and the circles in which they move are of great importance. It is proper, and I have never heard a conservative deny it, that the BBC programme staff should be recruited largely from young men and it is axiomatic that young men tend to mix in progressive circles. Great trouble is taken to make their contacts as wide as possible and the greatest care is taken when planning series of talks to consult experts with political sympathies of each kind.

This apologia for youth is an excuse served up even today. In this case Barnes can be seen to be deliberately shielding Burgess. It was untrue that political sympathies of every kind were consulted in these programmes, as he well knew. Burgess's recommendations, which of course would never have been seen by an outsider, show this beyond argument. Barnes ended on a note of challenging arrogance:

> To sum up: the great majority of our programmes have nothing to do with politics: criticism of political bias in the remainder must be directed to the responsible controller [i.e. of the relevant department rather than the BBC as a whole] *and the critic informed that ill-directed criticism merely indicates ignorance* [my italics].

This loyal backing of Burgess by Barnes, for that is what it was, probably stemmed from close personal friendship which developed between them through their common background of Dartmouth and Cambridge. I have found no examples of Barnes himself putting forward a Communist or far-left view.

Just as Smollett had difficulties with the PWE so Burgess found that his sympathetic view of Moscow did not meet with universal acceptance within the BBC outside Barnes's Talks Department or from Ivone Kirkpatrick. In particular the Home News Department took a more straightforward literal approach to news reaching it, from all sources, about events on the Russian front. The solution found, on which no doubt Burgess was consulted, although the exact mechanism by which it happened is not clear, was a savage attack on the BBC news, alleging anti-Soviet bias, sent to Brendon Bracken by the Soviet Information Bureau at the Soviet Embassy in London. Bracken forwarded it to Sir Cecil Graves, Director General of the BBC:

> The Soviet Information Bureau wishes to call the attention of the British Minister of Information to a number of incorrect statements made by the BBC during January and February of this year, in which attempts were made to anticipate the strategic moves of the Red Army in its struggle against the German invaders.

No more serious charge could be imagined, and there followed a long series of allegedly damaging remarks in BBC news broadcasts, with more than a hint that there might be some Nazi mole in the BBC deliberately leaking vital information to the Germans. The result sought was simply the BBC's strict adherence to the Moscow line. Bracken duly replied that the BBC had been suitably chastened, while denying all the allegations. We can imagine the reaction of Burgess and Smollett, who alone saw all sides of the episode. It is extremely unlikely that anyone in Britain would have been able to obtain strategic information about affairs on the eastern front, though the Russians may have had an exaggerated view of the abilities of the British Secret Service MI6. It is equally unlikely that any MI5 investigation would have been set afoot to see if such a mole existed in the BBC. Only once, on the outbreak of war, had the Special Branch under their direction entered the BBC in secrecy and removed suspects under the 18B regulations. These included two brothers and a sister of the famous William Joyce who wrote scripts for the German black radio station Workers' Challenge and also himself broadcast later in the war. In fact the members of his family working in the BBC all proved loyal citizens.

The atmosphere in Britain resulting from the efforts of Burgess and like-minded colleagues at the BBC and Smollett at the MOI changed rapidly towards one of growing sympathy for Russia. This was transformed into fervid support in many quarters when the Russian Army eventually moved onto the offensive. Simply to blame Hollis and others in MI5 for not keeping track of Communist sympathisers at this time is to overlook the basic fact that a great many members of the public would have had to be covered. In fact MI5, if they had persisted, could have laid themselves open to the suggestion that they had some actual sympathy with the Nazi enemy.

But the result was that Burgess and the others, including Sefton Delmer, the mole in the PWE, were all able to continue with their activities undisturbed, and confident that their cause was the right one. Burgess in particular was able to provide his Soviet controllers with information of great value obtained while he was at the BBC.

7

A Spy in Place at
the BBC

ROM the earliest days of broadcasting, its political significance
was obvious. The first move in any revolutionary putsch was to
seize the broadcasting station and hold it, even before confront-
ing the forces in power. In America, with its myriad private stations
all competing against one another, a simple coup of this kind would
not be possible. In Britain broadcasting was in the hands of the
state-appointed monopoly, the BBC, and the field, open to any
Communist agent who could get on the inside, was considerable,
whether a revolution was about to break out or not. It was logical
that Russia and any British Communists who thought that revolution was definitely a possibility should target the BBC. Infiltration
was the best way, and they succeeded brilliantly with a number of
agents of whom by far the most famous was Guy Burgess.

In all the furor over Burgess after his defection as a junior member of the Foreign Office, one thing had been almost totally ignored and that was the job which enabled him to gain the influence
he undoubtedly had. The answer was simple: Burgess was a radio
producer working in the vitally important Talks Department. In
the days before television, radio was immensely powerful. The
personalities it created dominated people's lives in much the same
way as television stars do now, and these personalities were largely

created by the producers who both brought them to the microphone in the first place and then shaped what they said over the air.
The work involved skills similar to those of an editor in a publishing house but with far greater demands on exact timing and the
ability to rewrite scripts to a close schedule. Many leading personalities such as Harold Nicolson were happy to place themselves in
Burgess's hands.

Burgess left the BBC before war broke out and joined a highly
secret black broadcasting organisation known as the Joint Broadcasting Committee, or JBC, as I have described in my previous
book *Truth Betrayed: Radio and Politics Between the Wars*. When he
rejoined the BBC it was to find even greater opportunities for doing
work which would be useful to his spymasters in Moscow. We saw
in the last chapter how he had gotten himself into a position to
write the paper that determined how Russia was to be handled in
broadcasts after she had come in on the Allied side. His success
here sprang from a new dimension to wartime broadcasting which
he was to master rapidly.

From the beginning of the war it had been realised that every
economy would have to be made in the use of raw materials and in
improving industrial and agricultural output within Britain as far as
possible to save on imports of food and manufactured goods. An
essential feature of the system evolved was the use of radio as a
substitute for the circulation of printed notices and information on
a wide range of subjects which affected farmers, for example,
thereby saving on the enormous cost of printing and paper, which
was placed on restricted supply as soon as war broke out. The
producer involved in the talks on agriculture was John Green, a
former President of the Cambridge Union and an early member of
the English Mistery (a patriotic movement) who had subsequently
developed an interest in agricultural affairs. In collaboration with
the Ministry of Food he soon established a *modus operandi* for what
was effectively a system of radio administration in his field. The
early morning programme "Farming Today," which still survives,
is typical of the kind of programme produced and stands as a tribute
to Green's initiative.

When Burgess returned to the BBC it was to restart his pre-war political programmes under wartime conditions. Burgess shaped his programmes along appropriate lines, which were an extension of ideas of a "radio administration" to the overtly political sphere. His role as an agent of influence in the BBC was important at a crucial time, but he was also an agent of a more conventional kind. There have been various accounts, drawn from defectors, of a massive output of information from Burgess. The assumption was that he knew nothing but "political gossip and tittle-tattle" of a kind similar to what he had gathered before the war at the BBC. In fact, as we shall see in this chapter, Burgess played a highly original and complicated role in wartime London which gave him close access to many Government ministers. Through his knowledge of the most intimate details of the war on the home front, which extended to advance information on budget announcements, and shortages necessitating emergency regulations, he would have been able to provide Russia with valuable insights into the reality of life in Britain at war. He would also have been able to provide answers on particular matters of fact through his ability to contact on a priority and highly secret basis virtually every ministry in London. In his dealings with the Army, which we shall examine shortly, he saw the Adjutant-General in person, and cleared a whole range of Army matters as they involved BBC coverage in talks or news through the Army security officers. One of his few failures was with the Ministry of Economic Warfare, where his hopes of establishing a liaison seem to have come to nothing.

To understand precisely what Burgess was doing at the BBC that gave him such access, and what he made of the wide remit he was given in the Talks Department, it is essential to understand that he could quite well form his own political theories on any subject, whether about the situation in China, or what was happening in Britain during the war. Zu Putlitz, describing Burgess after his defection as one of the most controversial characters in the history of modern England, attributed his initial fascination with Burgess in Cambridge in 1932 to the fact that Burgess was the first "young Englishman of good family . . . who seemed really to have made a study of Marxism and who frankly and brilliantly claimed definite left-wing ideals." The situation in wartime Britain caused him to think seriously about what was happening to Britain and where it was going. Not surprisingly he was infuriated by the bureaucracy, almost as bad as it is in modern Britain, that was strangling life everywhere. In 1941, ironically for a Marxist, although perhaps influenced by his profound admiration for Churchill, he thought that one way out of the problem lay through the broadcasting of Parliament in some form:

> In my opinion the present general and almost complete ad-ministrative totalitarianism covering every branch of national life, personal habits and freedom included, along with indus-try and wages etc., has enormously increased the desirability of covering Parliamentary debates more fully than we have ever yet seriously thought of doing. The House is the only place in which these administrative decisions are or can be questioned or discussed effectively. The Prime Minister has recognised this in his recent speeches. Historically speaking this is a new situation. I think it is important and possible to meet it—but it will require careful investigation and coverage in higher spheres than ours.

His hopes in this direction were misplaced, as he soon realised. Two years later an alternative system had been largely evolved by which the inevitable wartime regulations and administrative ac-tions could be tested and questioned, and if we look through all the papers we see that Burgess played a key role in creating it, and it was this that gave him his unique position. The basic idea he repeated in minute after minute over the years:

> May I be allowed the repetition of the general point. Our mobilisation of man- and woman-power has been in extent the most complete—and in speed the most rapid of all the bellig-erent powers. Our rationing, state-controlled and social schemes are probably the most complicated of all, partly from lack of unification. Between them these facts have created a novel and urgent personal *and* national need for a service that I am sure *broadcasting* and its logical extensions can alone and mostly cheaply perform.

And in a letter to his most important contributor he once wrote, at a difficult time: "I imagine somebody, sometime, as well as you and I will appreciate the role of broadcasting in administrative matters."

When the system that Burgess evolved with speakers that he had himself found and trained or collaborated with succeeded so well, the BBC naturally attempted to formalise it. A draft memorandum remarked, in an almost verbatim echo of Burgess:

> Since the outbreak of total war Government intervention has been extended to every detail of the daily life of the man in the street with the result that the public now depends upon an understanding of Government regulations in order to conduct its daily life and efficient adminstration depends upon the public being able to fill in correctly the official forms. Experience has shown the value of broadcasting such explanations and at present there are four weekly series of talks with this purpose: "John Hilton Talking"; "For Home Guards Only"; "Can I Help You?" and "Calling the Factory Front."

The first three of these had been set up entirely by Burgess, and their principles had been evolved by him in collaboration with senior officials in virtually every wartime ministry. The first two will be dealt with later in this chapter, but it is worth looking here at the series "Can I Help You?", perhaps the best of them, together with other programmes that Burgess produced almost in passing.

The way the system worked, and it was effectively a substitute for parliamentary representation, was as follows. Regular weekly broadcasts, normally on Saturday night, covered topics which were causing difficulty, or needed explaining, to the general public. A special link-up was established with the newly formed Citizens Advice Bureaux, and a close watch was kept on the effect of new regulations or newly drafted forms as they came out. When a difficulty occurred, which was usually obvious immediately from CAB reports, either the speaker or Burgess, as producer, was told of it. Burgess then either went to the relevant Ministry in person or established reliable contact by messenger with a senior official, and a rapid decision was taken on a way either of solving the problem or of changing the regulation. This was then conveyed to the broadcaster, who wrote a script incorporating the explanations or alterations which was then broadcast as soon as possible. The resemblance between this system of going to the CAB and the normal method of going to an MP's "surgery" was made closer still when correspondence was encouraged. Almost immediately ten thousand letters and more a month flooded in. All of them were answered with the advice of officials of the Ministry concerned, although in each case actually signed by the broadcaster.

At first Burgess had arranged talks in his pre-war fashion, ordering individual contributions from friends, as I have described in *Truth Betrayed*. Thus in January 1941 he got Aileen Furse, Philby's second wife (with whom he was then living, unmarried, with their family) to do talks in the "Kitchen Front" series about the community kitchens she had established in wartime London. It is worth remarking in passing that if the molehunters had gone through the BBC's archives they would have established, from details such as this, a more realistic idea of the wartime friendships and life of Burgess and Philby and the rest. Aileen Furse exists only as a shadow in their accounts; Burgess is always described in terms of the flat he and Blunt occupied in Bentinck Street, with the Philbys in a different world entirely. A glimpse of real life at the time such as this, a friend giving his colleague's wife some opportunity, and recognition, without any overtones at all is particularly revealing. It is revealing also that whereas the molehunters never got this close to the world in which Philby, Blunt and Burgess lived, Hollis was not only aware of it but part of it.

The realities of the war situation soon turned Burgess's energies away from his pre-war models to his new talks. The first serious topic was, prosaically enough, concerned with income tax. Before the war about a million income tax forms were sent out annually. The tax had evolved from the tax on "income" in the sense of unearned income; it was paid only by those of some means. The crushing financial burden of the war had brought about a decision to extend this "income" tax to ordinary working men and women—people, that is, who earned their wages, and who had no "income" at all. By 1941 over five million forms were going out, mostly to people who had never filled in a form in their lives, until the burden was shifted to employers by the PAYE system making them unpaid collectors of the tax. Burgess realised that there was an urgent need for someone to explain these things and reduce the appalling confusion being caused. Luckily he came across an officer from the Inland Revenue Staff Federation, who could speak on the wireless (actual officials were not permitted to do so) and who also knew the field.

The result in the "Can I Help You?" series was brilliantly successful. So original was the idea that the Chancellor of the Exchequer asked to see the scripts when he heard about it through Sir Gerald Canney, Chairman of the Board of the Inland Revenue. The stage was set for the closest collaboration at the highest level. Today even genial television broadcasts by Chancellors or their advisors are quite common; but then nothing like these talks on income tax had been attempted before and the impact was great. At one bound massive administrative problems which had been causing trouble to individual officers throughout the country were solved, as people listened in their own homes to simple explanations of forms they had in front of them. The system was soon extended and rapidly replaced the *ad hoc* issuing of instructions by Ministries, which might, or might not, be included in some news or feature programme. The old system of a Minister himself infrequently giving a talk on a measure he was about to introduce delivered in general terms, de-haut-en-bas, was displaced.

Apart from the Treasury and the Home Office, the Ministries with which Burgess dealt were those of Labour, Supply, Works, Food, the Board of Trade, then under Dalton, the Post Office and the Assistance Board. The specific topics dealt with were exceedingly numerous, and included the Fuel Economy campaign, Industrial Clothing Coupons and rationing generally, the Rent Restriction Act, the White Paper on War Grants, utility furniture, retail trade restrictions—concerned largely with small shops over which Dalton seems to have taken a particular concern—new legislation on Workmen's Compensations and so on.

At times the feedback was so direct that rumour of a new measure would reach Citizens Advice Bureaux before it had been enacted. As a result Burgess would find himself sitting in on discussions with his speaker and an Under-secretary deciding how to treat a particular problem. Even Budget strategy was not sacrosanct, as we shall see later here when the question of a possible raise in army pay was disclosed to Burgess and the BBC by the Treasury before the Army had been informed or had had time to inform those dealing with the matter in the field.

There were of course other producers involved in these series, but not many. The main one was Norman Luker, the friend who was later to throw a party for Burgess in New York before he came home to England for the last time from America in 1951. The work load on all of them was enormous. Occasional flashes of humour occur even in the drabbest paperwork: someone notices that the radio officer of the Price Regulation Committee was the appropriately named Miss Cutting; Burgess alerts a financial expert to do a talk on the Budget in 1942 and, without making any leaks, suggests he choose as his topic "austerity." Many of the issues had political overtones, though these were not often apparent at first. New regulations dealing with the relation of landlord and tenant having been announced, a suggestion from "Can I Help You?" that local Government officers or CAB officials would be able to assist with problems brought a speedy response from the legal profession, who pointed out that legal matters affecting two private parties such as landlord and tenant concerned them and that there was a not inconsiderable body of law on the matter which was outside the competence of the local Citizens Advice Bureaux, if they had any legal standing in the matter! It was gratifying to both Burgess and his speaker that they established their goodwill so well over this question that they were later specifically entrusted with publicity on the most complex matters of new Landlord and Tenant Law arising from the blitz which at first had caused great injustice and bitterness. A letter from the Lord Chancellor's Office is perhaps worth quoting at some length:

Dear Mr. Burgess,
    During our conversation on the telephone last night it was arranged that I should send you such material as I have in my

possession with reference to the Landlord and Tenant (War Damage) Amendment Act 1941 so that you should, if you think fit, draw the attention of your broadcaster to this. It is the view of this department that it would be helpful to the public, in view of the resumption of air-raids, if he could deal with this section in one of his talks. The Ministry of Health . . . are of the same opinion.

You will recollect that in one of your broadcaster's talks he explained the provisions of another Act for which the Lord Chancellor is responsible . . . the explanation which he gave of this Act seemed to us to be so satisfactory and helpful that we are encourged to think that this explanation of the effect of the War Damage amendment is likely to be as successful . . . If you and he think that this subject could properly be dealt with in one of his talks I am at your disposal for the giving of any such other information or explanation which you may require . . .

If we look at this situation through the eyes of the more naïve molehunters and their wilderness of mirrors we should perhaps be asking whether Hollis ought to have been aware that Burgess was gaining such detailed information with close access to a variety of leading figures in wartime Britain. On occasions when Burgess bumped into Hollis he would no doubt have bored him with his talk of Administrative Totalitarianism, and indeed if Burgess was sending *this* material to Moscow one wonders what they would have made of it, except to see in the changing patterns of events still more fuel for their speculations on how close the British revolution might actually be. There was, however, a more sinister, though never actually dangerous, side of Burgess's activity in this sphere, and that was in his dealings with the Army.

The longest-running series of talks put out by the BBC Talks Department, and those which its producer Guy Burgess regarded as by far the most important, were a continuation, in war dress, of a pre-war series on unemployment. The broadcaster was then extremely famous and the best-known microphone commentator on the harsh realities of the time—the first indeed to reach a genuine mass audience through radio. His name was John Hilton. Reputation is a notoriously fickle mistress, and by the time the molehunters and spy authors came to investigate the Cambridge intellectuals his name had almost been forgotten. He was even confused with an old school friend of Anthony Blunt's with the same name: in the index for the most recent biographical study of Blunt, *Mask of Treachery*, he appears in the same entry as Blunt's school friend, leaving the uninformed reader with a very odd idea of his personality!

Burgess first met Hilton at Cambridge. With George Barnes he attended his inaugural lecture as Professor of Industrial Relations, a chair founded by Montague Burton expressly for Hilton, and an extraordinary breakthrough because Hilton had never had any university education or, indeed, ever passed an exam in his life. He had begun as a mill apprentice at Bolton and had made his way, by sheer mental ability and a proficiency at statistics, to become an expert employed by the Garton Foundation and then a Government adviser on statistics in the First World War. He never forgot his roots, and was the person who suggested to the founder of Mass Observation, Tom Harrison, who had earlier investigated primitive tribes in their native habitat, that he go to Bolton and find out what life was really like *in Britain*. With the coming of the slump in the thirties Hilton began a series of talks on unemployment which were broadcast from factories and unemployed centres all over the country. It was introduced by a talk on unemployment by the Duke of Windsor, then Prince of Wales; it is probably this talk, and others related to it, that remain in the collective memory when references are made to the Duke's concerns with unemployment, at least as much as to the single remark "Something must be done" always cited as its origin. Hilton's early files at the BBC have unfortunately been destroyed—they are believed to have been lost in the bombing—but his files for the war years survive. They give a most detailed insight into the last years of his life, for, as we shall see, the enormous work load became too much for a man now no longer young, and he died while struggling with the tens of thousands of letters from individual soldiers and their families who so depended on his broadcasts.

Hilton's first broadcast to the Army was from France, where he had gone as a roving reporter with the British Expeditionary Force (BEF). He returned to Britain with them, and then in many hundreds of broadcasts covered every possible facet of army life as it affected the ordinary rank and file and their families. This early simple reportage was developed by Burgess into the sort of direct liaison with the authorities that we saw earlier in the chapter. From concern about the problems of families whose fathers were abroad, or even in POW camps, he was led to direct liaison which explained for the Army exactly how they were to communicate with the POW camps, where to write to and what their entitlements might be under rapidly changing regulations. Burgess, or his colleague Norman Luker, verified every detail with the Army departments concerned before Hilton broadcast them.

With hindsight, in the security world's wilderness of mirrors, the potential offered by this to Burgess would have been very worrying. It was well known that the entire order of battle of the Italian army at the time of their entry into the war had been worked out by Canadian censorship officials looking through intercepted mail from Italian soldiers to their relatives in Canada and America. Burgess had sight of mail, much of it uncensored, sent from every unit in Britain or from members of their families. Further, he was in liaison with the Army on matters of morale, as will be explained, and he was privy to a great amount of secret information about major events, such as the invasion of Europe, and many less important but embarrassing facts.

As an agent of influence his position was even more dangerous for, unlike Claud Cockburn with his foolish editorials in the *Daily Worker*, Burgess really was able, through Hilton, to influence what soldiers actually thought. However, while all this is no doubt true, it was not the whole story; we have already seen the distortions which can occur from this kind of logic, culminating no doubt in a suggestion that Hollis should have been alert to what Burgess was doing, or might even have been shielding him. In fact Burgess did not need actively to conceal his revolutionary convictions. The problems of life in post-war Britain, as embodied in the Beveridge Report, were as much a subject of discussion in the Army's Directorate of Welfare and Education as anywhere else, as a candid letter from an officer there, Major R.A.C. Radcliffe, who was in liaison with Burgess, makes clear in discussing proposed talks by Hilton on the report:

> . . . the Government should watch very closely to see what they can do after the publication of the Beveridge report. If they really do something concrete and adopt one or two of the many suggestions which will doubtless be made, I think they may allay the present suspicions about their intentions; if on the other hand they talk and do nothing, I think it will be generally felt that they do not mean business and the people will just watch until the opportunity occurs as soon as the war is over to turn them out and put in people who will take action.
>
> Whether this turning out will be achieved without trouble and bloodshed, and whether if it means bloodshed to any extent those who want the new order [sic: the German administration in Europe was referred to as the New Order] will be prepared to pay for it in that way is I think the big question for the future. I confess I do not know the answer. So by all means let us have John Hilton discussing the Beveridge Report and see what reaction we get.

This astonishing document shows that Burgess's views of a possible revolution were as nothing compared to some views current in the Army and freely expressed in the formal education side of the Directorate known as ABCA, the Army Bureau of Current Affairs, though not in such unguarded terms as this in their publications. Further, Hilton's broadcasts were definitely seen as a way of gauging the likely response within the Army to the actual possibility of revolution *tout court*, with "trouble and bloodshed."

In fact Burgess was circumspect in his actions, and did not rise directly to this provocative letter, at least in writing. The Hilton talks on Beveridge produced the usual crop of letters rather than any revolutionary demonstrations. The security aspect of having revolutionary opinions circulating within the armed forces must have taken second place to defeating the enemy, if Radcliffe's letter is any guide, for all Burgess's dealings with the Army were monitored by the Army's own military intelligence service. Radcliffe's letter for example had begun by thanking Burgess for two Hilton scripts, and the suggestion that the BBC should go ahead with them would only have been made after they had seen them. This is made quite plain elsewhere in the BBC archives, since Burgess and Luker frequently dealt directly with the security department concerned, a branch of Military Intelligence, "MI," but one actually coming under the DMI (Director of Military Intelligence) rather than the "covert" departments MI5 and MI6, so well known now, which had been hived off from Military Intelligence proper many years before. The relationship between these departments and MI5, and in particular the shadowy department known as MI(PW) (presumably Military Intelligence [Political Warfare]) remains a mystery; but if Hollis, or anyone dealing with the activities of the Communist Party, had been aware of Burgess's affiliations and conveyed the matter to their opposite number in the Army intelligence service, responsibility for lack of action would have been theirs. If Hollis or his colleagues deliberately failed to alert the Army, their action, as we have seen, was hardly likely to have affected matters one way or the other. However, that Burgess was able to gather valuable information concerning morale and probably lower-grade operational information is undeniable.

A crucial recognition of the position of Hilton's talks as being as important as it was perhaps natural for Burgess to suggest that they were came in April 1942. The Army had been considering appointing one of their own officers to take over from Hilton. Finally the Adjutant-General decided to interview Hilton personally, along with Burgess as his producer. Burgess's report of the meeting, as a result of which Hilton's broadcasts moved onto an entirely different plane, explains the position:

> The Adjutant-General stated that as as result of enquiries he had made he was satisfied that John Hilton's talks were performing a useful function in sustaining morale on welfare matters, [and] that they were a useful bridge between the authorities and the rank and file without being official propaganda.
>
> . . . one of the problems confronting the War Office was

how to get across the spirit of the new army to units whose officers frequently showed a desire and a tendency to live in the old. In particular there was the problem of getting the common sense of Army Council instructions put across to the forces which naturally had to be written in official language.

For these reasons it was intended not to proceed with the idea of seeking an official military spokesman to do tasks better fulfilled, informally and unofficially, by John Hilton.

The need to put Hilton's broadcasts on this sound footing had stemmed from the creation of a new committee, the Army Morale Committee. The secretary was Major John Sparrow, later to have a distinguished academic career as Warden of All Souls, Oxford. Burgess did not previously know Sparrow, and addressed him formally in correspondence, handing over day-to-day matters to John Hilton himself to settle directly with Sparrow. The actual need for any committee on Army morale had been made plain in earlier memoranda. Reference was made to a "growing browned-offness," which was obviously due, it was pointed out, to lack of action before the second front was established as a definite possibility.

As in industry, one of the natural focuses of disaffection was the question of pay. When in August 1942 it was decided to issue a White Paper on the subject, Hilton's broadcast was used as a frontline to put over a favourable interpretation, if possible, and to gauge genuine response among the ranks. This was considered so important that Burgess was summoned to the Chancellor of the Exchequer's office by the Chancellor's secretary to discuss exactly how Hilton should put the matter over. It was made clear to Burgess that the Government in fact proposed no actual changes in soldier's pay: "the Government simply sets forth certain considerations about the real rate of pay when allowances etc. are taken into account." This being the case, the Treasury clearly did not want Hilton entering into any discussions about the actual merits of the White Paper over the air, and that would appear to have been the central reason why Burgess was briefed at such a high level. With amusing understatement Burgess remarked to George Barnes in a memorandum that ". . . there may possibly be complications with the War Office who apparently do not see eye-to-eye with the

Treasury on the matter." His added footnote, "P.S. This is a matter of first-class parliamentary and political importance . . . ," at the end of a lengthy report was also an indication that he was fully conscious of all the overtones of the situation, even if everyone at the BBC was not. And it is clear from a security point of view that, if such situations had arisen at the time of the People's Convention movement, in the aftermath of Dunkirk, Hilton's broadcasts could have had a crucial effect.

The element, first noticed here, of the authorities' conscious use of Hilton for political reasons—Burgess and Hilton were in fact expressly informed of the contents of the White Paper in advance by the Treasury before the Army knew of it, so that the War Office would not have been able to give Hilton prior instructions on *their* view—was developed rapidly at this time. Sparrow's interest was handed over to another officer, Eric Maschwitz, who founded the Army's broadcasting section but is better known to posterity as the author of "These Foolish Things" and "A Nightingale Sang in Berkeley Square." He was far less guarded about the view he took of Hilton's broadcasts. In a letter of October 1942 Maschwitz first praised Hilton's talks and his reputation with the rank and file, and asked that he give two talks a week rather than one. But he then remarked:

> . . . the War Office . . . would not wish to "compromise" Hilton with his public by allowing any impression to arise in the listener's mind that he was in any sense the "Voice of the War Office" or being used in any way for "propaganda". . .
>
> Professor Hilton has for some time been asking for the assistance of a young serving officer as advisor on Army problems arising from his broadcasts and correspondence. The War Office does not favour this idea, it being felt that the association of a serving soldier with him would "compromise" him and lead to the impression in the public's mind that Hilton was himself, in fact, a "hireling" of the War Office.

This was an entirely new and offensive tone, and might even suggest that the Army Intelligence officers had gained some insight into Hilton's and, perhaps, Burgess's political background.

Hilton's talks continued at the new rate of twice a week. Considerable flows of additional mail were soon building up, particularly after military operations started again in North Africa with the Allied invasion. Then early in 1943 Burgess suddenly suggested to Hilton that he should go to North Africa and be with the troops, promising to deal with both the approach to the BBC and all the ancillary problems that would occur with mail arriving at his house during his absence at the rate of a thousand letters a week.

Burgess was as good as his word and, in a masterly campaign, launched the idea with the BBC and then with the War Office. He pointed out that Hilton had begun with the troops in France, and that, having an audience which listening figures suggested included "the families of almost all other ranks serving in the entire British army," it was only logical that he should go to where action was now taking place.

Hilton was duly dispatched in late May 1943. He returned in mid-June having seen thousands of troops and made some memorable broadcasts. The triumph was mixed with tragedy, however, as on his return he showed signs of illness. After a few talks he became very ill and died at his home in Cambridge, the strain of the journey having precipitated a dormant cerebral condition. Burgess was deeply shocked and wrote moving letters to his family and to Edna Nixon, his secretary, who was later to write the standard biography of Hilton. The shock must have been all the greater because Burgess had been responsible for the entire venture. But there was another, deeper level of guilt, for he may have had other clandestine motives for sending Hilton to North Africa. These motives he shared with Claud Cockburn who also went to North Africa, in his case apparently working with the GRU, who were now controlling Comintern members after the abolition of the Comintern itself by Stalin. The purpose of the two trips was far removed where John Hilton was concerned. He was simply going to make contact with the troops as he had at the beginning of the war and get material for his future talks so that the families of men in the campaign would feel closer to what was going on through listening to a well-known broadcaster who had actually been out there. But it is clear from BBC memoranda that Burgess's concerns about the trip were far closer to those of Cockburn and their Soviet controllers.

Before Hilton went on his trip, under the guise of obtaining introductions for him, Burgess had gone around the War Office and obtained detailed information about all the units in Africa, together with their most important personalities. In a memorandum to Barnes he couldn't resist running off a list of his triumphs:

> Informal introductions have been arranged as follows: *As regards the 8th Army*—the 2nd Rifle Brigade with its excellent Colonel Tom Pearson and its historic S Company under Martin; the 11th Hussars, the original earners, it is believed, of the title "Desert Rats". . . *As regards the 1st Army* to the Intelligence officer of the Guards Brigade—this man saw the serious fighting and the serious casualties of the Coldstreams. To a subaltern in the Gordon Highlanders who gave valuable advice on these talks when he was stationed in England; to General Eisenhower's very able Sergeant assistant . . . *As regards the Air Force* Hilton has a personal letter [obtained by Burgess] asking Air Marshal Tedder to give him every assistance.

Interestingly enough, the only branch of the armed forces which Burgess omitted was the Navy. He remarked to Barnes: "Past experience of which you are aware has lead us to omit it." The past experience was that, despite every attempt by Burgess and Barnes, the Navy steadfastly refused to have anything whatever to do with them or the programmes they tried to involve them in. Their position was that morale of the Navy and the families of naval men was best dealt with by the Navy, and Naval Intelligence concurred in this view. Whether they had any knowledge of Burgess's political views as a result of his early connection with them is not clear, but it still rankled as this memorandum shows.

The precise reason why Russia would wish to have detailed knowledge of the situation on the ground in Africa may not have been obvious at first, but Cockburn's visit made it plain, for it was concerned with the possible establishment of a revolutionary government there, as we shall see.

8
ETOUSA Catches a
Communist

WHILE Russia was regarded by many in America as a gallant ally in the fight against the Axis powers, there were those who never forgot the theories on which Communism was based and the aims it were still pursuing worldwide. This had been lost sight of by many in Britain where there was a growing enthusiasm prompted by skilled propaganda both for Russia and her leader, widely known as "Uncle Joe." When the first Allied landings in North Africa took place, there was some difficulty between the Allies on political questions, most obviously on how to deal with the Vichy French. There had also been a lot of Communist activity in Algiers.

The men in ETOUSA (European Theatre of Operations United States Army) seem to have been fully conscious of these issues in a way the British were not. The incident described here is important not only for what it tells us about the communist aims in Algiers, seen as part of France and the starting place for the next French revolution, but for the evidence it produces to once again link Hollis and Cockburn.

After the People's Convention Cockburn's file lay in Hollis's safe relatively undisturbed. Cockburn carried on with his organising for the Convention and general political activity, and returned to writing for the *Daily Worker* when the ban on it was lifted on 5 September 1942. Then in 1943 his file became "current" again in an extraordinary affair not involving matters in England at all.

On 18 July the Foreign Office were alerted through two independent channels to the fact that something had happened in Algiers which had angered Britain's American allies. At first it did not appear to be anything other than an over-zealous journalist managing to get somewhere that he shouldn't have, a matter for covert congratulation perhaps and mild rebuke rather than a telegram in cipher from Harold Macmillan, the resident British Minister in Algiers, and an irate letter from the United States Ambassador in Britain, John G. Winant, to Anthony Eden. This accused the British of "bad faith," a strong phrase in diplomatic use at the best of times, let alone when addressed to an ally in the middle of a war. What had happened?

From a number of contemporary accounts the sequence of events seems to have been as follows. The position in Algiers at this time, and the controversial deal struck with the Vichy leader, Admiral Darlan, in order to establish a stable situation, had caused outrage among many, not only those on the left. It led directly to the assassination of Darlan by a man allegedly using an SOE (Special Operations Executive) revolver, who was immediately executed. In an attempt to deal with the crisis the American forces kept a close eye on local political developments and raided a number of centres of political activity, one of them that of the local Communist Party. To their surprise, they found an Englishman there who said he was a political correspondent. He gave the name "Frank Pitcairn." There were not meant to be any political correspondents in the war theatre, and he was not one of the small group of war correspondents who had been allowed on a limited visit. He was therefore arrested while investigations were carried out. Harold Macmillan's assistant, Oliver Makins, now Lord Sherfield, was immediately able to identify "Frank Pitcairn" as Claud Cockburn. Having himself vetted all the war correspondents allowed in the area and cleared them with the Allied Force authorities and with ETOUSA, he knew that Cockburn was not one of them. Cockburn managed somehow to evade his captors at this point, but before he did so his passport was examined and was seen to contain a valid export visa issued by the Passport Office in London. As this must have been issued after clearance by MI5 and the Ministry of Information, it was obvious that Cockburn had not acted entirely illegally in coming to Algiers. The American authorities, however, said that they had earlier specifically refused a request for Cockburn to come to Algiers. Makins had no option but to send a strongly worded telegram to the Foreign Office asking for enquiries to be made. Unknown to him the American authorities, who perhaps knew more about the political side of what happened, had also complained. The result had been Winant's strong letter to Anthony Eden, which reached the Foreign Office at the same time as Makins's cipher telegram. The Foreign Office file on the incident is headed succinctly "Unsatisfactory Explanation of Mr. Cockburn's arrival in North Africa":

> From Mr. Makins. Is puzzled about Mr. Cockburn's arrival as Allied Force HQ were neither consulted nor informed and according to available information Ministry of Information arranged with Passport Office for Mr. Cockburn's exit permit contrary to the wishes of the War Office and Etousa. Feels the matter should be further investigated.

The formal investigation contained in the file was carried out by Sir Anthony Rumbold. It seemed to show that the mistake had been due to a concatenation of accidents. This anyway was the explanation given in letters sent to Makins and Ambassador Winant, and in the intense activity of the time the matter was allowed to drop with Cockburn's reapprehension and return to Britain. A reading of the papers in the file today, coupled with an analysis of what Cockburn said and did at the time and subsequently, shows that much more was involved than a journalist's chasing of a good story. Cockburn's purpose in going to Algiers was a political one, and, as we shall see, the Communist Party's intense desire to get Cockburn there had only been satisfied by the active collaboration of Cockburn's case officer in MI5, who was Roger Hollis.

The sequence of events began when the *Daily Worker* insisted that they should have a war correspondent at the front in North

Africa, naming Cockburn, or "Frank Pitcairn," as their man. The War Office immediately objected in strong terms, as well they might, since Cockburn was well known to Military Intelligence as the man who had encouraged mutiny in army barracks throughout the country at the time of the People's Convention. The Americans also objected, though ambiguously, unfortunately, as they also said that they would be able to provide a passage for him if he had an exit permit. MI5 also refused to recommend an exit visa, but only initially. The wording used by Rumbold is curious: "The Security Authorities had previously objected to Cockburn being given an exit permit but they . . . withdrew this objection provided the Foreign Office agreed." Rumbold later identified "the Security Authorities" as MI5, although he does not name Hollis, who held Cockburn's file. The circumstances in which Hollis changed his mind, an exceedingly odd thing for him to do, let alone passing the buck back to the Foreign Office, when MI5 were the authorities whose opinion was being sought, were created by the *Daily Worker* and the Communist leader Harry Pollitt trying a new tack.

Pollitt, faced with the refusal of an exit permit, wrote a disingenuous letter to the Passport Office expressing doubt about the reasons for refusal, and asking why the War Office was involved, as it was intended to send their man Cockburn as a *civilian* political correspondent. The Passport Office failed to see the illogicality of this remark—the War Office were involved because there was a war on in Algiers, not because the correspondent was a military one—and referred the refusal back to the Foreign Office. An official at the Foreign Office, who knew nothing about the previous correspondence, having been on leave, it was alleged, referred the matter back to the War Office who said that they had refused because of American objections while keeping their own reasons secret. The American authorities, naturally enough, declined to accept responsibility for refusing permission for a British *civilian*. The Ministry of Information was contacted and they too could see no reason for an exit permit not to be issued, if MI5 had no objection. At this point Hollis withdrew his objection if the Foreign Office agreed. The Foreign Office official, faced with this new situation and perhaps thinking it odd that MI5 should change their mind and place the final burden of decision on him, agreed to the exit permit, and the Passport Office duly issued it.

The central facts in this complicated story are that Hollis at MI5 and an MOI officer, *knowing* that the War Office and all other parties involved strongly disapproved, agreed to Cockburn's going to North Africa under the invented status of political correspondent—there were no such correspondents in North Africa at this time—and Harry Pollitt must have been fully aware of the nature of the approach he had to make to ensure success *in advance*. There can be no other interpretation, since the position of political correspondent was invented and there were no precedents; had Pollitt merely been following normal procedure there could be some residual doubt, but he was not. Officially he would not even have known that MI5 were involved in the process of issuing exit permits, let alone have relied on their changing their minds. This raises the obvious question, why was it that the Communist Party were prepared to risk the revelation of such collusion and the possibility of a fierce row when it became known? Why indeed had the *Daily Worker* and the Party been so intent on getting Cockburn to North Africa?

Sir Anthony Rumbold's file entry gives no answer to these obvious questions. It is in fact a wholly inadequate whitewash of what had clearly been a deliberate ploy by those involved, mainly Hollis and Pollitt, to get Cockburn to Algiers. The explanation given was in fact accepted and the risk that Hollis and the others had run did not lead to exposure. They cannot have known that Cockburn would be arrested in the circumstances that he was, or have realised that the entirely unique status which had been invented for Cockburn would mean that an enquiry would be inevitable if anything went wrong. It must have been a shock to Hollis when he was contacted by Rumbold, as he must have been; but his explanation of what had occurred, whatever it was, must have satisfied Rumbold and would be most unlikely to appear in Cockburn's file, which of course Hollis kept. The file may yet contain enough information to answer the question why such risks were taken to get Cockburn to Algiers. In its absence we have to turn to evidence provided by Cockburn himself.

Cockburn's arrest and final removal from Algiers was made much of by the *Daily Worker*. It completely misrepresented what had occurred, alleging that some important communiqués from their reporter had been banned, and that this was a reflection of the widely prevalent censorship designed to cover up the extent of the dealings with Darlan and other ex-Vichy officials. Cockburn published a pamphlet, *Where France Begins*, under his nom-de-plume "Frank Pitcairn" (see photo), containing much of what he would have said about his experiences. Taken with references to what he wrote years later, the overall conclusions to be drawn, in context, are reasonably certain.

In Algiers there were many French MPs from the pre-war Government who had been kept in Vichy prisons there and released when the Allies arrived. They included a large number of Communists and formed, in fact, the greater part of the pre-war French Communist Party. Their perspective on the international situation appeared to have changed little with the years, and their policy and view of the world were seriously out of step with current political wisdom as seen from Moscow. Cockburn's task, it seems, was to enlighten them, beginning with the official line on General de Gaulle which was at this time to cooperate fully with him and his group. The Communist deputies might have been surprised by this but would certainly have been flattered by the principal proposal outlined by Cockburn in his pamphlet, which was the setting up then and there of a provisional government not just for Algiers but for the whole of France. They were to become in Algiers what was in effect a National Committee for France somewhat along the lines of the Committee set up for Poland after the split with the London Polish Government in Exile which we shall mention shortly. Even in the guarded language of a pamphlet published in London Cockburn established the programme quite unambiguously:

> The Communist Party see as the first and foremost task the raising of the anti-fascist war spirit in North Africa which involves . . . the earliest possible establishment of a Consultative Assembly primarily representative of and responsible to the Underground resistance movements of France with North

Africa also represented—and not merely a North African Assembly with some representation of the French underground.

This Communist tactic failed, although their support of the Committee of National Liberation established in London under General de Gaulle and their infiltration of his organisation caused
continuing difficulties and aroused Churchill's direct intervention
and anger when they attempted to send delegates from Algiers in
1944, as we shall see in the next chapter.

Christopher Andrew has suggested to the author that there was
no great need for Cockburn to come to Algiers as a Communist
agent as they had their man Klugman with the SOE in Egypt,
where he was in liaison with Tito and others in Yugoslavia. But this
seems unlikely on two counts. First, Algiers was a theatre of military operations and a long way from Cairo; Klugman would need
both a good reason and time to get over to Algiers. Secondly,
although Klugman would undoubtedly have had some contact with
a Soviet controller, he can hardly have been in a position to get
full-scale instructions on such a complex question as the setting up
of a provisional National Assembly. On the other hand, it is certain
that Pollitt was not only fully informed of what was in Moscow's
mind, as was Cockburn, but was prepared to risk Cockburn's position in order to get him to Algiers. Although the "row" which
followed did not cause as much damage as it might have done,
thanks to the Rumbold report, Cockburn was never seen in the
same light again by the authorities. Hollis's role was never disclosed and has remained secret until now. It was not known to the
Fluency Committee.

The circumstantial case for direct Moscow involvement through
their agents in London is strengthened by the actions of Burgess,
mentioned in the last chapter, in fostering the project of Hilton's
trip to North Africa and then using this to obtain military information about the campaign there. It strongly suggests that this information was needed in order to give them essential grounding for
their projected move to establish a Communist Provisional French
Government in Exile. In fact Harry Pollitt did not approach the
War Office or the MOI about a passage for Cockburn until Hilton's

trip had been concluded, although the other military correspondents had actually departed two weeks before then.

When the reports Cockburn published in the *Daily Worker* on his return and his pamphlet reached Hollis for inclusion in Cockburn's file he would have been uniquely placed to make an assessment of their importance and their place in what has been called "Stalin's secret blueprint for post-war Europe." Anthony Glees has given an account of this matter in *The Secrets of the Service* unaccountably not mentioning Algiers; even more oddly, he does not seem to mention the very first difficulty between Russia and the West: the rupture between the Polish Government in Exile in London and Moscow caused by the horrific discovery in April 1943 of the bodies of 15,000 Polish officers in the Katyn Forest, where they had been massacred in 1941 by the Russians. The facts were hotly disputed by the Russians at the time and the Polish Government's task was not made any easier in London by the fact that it was the Germans who discovered the bodies and who announced the crime to the world. That their conclusions concurred with that of the London Poles was obviously embarrassing to the Poles in their arguments with the Russians. It has taken the passage of nearly half a century and the emergence of Gorbachev and *glasnost* for Russia finally to admit to Stalin's perpetration of the Katyn massacre.

The direct result of this event was the setting up of a provisional Polish Government in Moscow, but before we examine this there is one other factor which has not been noticed in the many accounts of what happened: a particularly unpleasant propaganda campaign run by the Communist Party of Great Britain. This suggested, in pamphlets and elsewhere, that the whole Katyn massacre story was a fiction invented by the Polish Government in London in active collusion with the Nazi Government in Berlin. It was seen, it appears, as the first stage in an attempt to forge a separate peace, Stalin's constant fear, no doubt echoing his own guilty conscience over the Nazi-Soviet Pact. What is astonishing about this campaign is that the pamphlets making the allegations were able to be printed in London for the CPGB and circulated without any interference from the authorities. It has been pointed out that Britain stopped examining Moscow's secret radio traffic to London after Barbarossa, but they seem also to have been given free rein to continue their propaganda on the ground through the CPGB against friendly governments in exile in London with whom they did not happen to agree. Hollis must have known of this. And it may be noticed in passing that his colleague Blunt's duties with MI5 included monitoring all communications of neutral and friendly governments and embassies in London. The Polish Government was foremost among these, and it can only be wondered whether and to what extent such events as the trials of Polish citizens in Moscow in January 1943 for treason and espionage stemmed from his activities. Certainly the Polish Secret Service was an extremely strong and well-informed part of the London exile community and their reports were valued by the Americans.

An immediate consequence of the falling out between the Russian Government and the London Polish Government in Exile over Katyn and the earlier espionage trials in Moscow was the creation in Moscow on 13 May of a "Union of Polish Patriots in the Soviet Union," whose newspaper speedily set out aims and purposes which led eventually to the creation of the Provisional Polish Government announced in Moscow in 1944 and set up in Lublin as soon as Soviet forces moved into "liberated" Polish territory. This was no isolated move, however, but the first step in a wide-ranging change in Soviet tactics that amounted to the much-discussed "secret blueprint" for post-war Europe. On 15 May the Comintern held a conference and announced that it was dissolving itself as the changing conditions meant that it was no longer appropriate to use it as "the directing centre of the international working-class movement"—the text of the resolution was broadcast on 22 May and widely commented on in Britain and elsewhere. To make the position quite clear Stalin took the unusual step of writing to Reuter's chief correspondent in Moscow, Harold King, explaining why it was thought that this was the "proper" move for him to make. His comments are illuminating because they show that it was motivated by Stalin's desire to conceal the existence of a Bolshevist secret plan for a take-over in liberated countries which was widely rumoured then, and not only among the Poles:

It [the dissolution of the Comintern] exposes the lie of the Hitlerites to the effect that "Moscow" allegedly intends to intervene in the life of other nations and "bolshevise" them . . . It exposes the calumny of the adversaries of Communism within the Labour movement, to the effect that the Communist parties in various countries are allegedly acting not in the interests of the people but on orders from outside . . . it facilitates the work of patriots in the freedom-loving countries for uniting the progressive forces of their respective countries, regardless of party or religious faith into a single camp of National Liberation . . .

Hollis must have been better placed than almost anyone to appreciate the significance of all these moves. Not only was he the person responsible for monitoring the CPGB, and therefore aware of the Polish situation in detail, including the pamphlet about the Katyn massacre. He also knew, through Cockburn, exactly what had been happening in Algiers and could not fail to link up the proposals, actually published by Cockburn, for a provisional Government for France acting as representative for the underground in France itself with the remarks made by Stalin on the closing of the Comintern. Here, clearly, was the new policy being put into action. And in fact Hollis was to spend the greater part of his time for the rest of the war dealing with the most important of the rash of organisations similar to the Polish Patriots, that of the Committee for a Free Germany which was set up in Moscow on 12 July 1943 and shortly afterwards in London.

Before going on to examine in some detail the work of this committee in Britain and what Hollis must have learnt from it, it is interesting to note how well the links established by Peter Smollett with *The Times* served Stalin in the days after the abolition of the Comintern. In an article on 24 May the paper remarked:

The decision to dissolve the Communist International is a wise step and one of the most important political events of the war. It removes the last remaining apprehensions, long unfounded but persistent in many quarters, that the Russian Government was pursuing through this policy a policy of world revolution . . . It destroys the last slender ideological basis of the Axis in the Anti-Comintern Pact and the last crumbling mainstay of Axis propaganda in the "Bolshevist bogey."

The echoing of the phrase "Bolshevist bogey" in Smollett's instructions to the BBC noticed earlier emphasises how completely the "open" channels of information had been infiltrated. Small wonder that the "moles" went undetected by anyone else in MI5, against this background and what was, in effect, the beginning of the Cold War.

9
The Cold War in 1943

THE Communist activities which America uncovered in Algiers—
and it is difficult to imagine that the British authorities would
have taken any steps at all over Cockburn, let alone create the
row that John G. Winant did with some courage at the highest
level—were only a small part of the political war the Russians were
waging with the exiled Allied governments located mostly in London. It has to be said once again that they were fighting what came
to be called in London at the time the "Cold War," with the
complete conviction that victory in Europe would be followed inevitably by revolution. The leaders of the Allied governments in
exile were acutely aware of the battle they were fighting; the Polish
government in particular knew that their enemy was in Moscow
just as much as in Berlin.

It is sometimes difficult to pinpoint with exact timing the shifts
in *realpolitik*, but it has become conventional to date any analysis of
the ideologically based conflict between East and West which has
dominated our time to the period after the end of the war. Winston
Churchill's "iron curtain" speech is seen as creating a watershed for
the suspicions about Russia which had been growing since the war
ended. In fact the roots of the Cold War, and the groundwork for
some of the most important early coups, such as the treachery of

Klaus Fuchs and Alan Nunn May, are to be found during the war itself, in 1943. MI5 were involved from the beginning in monitoring the activities of many of those involved, and these Russian successes were a direct result of their shortcomings. Hollis was a central figure in what occurred and, as will be explained, it is almost impossible to believe that he did not know what was happening and at critical moments actively cover up what he knew from his political masters.

That the conflicts between East and West were seen as just that by the Russians was obvious to commentators from the West in Moscow by the end of 1943. To the Polish and Algerian-French Committees had been added numerous others, including the Free Germany Committee. A telegram from the British Embassy in Moscow in late 1943 reported a Soviet official saying: "Anyway, we now have something that will prevent you from introducing 'Darlanism' all over Europe!" The official in the Foreign Office commenting on this remarked that it was "a possible indication that the Soviet authorities regard the Free Germany Movement among the captured German prisoners [mainly from Stalingrad] as possessing more than mere propaganda value."

The extraordinary naïvety of this comment is a measure of the failure of British Intelligence to alert their colleagues in the Foreign Office and elsewhere to what they perfectly well knew was happening. Although MI5 only dealt with matters within the United Kingdom, the presence of German Communist exiles in Britain with close links with Moscow meant that they were in a position to provide the fullest background information. They did not do so and in fact, in the case of Fuchs, Nunn May and others, enabled the Russians to gain a head start.

When the Free Germany Committee was announced in Moscow Hollis must have realised its significance, having dealt with the exactly similar event in Algiers involving Cockburn. His job at Blenheim, near Oxford, was focussed on the German Communists in Britain, who were always at loggerheads with the exiled Social Democrats. When the Communists approached the Social Democrats with a proposal for a similar committee to the Moscow Committee Hollis knew of it immediately and was in a position to see it for what it was. Its significance can be seen now from the name of one of the leaders of the Moscow Committee alone: Walter Ulbricht. When the first meeting of the British Free Germany Committee came to be held in London on 25 September 1943 Hollis had arranged for the fullest surveillance of all that happened and for a detailed breakdown of the political background of those involved.

Hollis did not himself prepare the report of the meeting. This was done in London by one of his officers, Captain S. P. Brooke-Booth, a fact which is not without significance, as will become clear when the final cases for and against Hollis are examined later. The two most interesting personalities mentioned by Brooke-Booth at the time were Hans Kahle and Professor Robert Kuczynski. Kahle, Cockburn's friend from Spanish Civil War days and now a fellow correspondent on the re-opened *Daily Worker*, addressed the meeting at length as a representative of the Moscow Committee. As MI5 knew, this was only a formal title, although part of the 400 invited audience may have thought from his enthusiastic manner that he had indeed just come from Moscow. Actually he had remained in Britain since his escape from Spain except for the brief period when he had been detained and deported to Canada. When he had first arrived in Britain he had stayed with the Haldanes, and on his return to Britain from Canada, with MI5's specific approval, he had immediately re-established contact and taken the job of military correspondent with the *Daily Worker*, as we have seen. Kahle's speech repeated the aims of the Moscow Committee and made it quite clear that their purpose was to establish a provisional Government against the day when Germany would be liberated and the Nazi regime removed.

Professor Robert Kuczynski, as chairman of the committee, was obviously an important figure, though he did not feature as prominently as Kahle and other speakers who were totally committed to Russia such as Siegbert Kahn who wrote pamphlets for a group called ING (Inside Nazi Germany) publications and put forward the orthodox line untroubled by any British censorship or, it seems, surveillance by MI5. Brooke-Booth reported the activities of the nascent committee and reviewed what was known of the participants. Clearly, to him, the committee had no obvious role, in the situation that its members found themselves, other than to attempt to forge links with Social Democrats and win them over to the Soviet view of things. Hollis would have seen more in the situation, having Cockburn's file and the full range of reports before him, including information on a brilliant young scientist Klaus Fuchs. He already knew Fuchs's case, as he had been responsible for vetting Fuchs when he first worked in Britain as a scientist, subsequently when he became a British subject to enable him to work on Tube Alloys (the Atomic Bomb project), and again at this time when he was cleared for the Americans, who insisted that all who worked on their end of Tube Alloys be thoroughly vetted.

The first link Hollis would have established between Fuchs and active Communists would have been the connection with Hans Kahle. When Kahle was sent to Canada he found himself confined with Germans who were mainly Nazis. Among the few Communists in his group of detainees was Klaus Fuchs. Kahle got to know him well, and when Fuchs returned to Britain he put him into contact with the Kuczynski family, first with Jürgen and then with Sonia. At the time of the setting up of the Free Germany Committee Kahle happily made use of Fuchs's presence in Birmingham when he set up a branch of the committee there. Astonishingly, while Fuchs was taking an open part in the Birmingham Free Germany Committee he was also sending out information on the Tube Alloys project and, according to Sonia herself, was doing so through her. She was a secret member of the Party and handling a considerable number of GRU agents, first from a cottage just outside Oxford and then from a new location within Oxford itself.

Despite all this Fuchs was cleared by Hollis at MI5. In chapter 12 we shall establish Hollis's precise role in this affair. For the moment it is worth emphasising what has been established here for the first time: namely, that Hollis knew of Fuchs's activities not only through surveillance of the committee but through his file on Cockburn which gave him an entirely separate bearing on all those involved—Fuchs, Kahle and the Kuczynskis—thus removing any doubt about what was happening.

After the inaugural meeting of the Free Germany Committee a

pamphlet was published by Siegbert Kahn, *The National Committee "Free Germany."* This revealed by chance another aspect of the affair which was of major importance and must have been known to Hollis and MI5. Kahn began by talking of the most convincing manifestation of the power of the new group—the fact that it had its own radio station:

> Since the middle of July [1943] a new radio station "Free Germany" has been speaking three times a day to the German people. Among the speakers are members of the German Army: plain soldiers, staff officers, doctors, military lawyers, NCO's of all the services and German writers, politicians and trade unionists. They all jointly exhort the German people: "Unite for ending the war by overthrowing Hitler! Put an end to this criminal war and the criminal Hitler gang! For the salvation of the German people! For a free and independent Germany!"

There is more than an echo here of the Algiers announcements, and even of those put out at the time of the People's Convention aimed at the British people. But the most interesting thing in Kahn's pamphlet is the mention of a radio station within Germany itself allegedly run by a National Peace Movement. He even quoted from a broadcast made from this station on 4 August 1943. In fact no such station was recorded by the BBC monitoring stations. This was not because the station did not exist, but because it was, almost certainly, a British "black" broadcasting station, one of many run by Sefton Delmer at Woburn Abbey.

Similar situations arose on a number of occasions when exiled governments enquired of the British authorities why there was no mention of, say, a Norwegian underground broadcasting station, which they could hear clearly every night, on the BBC monitors' reports. The reason for this was that since the stations were "black" it was decided that the BBC would ignore them rather than give the complete text, which could easily have been arranged. This would have involved the BBC having contact with the illegal broadcasters, which they absolutely refused to do in any shape or form. Sefton

Delmer's Peace Movement radio station flourished, and there must have been many Germans hearing it in Russia who actually believed that it was being broadcast from inside Germany.

Unlike the Norwegian Government in Exile the Russians and their German shadow administration in Moscow did not need to enquire about the station, because Sefton Delmer was putting it out as part of the war effort with their full knowledge; no doubt he provided Siegbert Kahn with his quotation! Viewed as an event in the cold war this was a remarkable coup, for the British had in effect been duped into broadcasting the most sophisticated propaganda for a post-war Communist Government in Germany by Sefton Delmer, acting for his Soviet masters. Many have doubted that Delmer, a *Daily Express* reporter later with impeccable *Express* views, could have been a Soviet agent as has been suggested. However, his loyalty appears to have been determined by a traumatic incident that took place when he was in Germany as a reporter before the war. One day, when he was unable to cover a Nazi demonstration, an impoverished colleague agreed to go instead. Later that evening the man was caught in a burst of gunfire from a Nazi machine gun. He did not die immediately. He tried to pull himself along the street away from the area; for hours no one dared risk help him and he finally died there. The shock of this incident was reinforced for Delmer when he was called upon next day to identify the body. Years later he was able to remember every detail of the scene, down to the holes in the soles of his friend's shoes. Readers of his autobiography, which gives a full account of his black broadcasting, may clearly perceive his loyalty though he does not explicitly state it.

The significance of these broadcasts for MI5 was not merely to emphasise the importance of the Free Germany Movement, but in the others involved in them. These included Philby, a regular visitor to Woburn, a friend of Delmer's and one better able to appreciate black propaganda than most, and zu Putlitz, a friend of both Cockburn's and Burgess's who returned from America towards the end of the war and immediately began working with Delmer on his broadcasts having been formally "introduced" by none other than Anthony Blunt.

The cold war as seen in Moscow, the fight against "Darlanism," did not stop with attempts to set up Soviet Governments in Exile for Germany and other occupied territories. It also sowed the seeds of a profound distrust between the other allies, notably Britain and America. Early in 1944 Fred Warner at the Foreign Office News Desk was asked by an American correspondent to comment on Russian allegations that Britain was deliberately releasing able-bodied German prisoners of war, and that these were then appearing on the eastern front where some had allegedly been captured, revealing what had been happening. Warner discreetly replied: "Such moves by the Russians are puzzling. I cannot explain them and can only say that they make me very pessimistic about the prospects of a really close co-operation with the Soviet Union in the postwar years" (17 March 1944). The most serious example of this kind of provocative remark by the Russians had occurred a few weeks before in what came to be called the "*Pravda* incident." This was described as follows by a well-informed observer, Sir Giffard Martel, present at the time, who had been Head of the British Military Mission to Moscow:

> On January 17, 1944 the Russian newspaper *Pravda* published a message which was alleged to have come from their Cairo correspondent on 12 January to the effect that a secret meeting had taken place between Ribbentrop and two leading English personalities at a coastal town in the neighbourhood of the Pyrenees . . . The aim of the meeting was to be the making of a separate peace with Germany, and the message added that the meeting was not without result.

There was, so far as is known, no truth in these rumours, which none the less created friction between the allies. On the ground in England the chosen avenue for this new Soviet cold war ploy that was to reach its height in the years after the war over the China question was, once again, Claud Cockburn's news sheet *The Week* and the other Communist publications. *The Week*'s first issue after the inaugural meeting of the Free Germany Committee came out with an explicit statement of the new policy: "Britain's only real card in standing up to the United States is the Soviet Alliance." This has remained in broad terms the Soviet policy for Britain from that day to this. The American authorities in London were incensed by this publication and sent a copy of it to Washington, who asked them to send copies of all subsequent issues. This they did until the magazine closed. As it was a paper with a considerable following among well-to-do supporters of the left and the media generally, the American authorities no doubt saw in Cockburn's outpourings a significant strand in British thinking. The Russians here scored a palpable hit in their new cold war tactics.

In order to make matters quite clear to the British, the Russians seem to have decided to sacrifice a pawn in their version of the "great game." While employing Cockburn for their overt campaigns they also stepped up espionage on a wide front. Their use of Fuchs and Nunn May and others was kept exceedingly secret, but in minor matters they continued on such a scale that discovery was almost inevitable. Knowing that their CPGB headquarters were bugged and that everyone entering and leaving the building was followed, they none the less used D. F. Springhall, perhaps the most immediately recognisable "high profile" British Communist, to run a series of agents in the field who were supplying military secrets. Inevitably Special Branch officers following Springhall on a routine basis discovered what he was doing. Arrests and prosecutions followed. With the British subjects involved, notably Captain Ormond L. Uren, an SOE officer, the matter was straightforward. However, Springhall was the National Organiser of the CPGB, and to prosecute him for engaging in subversive activities against the Crown when Russia was an ally greatly valued in military terms would have been extremely difficult politically. MI5 decided, no doubt after consulting their political masters, that Springhall should be prosecuted instead under the Official Secrets Act, which he duly was. He was given a long term of imprisonment. The Russians for their part sacked Springhall from the CPGB, claiming that his activities were illegal as far as they were concerned, and then retaliated in a mild way against the sentence by arresting a Russian secretary at the British Embassy in Moscow on a trumped up charge.

It is not easy to be exactly certain of the Russians' motives here. Whether they deliberately offered Springhall as a ploy, or whether they simply intended their adoption of all-out espionage to bring the new cold war "anti-Darlanism" message home to Churchill as strongly as possible, the desired result was obtained. Churchill was very angry indeed at what had occurred and in the following year sent his often reprinted telegram to Duff Cooper, the then resident in Algiers, protesting at his suggestion that some Communist delegates be included in a party with de Gaulle coming to London:

> I suppose you realise that we are weeding remorselessly every single known communist from our secret organisations? We did this after having to sentence two quite high grade people to long terms of penal servitude for their betrayal, in accordance with their communist faith, of important military secrets. If therefore the French Committee or any representatives sent here are infected with communism they will certainly not be made party to any British or, I expect, American secrets.

The Soviets' early moves in the cold war had indeed evoked the response that Churchill indicated here. Whereas the ordinary Ministries were left alone at first, the security services were looked at closely. In his diary entry for 13 August Alexander Cadogan noted briefly: " 'C' [head of MI6] about Communists in his organisation." What was actually done was to set in train a thorough check on MI6 staff, the pre-war veteran Valentine Vivian taking responsibility for the distasteful work involved. An anonymous ex-MI6 officer is quoted by Glees as saying that there was some check on Philby in 1944, and no doubt this was Valentine Vivian's investigation. Clearly it was not very effective; though some officers appear to have been moved to less secure posts, Philby himself was not suspected. There is no doubt that a similar exercise took place in MI5, but there has been no discussion of it in any of the books in the field drawing on recollections of former officers. The massive penetration of the organisation, which we now know occurred, seems to imply that the investigation was carried out by someone who was himself reluctant to point the finger at obvious suspects, although Maxwell Knight strongly suspected that there must be an agent in MI5 after Tom Driberg, his mole in the CPGB, had been identified by a leak. Hollis was the officer in charge of Communist affairs in MI5, and we have the direct evidence of Maxwell Knight's assistant that his paper "The Comintern Is Not Dead" and similar documents all reached Hollis's desk but got no further, as we have seen. Whether Hollis was the officer in MI5 given the task of removing Communists from MI5, as Vivian did in MI6, will probably never be known, but he would have been the obvious choice.

There is another pointer to Hollis's collusion with the Communist Party, and that is over the question of Niels Bohr, who was not a spy, and the other nuclear experts, Fuchs and Nunn May, both run by the GRU, already mentioned, who were. The Bohr affair will be examined in detail shortly, but for the moment it is sufficient to say that Bohr had approached the authorities, and even Churchill himself, with a request to be allowed to co-operate with ex-colleagues of his in Russia on nuclear questions. Churchill was outraged and threatened Bohr with internment, even saying in one memorandum that Bohr was on the edge of mortal crimes. The significant point is that Bohr had previously told MI5 of the Soviet approach to him, and they were fully aware of what he was doing and Churchill's subsequent reaction to it. Whether the officer who dealt with Bohr was Hollis directly or someone in his department, he cannot possibly have been in ignorance of Churchill's views. Yet he did nothing to draw attention to the cases of Nunn May and Fuchs, and no doubt others, who he knew perfectly well were engaged in exactly the same work as Bohr and were active Communists.

As the Springhall affair developed, the American authorities in London were kept informed of the case and were specifically asked if there had been any similar outbreak of espionage in America. They must have been amused by this request, since by this time they had already begun to realise that the British security service MI5 was not entirely realiable. In one important report to Washington the Embassy in London actually quoted an extensive report from the Polish Political Intelligence Service in London on the activities of the Communist Party in Britain, which they had observed was becoming very active long before any of the British authorities commented on the fact. By chance the Polish report had come to the American Embassy two days before the British section of the Free Germany Committee was established, adding weight to their conclusions. The report is of particular interest since it does not deal with Communist activity among the various exile groups but with activity in the native community. A main feature of their findings, which would have escaped Churchill's personal attention, absorbed as he was in the most complex problems prior to the second front, was the establishment of a chain of Communist bookshops in cities throughout the country from Exeter to Edinburgh. These were being used as the front line in a new campaign for all the far-left groups, not just those that were openly Communist. They displayed an enormous variety of pamphlets, including many of those mentioned here by Cockburn and others. The Polish intelligence officers had examined these in detail and realised that it was quite impossible for them to have been printed and distributed with the paper rations and funds available to the CPGB, the nominal publisher of most of them.

Although the Communist Party did not field many candidates at the end of the war, the general propaganda campaign for the far left, focussed on these outlets from 1943 onwards, must have affected the climate at the time of the election in 1945. With his known feelings about Communist activity Churchill would no doubt have been very interested to know what was happening at the grass roots, if MI5 had ever informed him. As it was, the report came from the Polish side, who were known to be at loggerheads with the Russians.

If the American authorities had pressed for action over the fierce anti-Americanism seen in Cockburn's paper and everywhere else on the left, they would have faced a united front arguing for freedom of the press, particularly a press sympathetic to Russia which was bearing the brunt of the fighting. MI5, in the person of Hollis in charge of Communist affairs, also took this view it seems. Understandably, the public would have been incapable of taking in any news or propaganda dealing in an unfavourable way with Russia, especially when every newsreel was filled with coverage of fighting on the eastern front and the walls throughout Britain were daubed with the slogan "Second Front Now!"

It was for this reason no doubt that the purge which Churchill described as "remorseless" in the security services was so weak in MI6 and almost non-existent in MI5. None the less it did expand from this small beginning in the secret heart of the Government services to take in a number of other particularly sensitive Ministries, mainly the MOI. We have already seen how Peter Smollett used his position at the Russian desk there to call up crucial editorials in *The Times*. This process continued right through 1944 and seriously distorted the establishment's view of Russia in the build-up to the great conferences in Moscow and Yalta which were to determine the outcome of the war and the shape of Europe after it. Giffard Martel, commenting in 1946 on a *Times* editorial on 3 February 1944 dealing favourably with a new Soviet constitution, realised that something was amiss in the paper's line. He quotes the central theme of the *Times* article at length. The writer had received with enthusiasm Russian proposals for decentralisation and devolution of powers to each of the sixteen Soviet republics, though this might mean Russia's sending sixteen delegates to each conference, saying that they would be "received with particular interest and sympathy in this country, owing to the interest which it obviously owes to the flexible framework of the British Commonwealth of Nations [sic]." Martel remarks that at the time those in Russia realised that this was simply propaganda, and his analysis begged the question of how such propaganda had got into *The Times*.

Whether or not Churchill ever discovered how this was done in detail, through Smollett and his creature E. H. Carr, the MOI did indeed begin to feel the effects of a purge, combined with the application of security measures which had never been extended to it before. At crucial meetings prior to the landings in Europe Brendan Bracken himself was denied access to the Cabinet and complained bitterly to Churchill in writing. Churchill replied movingly, saying that Bracken could see him any time he liked and blaming him for "beating me up on paper," telling him not to do it again.

But Bracken was still kept from secret meetings. He even had the chagrin of having to listen to complaints from his censorship chief Francis Williams that American papers were carrying reports of material not released in Britain, or banned by Foreign Office censor stops even when it had leaked out.

The fierce battle within the MOI which developed as a result of these events has not received the attention it deserves. The papers released into the Public Record Office are incomplete and disordered. But some incidents have become widely known, though without their significance in this cold war being seen till now. The best example is perhaps that of the MOI's banning of George Orwell's *Animal Farm*. Written sometime between the end of 1943 and early 1944 it was easily recognisable as a savage attack on the Soviet Union. Orwell had been forced to leave the BBC after making an uncensored broadcast referring in cynical terms to the abolition of the Comintern. His revenge, one of the most brilliant satires in the English language since the days of Swift, was also an unmistakable blow in the cold war.

The MOI faction associated with Williams knew immediately what Orwell's book was and took the opportunity to strike a blow for their side which was also undeniably in line with formal Government policy of support for Britain's ally. When a publisher approached them for "advice" on whether to publish the book or not—censorship was a very gentlemanly business then, when it affected books—they unhesitatingly banned it and Francis Williams, head of censorship, was directly responsible. Orwell had set great store by the book and when its publication was stopped he was obliged to seek his living as a journalist, appropriately enough on *Tribune*, which had carried his earlier bitter attacks on the People's Convention. When the book finally came to be published it was seen by the general public as one of the most effective blows struck in a cold war which they were just becoming aware of; in reality it owed its force to the bitter struggle which had started in 1943/4, at the time Orwell wrote it.

Francis Williams's threat to resign came over the question of censorship of news reports of the civil war in Greece. Williams was responsible for all censorship, but he discovered to his acute annoyance that all information reaching the MOI was being censored in Cairo before it reached Britain. There is as yet no direct evidence linking Williams's stand with the Communist secret activity in Britain. In view of the almost universal outcry on the left against the suppression of the Communist Greek partisans there may have been no need for any. It was sufficient no doubt that Smollett exerted his influence on *The Times* to produce one of the most famous and most frequently cited editorials opposing Churchill's line. Williams's own protest was directed more against the Foreign Office, whose Press Department co-ordinated the pro-Churchill line and ensured that Williams received nothing but pre-censored information. Williams found again that information which had had censor stops placed on it at the request of the Foreign Office was published with impunity by the American press, and it may well be that his anger was fired more by the affront to his *amour propre* than by any active subversive intention. Further, although he did not carry out his threat of resignation, and went on to become Attlee's public relations officer in the immediate post-war years, he never won his war with the Foreign Office Press Department, as MOI papers released in the Public Records Office make clear. The solution to that problem was yet another classic example of infiltration by Guy Burgess who, as we shall see in the next chapter, arranged his transfer to the Press Department after carefully cultivating a connection with the head of it while he was at the BBC.

Hollis's brief as an MI5 officer watching the activity of all Communists in Britain gave him a ringside seat at these early stages of the cold war. There cannot have been one of the vitally important areas which we have looked at here that he did not have direct information on, either through Cockburn or known Communists such as Hans Kahle and the Kuczynskis. He collaborated on an almost daily basis with Philby in MI6 on Soviet matters after the anti-Soviet section there was set up with Philby as its head. Even before, he worked closely with him and would have known all about the black propaganda broadcasts, for example, and been responsible for the vetting of men such as zu Putlitz who worked for the stations controlled by Sefton Delmer.

Particularly damaging was Hollis's clearance of all the Soviet agents so far known who were infiltrated into the atom bomb project. We will examine his response to them in chapter 12, but it will already be clear that he did nothing, although fully aware of his Prime Minister's vigorously expressed fears about the dangers of Communist infiltration and espionage. The fact that the detection of Communist infiltration was more than a theoretical possibility at the time was revealed after the war when Churchill disclosed the purge of the security services in his history of the war. But there was an even more pointed revelation of it in 1955 when the then Chairman of the Parliamentary Labour Party, Maurice Webb, revealed in an article in *The People* that he had denounced Guy Burgess as a Communist in 1944 and had been in some way responsible for his "removal" from the BBC.

It has never been clear before why Webb should have made such a denunciation at a time when Russia was Britain's ally; it can now be seen as entirely plausible within the framework of the emerging cold war described here. If what Webb said was true—and there are good reasons for questioning at least some of the facts related to him—and the BBC had a record of Burgess as a Communist, the close links between the BBC and MI5 would inevitably have meant that this information would have reached Hollis's desk. If there had been an actual dismissal, the most unlikely part of Webb's story, this would only have been after direct discussion with MI5, who monitored all security aspects connected with the BBC's staff, as they do to the present day. Hollis would have known that there was already a file on Burgess as one of their agents who was "running" some useful sources of information. He could have safely discounted Webb's denunciation in terms of a misunderstood meeting in connection with Burgess's MI5 alter ego and left it at that. If he was acting to protect Burgess more directly, he might perhaps have taken the risk of destroying all reference to the incident. Whichever action he took, it is unlikely that he realised that this move of Burgess from the BBC at the very beginning of the cold war was to be the prelude to his defection less than a decade later.

10
The Red Dawn
in China -
Prelude to Defection

THE attempts by European Communists to bring about revolution failed except where their countries were in effect occupied by Soviet forces. The cold war scenario, begun as the war was within sight of its end, settled down to become the norm of the postwar world. The Iron Curtain did indeed descend as Churchill said, with a divided Germany its main feature. Almost from the beginning America gave effective backing to countries on the free side of this curtain, including Britain despite the shock of its socialist postwar government.

In the Far East, and especially China, there was no Iron Curtain; Mao Tse Tung and his Communist cadres became the masters of the entire mainland of China. Before Mao Tse Tung was recognised there developed a distinct difference of approach between the American and British governments. Whereas America continued her involvement in Europe and supported Britain, in China Britain developed a policy which led to her recognising Mao as the ruler of a new Communist China. Astonishingly Burgess was much involved in moving British policy towards this end. It is amazing that one man could find himself in so many different positions, and even experienced journalists have said that his junior post in the Foreign Office meant that he could not have had much influence. But in fact, Burgess held the China desk and prepared the papers that formed the basis of advice given to Ministers, which became the British line.

Perceptive American commentators have thought that Burgess played some part in the China fiasco, notably General MacArthur's biographer C. A. Willoughby. To establish how true this suspicion was, it is necessary to work back through Burgess's career from that last act which made him known to the public.

The circumstances of Guy Burgess's defection to Russia with Donald Maclean in 1951 have been analysed by every writer on the subject, from leader writers immediately after the defection to scholars dealing recently with espionage. A consensus has emerged that Burgess was not supposed to defect and only did so on the spur of the moment. There are many reasons for believing this to be true as will become clear, but what has not been remarked is that a corollary of the theory that Burgess's flight was a last-minute decision must be that he was sure that he himself was not in any danger from M15. The same applies even more strongly to Anthony Blunt who, by his own account, was ordered by his Soviet controllers to defect also but declined to do so, as seems to be confirmed by the very first news reports of the defection published in the *Daily Express*, which made mysterious reference to a third possible defector:

> According to a friend, [Burgess and Maclean] planned the journey to "serve their idealistic purposes" . . . News of their plan was given to the authorities by [the] friend who said they expected him to go with them. They were to go to France as if on holiday and then make their way behind the Iron Curtain. The friend backed out.

Burgess's certainty on this is the more remarkable since, as we have seen, it has been alleged that he was denounced as a Communist in 1944 and obliged to leave the BBC because of it. As the prelude to Burgess's defection undoubtedly began with his move from the safe haven of the BBC, under the wing of George Barnes, Maurice Webb's allegations in *The People* newspaper are the most logical place to start in describing the stages on Burgess's "long road to Moscow."

Webb's claim that he had denounced Burgess on at least two occasions was made when the 1955 White Paper on the defection, prompted by allegations by the defector Vladimir Petrov in Australia, looked like bringing the whole Burgess question out into the open. There was talk already of a "third man," said by now to be the person who had warned Burgess and Maclean rather than the person who refused to defect with them, and the most likely reason for Webb's speaking out was that many in Parliament knew that he had been a close working colleague of Burgess's throughout the war when Burgess had been at the BBC. A good deal of what Webb had to say suggested that Burgess had attempted to use him in order to obtain confidential information, implying that Burgess's post at the BBC was not of any great importance, a myth which has survived to the present day. In reality Burgess knew vastly more than Webb, who was in fact no more than a parliamentary correspondent, with a leading position in the press lobby. At one point Burgess tried to get Webb the job of sole parliamentary reporter for his programme "The Week in Westminster," in place of the medley of MPs who normally did the commentary. He failed, but he did get him a part-time job doing talks when he left the BBC for the Foreign Office. Webb's anxiety that this might come out, and that it would ruin his position as Chairman of the Parliamentary Labour Party, was justified. If he had been thought to have been a recruit of Burgess's, this would indeed have been the end of him, particularly as he took a leading role in a campaign to oust Attlee from the leadership of the Labour Party and replace him with someone more useful to the far left.

Webb's account as reported in *The People* was not merely couched in general terms. Two instances are described that ring true. The first concerns a conspiratorial incident that took place in a pub after a broadcast he had done for Burgess:

> As they were talking a man wearing a gaberdine overcoat came into the far corner of the saloon. Thereupon Burgess's manner became tense. "He's one of our chaps," Burgess said as he

went across the room to speak to him. A few seconds later he
came back and told Webb that he would have to leave at once.
Webb followed Burgess and his companion to the door and
was interested to see that they went back not to the BBC but
into the Oxford Circus tube station. Webb was interested because he recognised Burgess's friend as one of the organisers of
a Communist sponsored pacifist People's Convention Webb
had attended four years earlier.

The identification of the People's Convention as pacifist is of course
disingenuous and can only reflect the total oblivion into which that
event had fallen when he mentioned it in 1955. Webb does not
explain his own presence there or divulge who the organiser was.
There is also, more telling than anything else in the story, the
vastly improbable action of Burgess in identifying a fellow Communist to Webb unless Webb was also included in the description
of "our chaps." It seems clear that Webb knew that there had been
a purge in 1944 and decided to use it as a peg on which to hang his
story. There is no other evidence to indicate that the cold war
reached the inner circles of the BBC as Webb implied, and all
Webb succeeded in doing by making the allegations he did was to
draw the spotlight on himself, for no other evidence on the matters
he disclosed came to light until my own researches in the BBC
archives in the mid-1980s. Webb may have remembered making
some objection to Burgess's behaviour at the time that he could
have used as a cover if the BBC denied publicly that he had ever
approached them which, with Burgess's skeleton in their cupboard,
they were most unlikely to do.

There is of course an alternative explanation of how Burgess
came to leave the BBC and go to the Foreign Office News Department, which now follows. It was necessary first to explore
Webb's claim. If true, it would have meant that MI5 knew that
Burgess was a Soviet agent in 1944 and then covered for him when
he moved into the Foreign Office, which had not been entirely
unaffected by the purge initiated by Valentine Vivian in MI6. We
have seen already how the activities of the Foreign Office News
Department were blunting the almost totally pro-Soviet line being
furthered by the MOI's Russian section. As the fight against "Dar-

lanism" grew, the Russians' need for someone in the FO News Department in Britain must have become more and more acute. Papers in the BBC archives establish beyond doubt that, from the earliest days of the cold war, Burgess was paying special attention to the head of the News Department, William Ridsdale.

In May 1943 Burgess approached Ridsdale with the suggestion that a more adventurous kind of programme dealing with foreign affairs would become highly desirable, particularly on postwar Europe, as the war drew to its close. In the formal report Burgess made to George Barnes, Poland was one of the questions discussed:

> It was agreed that controversial issues were likely to arise, and must be dealt with in these talks. We took the Polish/Russian dispute as an example, and Ridsdale said that had we had a commentary during the week in question this matter would certainly have had to be dealt with. I said what about the Foreign Office stop [the Foreign Office censorship over the BBC foreign affairs operative during the war] which had existed on subjects of this kind and Ridsdale said the matter would have to be taken on a sufficiently high level for such stops to be got round. He was confident in this case he could have done this—if necessary by going to the secretary of state in person [Anthony Eden] . . . Ridsdale . . . said that though the talks might well be subject to criticism and attack from various vested interests (e.g. over Poland) this could, in his view, be faced. It was important that the BBC should give such talks as otherwise the public field was rather open at the present for agitation run by interested parties. This situation was likely to develop and he personally hoped that an early start would be possible.

By "interested parties" was presumably meant the Polish anti-Communist exiles in London. Even allowing that the report was by Burgess himself, it is quite clear that Ridsdale was already very much of his way of thinking on the Polish question, and it would have been but a short step to getting programmes on such questions put out with Foreign Office backing. Later, in 1944, Burgess's move to the News Department seemed simply a logical progression. The exact details of how Burgess put that to Ridsdale is not known, but obviously Ridsdale would not have objected and would probably have found someone with Burgess's wide knowledge of the inner workings of the BBC and Government ministries a desirable asset. For his part Burgess would immediately be able to discover the Government line on controversial events such as the fighting in Greece, and also steer the departmental view more in the direction favoured by the MOI Russian desk and Stalin.

When Tom Driberg visited Burgess in Russia after his defection he discussed with him every aspect of his work in the Foreign Office and the BBC. He discovered that Burgess had greatly enjoyed his time in the News Department with his colleague Fred Warner, who subsequently accompanied him when he moved to Hector McNeil's office in the post-war Labour Government. Driberg wrote later:

> This was perhaps the happiest period of his career in England. When we were talking about it he said: "I was tremendously patriotic about the News Department, as a department, and I still am."

Burgess's use of the word "patriotic" was not necessarily ironical. The News Department of the Foreign Office was very much a twentieth-century creation. It combined the vast diplomatic experience of the Office gathered over hundreds of years with the world of press, radio and propaganda that created the patriotic image of Britain during the First World War and between the wars. It was always at the centre of matters involving the newer diplomacy created by the media of press and radio, which earlier generations would have ignored entirely. We have already seen it in action in China when it suggested and approved a "leaked" article by Peter Fleming on BAT's troubles. Burgess would also have found that such coverage as there was of his Joint Broadcasting Committee (JBC) activities, and the radio war that was so important in the lead-up to the Second World War, would have fallen to the News Department, with the files being under their code number. It is indeed true that for the twentieth century, vast though the series of files of Foreign Office general correspondence are, they often cannot be properly understood if not read in parallel with the News Department files for the same period. Exactly what, in detail, Burgess did in his years with the Department will have to await close study by a future biographer; but he would have seen every action of the war up to the surrender of Nazi Germany, both as they appeared to the Foreign Office when the news arrived and as they were released to the public after the politicians had decided on their policy over them. As the cold war came into the open with the seizure of parts of ruined Germany by the Allies and its rapid division into zones, Burgess would have been able to follow in the greatest detail exactly what was happening, without actually gaining access to the centres of policy-making. His position can perhaps be illustrated by what happened when news of Churchill's Fulton speech which first gave wide currency to the term "Iron Curtain" was released, as Burgess told it to Driberg:

> Guy was on duty that day [5 March 1946] in the Foreign Office News Department [i.e. was holding the Press briefing]. The more perceptive correspondents asked him if Bevin had approved the text of the Fulton speech. Guy went up to the private office and consulted Bevin's secretaries. "Look here, old boy," said one of them, "you just tell the press he hasn't even read it yet—it's only just coming through on the tape— and what little he has seen he doesn't think he agrees with." Then he added: "Between you and me, of course, Winston showed him what he was going to say before he went, but don't you tell them that!"

Leaving aside for the moment the question of whether this story is true in itself—Driberg's book and its authenticity, after it had been vetted by the KGB and by Hollis at MI5, will be examined in the final chapter—it is quite clear what Burgess's job entailed. The fact that among the "more perceptive" journalists were many who had known him in his previous job as a man with the BBC who was always in the House of Commons press lobby was significant, for it was they who first thought that Burgess must have been part of some inner circle whose overall power could be the only explanation for his almost unbelievable ability to move across normally inviolate boundaries between departments such as the BBC and the FO, from one plum job to another.

The general election of 1945 produced one of the classic upsets that show the advantages of the democratic system in recording the true state of a nation's mind. Churchill, the great war leader, was rejected by the electorate and a Labour Government under Clement Attlee set up in his place. Many electors were looking to a socialist future which they mistakenly believed to be already in existence in Russia. A few members of the Labour Party, notably Harold Wilson, clung to their wartime belief in Soviet Russia and its growing scientific and industrial achievements. Attlee and in particular Ernest Bevin saw the Soviet menace for what it was and fought against the forces pointing to moves towards a Communist Britain. A major factor in the election was the part played by radio. Throughout the war people had come to rely on the BBC as their main source of information, and it was largely due to this that a report such as that compiled by Beveridge became universally known and could come to be seen by the electorate as a model for a future Britain. We have remarked how Hilton's broadcasts on the report were seen even within the Army as testing the waters for the most radical post-war changes. For Burgess the effect of radio and his part in the wartime political broadcasts was even more direct, for two of the "radio personalities" he had created, Hector McNeil and John Strachey, both obtained office in the new Government. Strachey was already well-known in the Labour Party, although his radio personality as "Wing Commander Strachey" no doubt gained him greater recognition with the public and led directly to his choice as Air Minister. McNeil, on the other hand, was an almost unknown quantity. It was Burgess who had seen McNeil's potential as a public personality and shaped both the form and the content of the talks he gave over the air. Burgess's detailed editorial work made him, in fact, closer to the American idea of a personal assistant and speech writer.

When he entered the Foreign Office under Bevin, McNeil soon began to feel the need of Burgess's help on a wide variety of matters—help which Burgess happily gave, unofficially, in spite of his relatively junior work in the News Department. The situation

was clearly irregular, and McNeil soon realised it. After two months
in office he persuaded his staff to allow him to appoint Burgess
formally as his personal assistant. At the same time Warner, the
senior official in the News Department below Ridsdale, was made
McNeil's private secretary, no doubt to keep an eye on Burgess.
Although the creation of this post was irregular, it was not without
precedent. A notorious example was that of Francis Williams, who
occupied an exactly similar post under Attlee himself in the years
after the war. Williams, who was later to write a biography of
Attlee, was soon rumoured to be the *eminence grise* at 10 Downing
Street. His role was greatly exaggerated at the time, but Burgess's
situation vis-à-vis McNeil was indeed that of an *eminence grise*. He
did a great deal of McNeil's work for him and was in a position to
see all but a few of the papers that crossed the Foreign Office
portals on their way to Bevin's desk. When Bevin was away McNeil
became the acting head of the Office. Burgess then saw everything.

Those who have speculated in later years on which of the Soviet
agents so far revealed caused the greatest damage have tended to
concentrate on Philby and Maclean. This has suited those who
have wished to preserve the *amour propre* of the security services,
for both were not in the least obvious externally and were difficult
to detect, even when their loyalty was in doubt. Burgess did not fit
into the pattern of a secret agent. His position and role in contemporary affairs were all too blatantly clear to those in authority, and
to a great many in the journalist world and beyond. This was why
the most determined effort at a "cover-up" was made after Burgess's defection. His well-known eccentricity was played up for all
it was worth, while the secret activity he had been involved in
before the war remained unknown. His position on McNeil's staff
was unusual, and his actual position was concealed by describing
him as a relatively junior member of the Foreign Office, which was
literally true. But when Petrov defected in Australia in 1954 one of
the stories he told which helped produce the White Paper on Burgess and Maclean's activities was concerned with what Burgess had
actually been doing. He described how the staff at the Soviet
Embassy in London had been kept working right through the night

coding and transmitting the vast amounts of material Burgess was supplying every day. What exactly was this material?

The scholar or researcher looking through Foreign Office papers of the time will find Burgess's notes or initials on countless documents of vital importance to the shaping of the post-war world. These range from material gathered when he was the secretary responsible for drawing up accounts of meetings prior to the establishment of the "Brussels Treaty Organisation" to an hour-by-hour knowledge of the British position during the Berlin airlift. Details of both were provided in Driberg's book and seem to have been correct; we shall examine shortly Burgess's role in the evolution of Britain's policy towards China in which a fresh study of the relevant Foreign Office papers, revealed here for the first time, establishes that on that question he was consciously misleading, while Driberg, and Hollis who authorised the publication, apparently connived at it. Petrov's account of the mass of material that was to be copied suggests that Burgess was literally taking every paper of interest out of the office for copying. There is a pointer to this being so in some cases, where he apologises for keeping papers unduly. In one of the most important, involving the China question, he kept papers for over four months. The delay itself significantly affected policy, as the paper was vital and its circulation at Cabinet level could have caused changes in British policy.

With such intense activity it is more and more surprising that the security services did not gain some inkling of what Burgess's position was. But defenders of Hollis have pointed out that without some initial clue such activity is exceedingly difficult to detect. With this in mind it is odd, to say the least, that Driberg happily described Burgess in these years as discussing questions of foreign policy with friends of his such as zu Putlitz. Hollis knew that this was in the text and passed it, and yet the text makes it quite clear to us in retrospect, as must have been clear to Hollis in 1955, that Burgess after the war was still closely involved with the group we have looked at during and before the war, all of whom were known in the final analysis to be Soviet agents. Only Cockburn was absent, "burnt" by his wartime activities and spending much of the im-

mediate post-war years behind the Iron Curtain before finally set-
tling in Ireland.

The personal strain on Burgess caused by his double life began
to tell at this time. McNeil used to claim that he never knew
Burgess to be under the influence of alcohol before six in the
evening; but as an habitué of his social circle as well as his Minister,
he might have added that Burgess was never anything like sober
afterwards. Burgess may have sensed that his position was being
questioned, or he may even have created the situation himself, as
he was to do later to initiate a move he wished to make. However
it was done, he terminated his extremely important position, from
his Soviet controllers' point of view, as McNeil's assistant with a
move to an entirely new department in which they were greatly
interested, the Information and Research Department, formed by
Christopher Mayhew.

Although Britain under a Labour Government was transformed
internally into something resembling a socialist state, her external
affairs remained relatively unchanged. Burgess must have felt the
position acutely as Britain fell more and more under American
influence. The situation in post-war Germany, after the brief fu-
sion of the British and American zones of occupation into the arti-
ficial state of Bizonia, rapidly moved towards an American rather
than a British, let alone a Soviet, model. Whereas the British steel
and coal industries were nationalised along with many other
branches of the economy, in Germany they were set up as capitalist
enterprises under the umbrella of great American business em-
pires. These developments were highlighted by a barrage of Moscow propaganda and espionage which Mayhew felt needed to be
countered, especially as they could well have had effects in Britain
which the Labour Party, particularly old union men such as Bevin,
wished to avoid at all costs.

Mayhew's idea was to set up a department that would mount an
"ideological offensive against Stalinism." It had been taken up by
Bevin, and at Attlee's suggestion a paper was submitted to the
Cabinet, where it was received with approval. Its activities were
secret, some so secret that the relevant entries have even been
removed from the printed Foreign Office indexes. A pointer to

what these may have been can be seen in the title of the organi-sation, the IRD, or Information and Research Department. Al-though Lord Mayhew was not aware of it at the time, one of the most feared and secret of the internal security systems during the war had had a very similar title. The head of this department had at one point attempted to resign, saying in a letter that if it was ever discovered what the department was doing it would be called the English Gestapo. Its actual activities were not in fact quite so terrifying, but every civil servant during the war years would have known of them. Mayhew placed at the head of the new IRD Ivone Kirkpatrick, who was fully aware of the wartime IRD, and it may have been he who gave the new department its title. Bur-gess, who was later to refer to Kirkpatrick as a "black catholic" who gave the world Adenauer, was intensely interested in what the IRD was doing, and it was to this department that he now moved.

Lord Mayhew has candidly remarked in his autobiography:

> IRD seemed to have made a good start, but I now made an extraordinary mistake. One day Hector McNeil came into my room, congratulated me on the progress we were making and said he had someone available who was uniquely qualified for IRD work. I replied that I was now only taking on people with exceptional knowledge of Soviet Communism. Who was his candidate? "My personal assistant Guy Burgess. Just your man." I interviewed Burgess. He certainly showed a dazzling insight into Communist methods of subversion and propa-ganda and I readily took him on.

There can be no doubt that Burgess relished the task of getting the better of Kirkpatrick, just as he had during the war with the help of Smollett at the MOI. But the job also marked the beginning of his complete disintegration, which in the end was to reveal the full extent of Soviet penetration in British institutions. Clearly he saw the IRD in a similar light to the JBC of his pre-war days, and gave himself the task of going round Europe and the Middle East to acquaint diplomatic, and even MI6, officers with exactly what it was that his important new department was doing. But ten years had passed since his JBC days and they had taken their toll. By the time he reached Istanbul, where he had arranged to call on Philby, he was existing on alcohol and a wide range of drugs (which had become available after the war largely through American sources). His conduct was blatant, and produced a string of telegrams complaining of his behaviour, which included joking references in public bars to the identity of MI6 agents. In Istanbul he did relax while giving Philby the fullest possible breakdown of Mayhew's attempts to counter the Communist menace and the methods he was using. According to an FBI report released in America under the Freedom of Information Act, he also became close to Philby's secretary during his stay. He was to meet her again when he moved to Washington and stayed with Philby.

When Burgess returned to London Mayhew had already been alerted to his behaviour. He removed him from his post, marking his file "Burgess is drunken, idle and dirty," as damaging a reference as could be imagined. Nevertheless Burgess was kept within the Foreign Office and moved to yet another department. This seems now to be incomprehensible except in terms of a great department looking after its own. Yet there were other factors. There is no doubt that Burgess's knowledge of Britain's pre-war activity in Germany on the ground, involving illegal broadcasting against the Nazis, placed him in a powerful position despite his lowly place in the hierarchy, particularly since the Nuremberg trials when such activity had been ascribed as a War Crime to Goebbels and his men. In addition he unquestionably did have great brilliance and knowledge. Expanding on the brief remark about his interview with Burgess cited here, Lord Mayhew has observed that you only had to listen to him for two minutes to realise that he knew an exceptional amount, particularly about modern history. Thus it was Burgess who actually wrote the article on the Labour Party between the wars ascribed to McNeil in a widely circulated history of the Labour Party. This incidentally showed how easy it was not only to infiltrate the Labour Party, but to rewrite its past. In a broader perspective he was an authority on the great Lord Salisbury, of whom he contemplated a biography, discussing it with the then Headmaster of Eton on the very day before he defected. Nevertheless it must have taken the most extraordinary powers of persuasion to talk himself into his next post in the Far Eastern Department dealing specifically with China.

The day Burgess took up his post at the China Desk, 1 November 1948, was the day Mao Tse Tung's troops overran Mukden. In a story filled with ironies and strange, often incomprehensible, conjunctions, this is perhaps the most unusual. Barely a decade previously a Communist ring had been discovered in Hollis's firm in Mukden. Now Burgess, a Communist agent, was the Foreign Office man dealing with affairs in Mukden and their implications for Britain, while Hollis was part of the British Security Service MI5 dedicated to tracking down his own colleague in the Foreign Office! It is even stranger that both before the war and later while the molehunts were in progress Hollis would clearly have agreed with Burgess's view of the situation there.

The importance of China in the postwar world was vital, and the divergence of views between Britain and America which took place at this time was of the greatest significance. General MacArthur's biographer, C. A. Willoughby, alleged that Burgess materially affected events leading up to the Korean War and its progress by leaking vital information to the Chinese. Driberg was at pains to convey Burgess's explanation of what occurred. While this is plausible, in fact it draws attention away from Burgess's actual role before the vital recognition of Communist China by Britain. Burgess contributed largely to Britain's decision to recognise China when the Americans were adamant that they would not, which in turn led to insufficient attention being paid to a warning that China would intervene in Korea. That Burgess and his controllers at the KGB took the matter seriously is obvious from the prominence given it in Driberg's book, but later commentators have cast doubt on it. Indeed it seemed odd that someone as lowly in the Foreign Office as Burgess could, among so many other things, have been a commentator on China or, if he was, that anything he said could have had the influence suggested by MacArthur's biographer. We shall now examine one of the key position papers prepared by Burgess, to show that Willoughby's suspicions, with only slight alteration in detail, were correct.

The file examined here, containing some of Burgess's most revealing comments, is based on a paper sent to the Foreign Office from China by the Indian Ambassador to China, K. M. Panikkar. The burden of Panikkar's analysis, repeated on a number of occasions, was that the revolutionary movement in China under Mao Tse Tung should not be seen as an equivalent of the Soviet movement under Lenin and currently under Stalin. He suggested that in reality it was an agrarian reform movement, and that only Mao and a few of his colleagues had any knowledge of Leninist writings and theories. Indeed it is clear now that few of the central works of the Leninist canon would have been translated at this time, and that such as existed were not widely understood. Panikkar's position was unusual in that he was a central channel of communication between China and Britain and America at a time when America had no effective mission and Britain's officers on the ground were not in close contact. Panikkar was an Oxford man, an able historian, who took a double first at Christ Church. His paper was perhaps theoretical, but it provided vital clues to what was going on in the minds of the Chinese.

It was this paper that Burgess detained for four months, thereby preventing discussion of Panikkar's thesis, which was very close to the American view. Burgess did make a fleeting apology for "holding this up very badly" and the next official to comment remarked on the fact, though without fully understanding what had happened. Burgess's position is given here, followed by his detailed comments on the paper.

> The paper is . . . well worth reading as one of the completest statements of illusions as to the "special" nature of Chinese Communism and why it will be "different" that we have yet received. We knew that these illusions were particularly cherished in India and particular attention has been devoted to combatting them there. The case is argued at greater length within and with a greater display of illustrative reasons than elsewhere but the very display of the arguments reveals their weakness. Some marginal comments will be found within [extracted and printed below] on these points of detail. They were written at the time of receipt of the memorandum. Sub-

sequent events and speeches by Chinese Communist leaders have only reinforced the rigid and essential orthodoxy of Chinese Communist policy and further exposed the illusions within.

The Indian Ambassador has two main lines of thought. The first is to differentiate sharply between China and Russia and to maintain that because of these differences China will not go Communist. Pushed to its logical conclusion this means that no other country can go Communist since no other country is identical with Russia. In fact the social differences between China and Russia are less marked than in many other cases and one would have thought, therefore, that Marxism being a social theory similar results might have been expected. However that may be, the main differences between the two countries (degree of industrialisation etc.) have for long been taken into account in formulating the orthodox policies recommended by Russian and Chinese Communist leaders. Stalin formulated them very precisely in 1927 and the CCP has since followed his line. In Mr. Panikkar's eye, however, this differentiation finally leads, though via more sophisticated hoops than others go through, to the familiar and dangerous wishful thought that Chinese Communism is basically a movement of agrarian reform.

The "turn to the cities," the advocacy of the building up of Chinese industry as the primary task of the Chinese revolution, the insistence that the Chinese dictatorship is "led by the working classes" that has featured in all recent Chinese Communist pronouncements since this analysis was written, shows that whatever relevance it may once have had no longer exists. H.M. Ambassador indicates one of these developments in his paragraph 4 within as modifying Mr. Panikkar's conclusions. Subsequent developments have abolished them.

We can, of course, agree that because of the difficulty of their task the Chinese Communists may in the long run fail just as for very similar reasons it was always said that the Russian leaders would fail in their task of imposing Communism in Russia. But I do not think this conclusion helps very much.

Mr. Panikkar's second preoccupation in his short concluding

section is the impact of Marxism on Asia. Undeterred by the fact that he has earlier said Marxism is not applicable to China he concludes that Marxism "has come to stay" for no acceptable alternative has been offered to the Asian people. From this conclusion he however partly excepts India. Here he traverses familiar ground and in his differentiation between Chinese and Indian conditions his short restatement of the position as outlined sometimes (but not always) in Nehru's books and more confidently in Nehru's recent policy, is one that it can only be hoped is sounder than is the previous differentiation between China and Russia.

G. Burgess
5th August, 1949

Panikkar's paper that followed was entitled *Karl Marx in Asia, or Chinese Communism in its Relation to Asia*. The extracts are set out here as though part of a dialogue:

Panikkar: It is safe to predict that no political doctrine however clearly planned beforehand and however rigid its dogma can remain unchanged or unaffected when it spreads over so vast a territory . . .

Burgess: One of the tenets of the dogma in question is that it is altered to suit circumstances.

Panikkar: The geographical character of the Russian Empire has had an influence in the development of the Leninist doctrine which is but insufficiently appreciated.

Burgess: Not by Lenin.

Panikkar: The economy of China as in the rest of Asia is predominantly a small peasant economy . . . Capitalism is mainly foreign, compradore or bureaucratic and therefore not national. The anti-capitalist feeling is *therefore nationalist* and not based on a class feeling . . .

Burgess: No; the peasant question is in China as in Russia a class question. Industry it is true is partially foreign, and the question therefore national. But so it was in Russia [with] French capital etc. "Russia is a semi-colonial country": Lenin.

Panikkar: The problem of liquidating the *kulaks* does not exist in China for the *kulaks* do not exist as a class.

Burgess: In Russia this was not raised until the late 1920s. And many Russian Kulaks had been *created* by the 1917 reform.

Panikkar: The peculiarities of [the Chinese ideographic] language considerably change the thought of other countries when it is conveyed through its medium.

Burgess: Mao's utterances in translation read pretty familiarly. Marx does not appear to have been much altered by translation into Slav.

Panikkar: The terms Marxist-Leninism and Leninism and Leninist-Stalinism themselves go to prove that Communist doctrine is a changing one.

Burgess: As Lenin always said it should be. Hence it can be applied to China.

Panikkar: Essentially what has been achieved in the Eastern European countries is a national revolution under Communist leadership and not a Communist revolution.

Burgess: No. An imposed revolution with Russian force behind it.

Panikkar: *Today China is dependent on the sea for her life* and this must inevitably modify her approach to the *continental* interpretation of Communism as favoured in Moscow.

Burgess: Tho' conceived in England.

Burgess's annotations dispel once and for all the attempts made in the 1955 White Paper (see p. 285) to suggest that Burgess tried in any way to conceal his Marxist-Leninist views. Not only are his remarks couched in Leninist terms, they are resolutely and determinedly partisan. Moreover this vital paper of Panikkar's and others like it did not come to him by chance but because he was the person who dealt with such matters and was regarded as the authority. His line, that Chiang Kai Shek was finished and that Mao was to be recognised as the leader of a Soviet revolution in China, was also the British line followed by his department heads Sir Peter Scarlett and Sir Esler Denning. As Burgess remarked to Driberg, his superiors had "got the whole thing taped" and "persuaded Bevin to recognise the People's Government in Peking." But they were relying on Burgess's position papers. He then followed this up with a collective pat on the back that must have infuriated his old colleagues when they read it:

> Anyone could be proud of the wisdom, the knowledge and the lack of prejudice of that department, and the people in it. It was also agreeable to find that all but one of [his] colleagues in the department were old Etonians.

The denigration of Panikkar's views continued in the Foreign Office, where the joke was "Ah yes! Panikkar! Aptly named, we always thought!": precisely the attitude that Burgess and sympathisers of Mao Tse Tung and the Soviet view of him wished to encourage. Peter Lowe, an authority on the origins of the Korean War, has remarked that Panikkar's opinions were indeed suspected by the Foreign Office. This became particularly important when the question of possible Chinese involvement was considered.

Initially Panikkar thought that the Chinese would not become involved, basing his opinion on an interview he had had with Chou En-lai in September 1950. But further investigation swung him round to the view that they would indeed act. As Lowe remarks:

> Panikkar had seen Chou En-lai on 21 September and had deduced then that China would adopt a more aggressive policy. . . . The British felt Panikkar's appraisals had to be viewed with caution given his volatile and not always reliable nature. At the same time, the warnings must be given serious consideration.

In fact, while the British Chiefs of Staff appreciated the position, the Foreign Office and Britain took the view that Panikkar's opinion was wrong. "Panikkar panicking again," with the now well-known consequences. There is no doubt that Burgess's view was echoed widely on the left of the Labour Party; as we have seen China had been a rallying cry from the days before the war and there were those who saw the cradle of that conflict there. The other major area in which Burgess's knowledge of Foreign Office policy was of use to the Chinese, and in real terms by far the most important, was over the question of the major trading firms in China. Burgess referred to them in Driberg's book:

> The Ambassador also sent admirably objective reports, not concealing his conviction that Chiang Kai Shek was done for. This—and the corollary that the communist regime must be recognised—was the established British line; and the "old China hands" of the China Association, the capitalists concerned with the £300 millions of British Money invested in China, worked loyally with the Foreign Office and (unlike the China Lobby in Washington) did not attempt to dictate policy.

This statement was as far removed from the facts as possible and reflects little more than Burgess gloating openly over one of his major triumphs, a direct blow at the capitalists he hated. The fact was, as he well knew, that the British companies involved, of which the largest was BAT, Hollis's old company, suffered grievously over their withdrawal from China and had made every effort to come to a compromise solution, as they had in the past wherever they traded. Unknown to them, Burgess had been closely involved in the negotiations throughout. He was, in fact, the person who actually transmitted BAT's own communications to and from its employees, and saw the censor intercepts of all cables sent privately from Shanghai to their Directors in London. He frequently wrote the position papers needed, and there can be no doubt whatever that through him Mao Tse Tung must have been completely informed of all the moves the company intended making. The idea that there was no China lobby in London was the sheerest nonsense. The astonishing thing is that Hollis, an ex-BAT man with many senior employees among his friends, had complete control of

Driberg's book, as we shall see, and yet he let these statements pass. Burgess's view expressed in these papers, and his action as an "agent of influence" must have been at least as important as the fact that he was able to keep the Soviet Government informed of what Britain's intentions were.

It has always been suggested that Burgess in some way dissembled his political views. His defenders have said that he made no secret of his beliefs. We can see that the latter view is unquestionably the right one, though there is no doubt that his earlier memoranda were less frankly Leninist in their terms. The comments we have examined in detail were Leninist, and the fact that he was moving more and more towards open avowal, as, in general terms, Britain moved more into America's orbit and the likely alignment of the post-war world became more evident, must have placed an intense strain on Burgess. His behaviour, never good, deteriorated so badly during one holiday that on his return he faced a full-scale inquiry into his actions from which he barely emerged unscathed.

Washington would hardly seem the sort of posting for a man who had just survived a disciplinary hearing by the skin of his teeth; but Burgess showed once again his old flair for falling on his feet and getting the job he would have wanted, that of China expert, given the limited options open. A major factor in his move must have been Philby's intimation that he would keep an eye on Burgess, who was known to be an old friend. In fact when Burgess arrived in Washington he moved into Philby's basement. This was also home to Philby's secretary whom, according to FBI files, Philby had brought with him from Istanbul, where Burgess had also stayed.

If this posting was indeed a last effort to get Burgess back on the rails, using his undoubted knowledge of Chinese affairs and of precisely how Britain's views differed from those of the Americans, it failed. Apart from his drinking, he also found the temptation of fast cars and American roads irresistible. It is ironic that the Lincoln cars which were used in Russia to sweep Intourist guests around the country, and which Hollis had remarked on in his letters home, were to be Burgess's downfall. He chose a massive twelve-cylinder Lincoln convertible shortly after he arrived and then began to collect speeding tickets with tiresome regularity. Despite warnings he was finally brought down when he got three tickets in one day in a state where another diplomat had recently killed someone by dangerous driving and then claimed diplomatic immunity. Later attempts have been made to link this with the chain of events that led to Burgess's subsequent defection with Maclean. But even spy writers would not invent such an absurd scenario. In fact, as has been shown convincingly by Knightley and others, the dates were entirely wrong and Burgess remained in America for a considerable time after the incident. An added detail from FBI files released under the Freedom of Information legislation was that a tape recording of Burgess giving an account of Churchill's presentation of a book to him was made openly at a party given for him before he left by his old friend Norman Luker, hardly the action of a man embarking on a clandestine operation.

Much attention has been paid to the exact sequence of events leading up to the actual defection. There is no doubt that Maclean had learned that he was under suspicion. The fact that he and Burgess had defected on a Friday, when the order for his interrogation had been signed that very day, seemed to point to a tip-off by a third man—later thought to be Philby. On the other hand, it has been pointed out that, if Philby was the third man, he had no time to get the relevant message to Maclean, or to his Russian controllers.

The fallacy in these analyses is that the actual signing of the order was only the last stage in a relatively complicated process which had been going on for months. There were other people who knew what was happening and would have known that the precise moment of signing would be the very last moment *by which* all relevant arrangements would have to be made. Philby has said that he sent a letter to Burgess warning him that moves against Maclean were imminent by a reference to his car, which Burgess would have understood. Blunt learned of this through Burgess and may have informed Maclean, but there were other possible routes which it would be impossible now to test, including a leak through politicians who knew of the impending action.

The choice of Burgess to accompany Maclean is not to be explained by any danger to Burgess himself. Burgess hardly knew Maclean and had not seen him for years, which meant that he would not be known to Maclean's wife or anyone they might meet. More important, he was capable of carrying out the difficult job of getting Maclean out safely. There is a great difference between going abroad with a post to go to and everything arranged, as Maclean had always done, and going illegally with every chance of slip-ups and the need for rapid changes of plan. Burgess in his pre-war days with the JBC was quite familiar with such escapades. When the day came, Burgess moved according to plan and got Maclean clean away.

The evidence that Burgess was not intended to go with Maclean, apart from the mention in Philby's autobiography of his last remark to Burgess, "Don't you go too!", is apparent in details such as Maclean's giving Burgess a false name when he telephoned his wife the previous day to say that he had invited a friend down for a meal that Friday evening. He and Maclean suspected, correctly, that Maclean's telephone was bugged. The only reason for giving a false name would be that, when Burgess returned to England, it would not be known that it was he who had been the escort. When Burgess came back from the visit to Wystan Auden in Italy, which he had apparently planned, there would be no link with Maclean's move at about the same time. Burgess was already under suspension from the Foreign Office after the debacle in America, and a visit to consult an old friend on his future would have been entirely understandable. In fact he obtained all the consultation he needed in conversation with Maclean just before the defection who, independently, had come to precisely the same conclusion about the hypocrisy and dishonesty of the Labour Government as Burgess. One old friend of Burgess's has suggested that he may also have made a fundamental misinterpretation of the political state of Britain and envisaged returning after none too long a period to a Titoesque regime, perhaps under Aneurin Bevan whom he regarded as a promising young leader. Whatever his reasons, the defection proved to be the single most important action of his life. It is clear too that in following the logic of his position he precipitated the extended analysis of the political establishment in Britain of which this book is a part. If Maclean had gone on his own, a spy—albeit one with an ideological motivation—it is inconceivable that the event would not have been forgotten within a decade. Burgess's career if he had remained can only be guessed at, but we would not have learned even a fraction of what we now know about the Communist loyalties of many in high places in British life. It is an irony that the elitist attitudes epitomised by Anthony Blunt would have seemed the very hallmark of an upper-middle-class establishment figure and that Blunt should have been exposed, finally, as a result of the chain of events caused by Burgess's move. There was a fundamental political honesty and seriousness in Burgess which led him to act as he did and this both defeated the devious purposes of his Soviet spymasters and exposed the hypocrisy of Blunt.

11
The Great Mole Hunt – From Burgess and Maclean to <u>Spycatcher</u>

WITH the full panoply of state secrecy brought to bear on anything to do with Burgess and Maclean, or later Philby, Blunt and the procession of scandals and spies, it was left to the long-sustained researches of journalists to discover what had been going on. That process is still continuing, but initially it went against the grain. Britain had no great tradition of investigative journalism of the kind that flourishes in America. The large papers were all in the ownership of great newspaper barons who had a firm eye on their main aim—political power with a seat in the House of Lords and no nonsense about democracy. Anything other than a conventional "scoop" was unwelcome, particularly if it offended powerful figures in the British establishment.

The spy stories that followed after Fuchs and Nunn May slowly broke down this restricted view, and there was a period when journalists such as Chapman Pincher made remarkable break-throughs. As we shall see, without Pincher the *Spycatcher* case would never have happened and in all likelihood the book would never have been written. Ironically the situation today has almost come full circle. The "espionage" reporters of the great papers all now work hand in glove with the security service, and with the Left factions in it for preference. Woe be to any civil servant or member of the public who comes to one of these men in person with a story, for both the story and the informant will be traded in immediately in exchange for some mild scoop of the old kind. Even anonymous handing over of incriminating documents can no longer be guaranteed to produce an investigation. But this is a sad decline. The great mole hunt in its heyday was a triumph for British journalism and it began with Burgess's heroic, or foolhardy, act of following into exile the man he was escorting.

Among the journalists whom we have seen listening to Burgess as he announced Churchill's Fulton speech at the Foreign Office news briefing, and who remembered him swanning through the press lobby at the House of Commons during the war, there was little doubt when Burgess defected that the story when it was told would be the spy story of the century.

It was obvious from his risqué life style and the ease with which he got any job he wanted that Burgess was part of some inner establishment, and that his defection would be the subject of a cover-up on a scale never before known. It fell to Chapman Pincher to deliver the most comprehensive indictment of all:

> . . . Parliament and the public have been systematically mis-
> led by official statements and reports on security and espio-
> nage affairs . . . the truth has been repeatedly suppressed,
> distorted, manipulated and, on occasion, falsified on spurious
> grounds of "national interest" while the real purpose was to
> prevent embarrassment of departments and individuals . . .
> British governments hate to be accused of cover-ups but there
> is nothing of which they are more consistently guilty, largely
> because of their dependence on the advice and testimony of
> officials over whom there is no effective oversight.

It is appropriate that it should be Pincher delivering this verdict more than thirty years after the defection, because it is he who has perhaps done more than any other journalist to keep that earliest suspicion alive and bring out the truth. An earlier book by a fellow journalist, John Fisher, perhaps the best before the cover-up of Blunt's treachery began to break down, had introduced two chapters entitled "The First Cover-up" and "The Second Cover-up," referring to the initial response to the defection by Labour Ministers in the House, and the clearing of Philby by Macmillan. In fact the propensity of successive British Governments to take the easy way out and issue warnings and immunities had already become apparent to the Canadian and American authorities from the first denunciations caused in 1945 by the defection of the Soviet GRU cipher clerk Gouzenko in Ottawa. In Canada an entire GRU spy system had been rounded up, and a wide range of academics, scientists and Government officials had been put on trial without fear or favour. Some received substantial sentences, others shorter terms of a year or so resulting in almost immediate release. In Britain it was obvious that only Nunn May, against whom the strongest indications of guilt had been obtained and who had made a full confession, was to be prosecuted. The sense of unease both among knowledgeable members of the public and the press laid the ground for the scandal that broke with Burgess and Maclean's defection. It then became clear that many establishment figures must have been closely associated with the spies and that, as in the Nunn May case, all were to be protected. Disgracefully it was in the erstwhile "colonies" that an honest clean sweep was attempted, while in Britain the discovery of the truth was left to hard-won discovery after many years' work at the frontiers of journalism. As Burgess had spent much of his working life in the company of newspapermen and Philby was himself a working journalist both at the beginning and the end of his career, first with *The Times* and finally with the *Observer*, this is perhaps appropriate.

Initially the stories were simply factual ones. Later, as revelation succeeded revelation and each time the authorities merely moved their defences back an appropriate distance with yet another off-the-record briefing which could be denied as soon as given, it became obvious that the "cover-up," if that is what it was, could only be broken by the most determined efforts of investigative reporters. Unbeknown to the reporters the cover-up had gone on within M15 itself, both to protect Britain from American wrath at the security breakdowns and, it seemed, to protect senior officers within the service. While journalists outside were trying to find out the truth about Philby and seizing on the fact that he had been head of the anti-Soviet section of M16, within M15 teams of men were going over the slightest actions of their colleagues to discover whether one of them had been a spy. Eventually, as the years passed, these two separate quests grew into one. The early reports gave way to inquiries by the investigative teams of the great Sunday papers. These in turn were overtaken by the triumphs of Chapman Pincher which finally brought the truth about M15's internal war out into the open. This we shall examine, with the main defence of Hollis, in the next chapter.

The press stories dealing with the Burgess and Maclean defection alone would require a substantial index if recounted fully. What is intended here is simply a presentation of the key events as they became known for certain through the press investigations, with an account of the most important books published in the field, culminating in the few from the universities, which began to show interest as the thirty-year-rule passed relevant documents into the Public Record Office.

The stories of Nunn May and Fuchs, the "atom spies," were superficially not unlike the classic spy stories of William le Queux and John Buchan, but the reporters with scientific training soon pierced the surface and wanted to know how two men with Communist backgrounds had managed to get through security checks to work on the most secure project of all. Though they did not know it, the American authorities were equally keen to find out. The final answer has only now become clear, but at the time there were clues enough, if the molehunters and the press had been able to see them. One clue the significance of which was not to be apparent for decades was connected with the arrival in England of the Canadian Prime Minister, Mackenzie King, shortly after Gouzenko's defection. Roger Hollis had boarded King's boat as soon as it touched shore to give him an urgent message, and also to obtain the latest information he had from the defector. It was Hollis also who had gone over to Canada to interview Gouzenko, however briefly. These two incidents would have pointed to another: that Hollis was the M15 officer who was dealing with Communist matters for M15, and that it was he in fact who had cleared May and Fuchs.

The press men who followed the aftermath of the Gouzenko en-quiry in Canada awaited similar developments in Britain, but noth-ing happened. Further progress, it seemed, would have to wait on the next defector with fresh information. But when the next de-fections took place the defectors were going the other way.

The news that two diplomats were missing was first broken by the *Daily Express*. Others soon followed, and the great era of the cover-ups was under way. This was said to be the first time that anything like this had happened in the closely knit world of the higher civil service, and the effect was particularly traumatic. But the main lines of defence were soon laid down and were used to brief the Labour Ministers who had to make the necessary state-ments in the House of Commons. Understandably they were wor-ried that there might be a scandal of very large proportions, along the lines set by the Zinoviev letter affair, if too many questions were asked suggesting that Labour had let Communists into posi-tions of power. It is now clear that Ministers, such as John Stra-chey, Hector McNeil, Maurice Webb and others, were only too well aware how close Burgess was to them, although the security services themselves, without access to BBC papers, may well not have understood exactly how thorough the infiltration was or how it had been carried out.

The line of defence in the House was to deny even such sug-gestions as those of Duncan Sandys that Burgess had been a well-known Communist sympathiser or, most embarrassing in retro-spect, that there was any real evidence that there had been a defection. One Labour MP even tried to suggest that there was no evidence connecting them with Russia at all. Neither the press nor the American authorities believed this for a moment. The Ameri-cans in particular knew that Philby had probably been involved, and insisted that he be withdrawn from his highly sensitive security posting in Washington. If an enquiry at this level had been set on foot in Britain, much more of the saga would no doubt have come to light. As it was, the cover-up worked, as it had with Fuchs and Nunn May.

Two years later Melinda Maclean was spirited away behind the Iron Curtain to join her husband, and her defection was followed by the publication of the first important book about the affair, Geoffrey Hoare's *The Missing Macleans*. Despite its early appearance Hoare's book still retains interest and is the source of a number of facts not found elsewhere.

The next development came with a defection in Australia in April 1954 of a senior Soviet security officer, Vladimir Petrov. The story broke as news in Britain, but Australia was still seen as a long way away and there was no great sensation. This would have pleased the authorities, but the press intervened and effectively lit the fuse which has been burning ever since. *The People*, which shared the main honours in the story with the *Express*, arranged for details of Petrov's story to be serialised in Britain, and this was to coincide with publication of a book, *The Petrov Story*, written by a man with security service connections who was closely involved, Michael Bialoguski. The most important of Petrov's allegations was that Burgess and Maclean were not merely defecting diplomats who had been cornered in vulgar mercenary acts of espionage—the Government line—but convinced Communists who had been agents since they were recruited as undergraduates at Cambridge together.

Here at last was the first hint of the cover-up that the press veterans knew must have taken place. They were not the only ones to realise it, and the Government decided that it would have to issue a White Paper on the defection in an attempt to answer some of the most obvious inconsistencies in the story they had peddled so far. This paper precipitated the next stage in the affair. J. Edgar Hoover at the FBI saw an advance copy. He was so enraged that no mention was made of Philby that he set in train a series of leaks to ensure that the allegation did become public knowledge. The route he chose was complex and involved the press—the *Empire News*, whose editor Jack Fishman had good security service contacts. The story was finally leaked through his contacts in the New York press, to headlines screaming ALL THAT IS NEEDED IS THE HARRY LIME THEME MUSIC "WHO WAS THE THIRD MAN"? The story revealed that the defectors had apparently been tipped off and that Philby was the most likely suspect. The day after the news broke in New York a Labour MP, Marcus Lipton, named Philby in a question in the House. Not the least surprising reaction was that of Hollis, by this time Director General of MI5, who *personally* approached Lipton in the central lobby of the House and asked him for his source of information.

While the story was developing at the highest levels *The People* kept up the running with stories such as that of Maurice Webb, already noticed, whose significance has only now been made apparent. The publication of the White Paper and the sequel to the questions about Philby was finally to produce two of the classic pieces of theatre in the spy saga. First was the clearance of Philby by Macmillan in the House of Commons, a move thought only correct since there was in fact no evidence against him that could have been used in a court of law that did anything other than suggest that he had not chosen his friends wisely. Then came the press conference stage-managed by Philby and held in his mother's London flat, at which he convincingly lied his way around all the issues and suspicions under the eye of a television film crew. His performance was so convincing that he only needed to put his tongue in his cheek once.

The next major news break came from Moscow when, in answer to a journalist's request, the *Times* and *Reuters* correspondents were called to Room 101 of a prominent hotel—no doubt an Orwellian joke—and there found themselves face to face with Burgess and Maclean. They handed out a press statement (see Appendix 2 [iii]) and after brief courtesies left. An intense flurry of journalistic activity followed, Burgess even writing a story and offering his fee to the Royal National Lifeboat Institution, which patriotically declined it. When this died down there was a possibility again that the story would now finally sink. Instead there followed an extraordinary incident which, for those who knew it, showed Hollis's hand clearly at work.

One of Burgess's wartime broadcasters who was still keen to keep in touch with him was Tom Driberg, now a prominent journalist. After Burgess's reappearance Driberg wrote suggesting an interview. This Burgess agreed to. Some months later the visit took place, and Driberg returned, bringing with him not merely material for an article or two but an entire book. The text was of course vetted by the KGB and was in any case written by one who was deeply sympathetic to Burgess, as his introduction made clear:

> In common with millions of other British newspaper readers I had found the Burgess and Maclean story one of the most fascinating news-stories of the century: doubly so, for it was not only a story of pursuit and escape, almost in the classic tradition of the "Western" films; it also had a much deeper personal dilemma of two intelligent and gifted men, the plight of a whole generation caught in the confusions and contradictions of mid-century Britain, with its chronic lack of philosophic purpose and its "mixed"—or muddled—economy.

But what has only recently become obvious is that the book *Guy Burgess: Portrait with Background* also received the imprimatur of Roger Hollis. The significance of this will be dealt with in the final chapter. It will be suggested that this was M15's first determined attempt to muddy the waters to prevent further developments in the story, most obviously by an extension of it to Blunt—at this time not known to have any connection with the affair at all—and, beyond that, the ghastly possibility that the press might sense that the most senior figures in M15 were not without stain. Again it was the press who wrecked this carefully laid plan. *The People* arranged to publish a series of articles by a friend of Burgess and Blunt's, Goronwy Rees, a Welsh academic. There was no vulgar naming of names, but the story made it quite clear to those in the know that a serious break had occurred in the wall of silence. Rees found himself disgraced and removed from his academic post, an astonishing example of power in Britain, for Rees had committed no offence. His purpose in getting his story printed had been to forestall any verdict that might have been in Driberg's book—or so it was thought. In fact, like Maurice Webb, he had little to fear but fear itself.

The impact of Driberg's book was considerable, and it did have the effect of drawing a line under one aspect of the story, for clearly no other book with this level of authenticity could be expected. The question of Burgess did not arise again until 1962, over his possible liability for prosecution, when it was suddenly made known to the press—ten minutes before the London *Evening Standard*'s deadline—that warrants had been issued for the arrest of both Burgess and Maclean, who were rumoured to be thinking of returning from Russia. An explanation for this bizarre incident, a mystery at the time, will be suggested shortly, but it had the effect of providing a peg on which was hung yet another book on the spies, by Anthony Purdy and Douglas Sutherland, entitled, appropriately, *Burgess and Maclean*.

The year that saw the publication of Purdy and Sutherland's book, 1963, also saw the first of a new kind of book—an account of M15 itself written by the distinguished Foreign Correspondent John Bulloch. Called simply *M15*, it was only published in a censored version approved by Hollis (see p. 231).

The first sign that Philby might be playing a constructive part in the literary spy game, apart from being de-briefed on a massive scale, was a story that he had ghosted a book by Gordon Lonsdale. The rumour reached the ears of a *Sunday Times* man, David Leitch, who had made an attempt the year before, while in Russia, to interview Khrushchev in order to see Philby. Bruce Page, editor of the *Sunday Times* Insight team, was aroused, and a two-year secret project investigating the life of Philby was set in train. In 1967 news reached the *Sunday Times* that their rival paper the *Observer* was working on a book with Eleanor Philby, and a classic Fleet Street struggle began which ensured that as much as could be known about Philby and his circle would be known. A not inconsiderable element in the puzzle that made such investigations easier to undertake from this time on was that one of the most important senior figures who had been handling affairs from the official side, Roger Hollis himself, had retired in 1965.

The investigation that produced *Philby: The Spy Who Betrayed a Generation* was thorough, but there was a single breakthrough which remains one of the great moments in the trail through the wilderness of mirrors: whereas Philby had long been known to have worked for M16, still a shadowy organisation whose existence was officially denied, it was now discovered that he had in fact been the head of its anti-Soviet section! Here was evidence of incompetence that would have been grounds for any kind of cover-up. It was also, though this was not understood fully at the time, an indication of the profoundly political nature of the struggle which had been going on rather than simple "spying." Knightley's description of how he found his source for the story is worth giving, not only in itself, but for its uncanny foreshadowing of a later informant, Peter Wright:

> Trying to find former colleagues of Philby's I managed to track down Leslie Nicholson, an old time SIS [M16] officer who had fallen out with the service over his pension and who had written a book about his career, *British Agent*, under the name of John Whitwell. Nicholson was broke . . . and living in reduced circumstances in a room over a café in the east end of London.

Although largely forgotten now, Nicholson's book had included a preface by Malcolm Muggeridge, himself an ex-M16 man and one of Philby's staunch defenders before his defection, and an epigraph on its half-title page by Captain Henry Kerby MP which proudly, and provocatively, stated:

> This is a piece of publishing history. For the first time ever a senior member of the service which officially does not exist tells the true facts of life as a secret agent.

It was a precedent which others were soon to follow, notably Philby himself, who, as we shall see, was provoked by the chain of circumstances which this book set off. As we shall see as well, Henry Kerby was to play a key role in the final stages of the Profumo affair which ensured that a game started by Hollis was played out to the bitter end.

The Insight team's book began to be serialised in the *Sunday Times* at the end of 1967. The first response, fortunately for the team, was a letter that gave them a vital clue to Philby's first serious problem, the now well-known affair of the planned defection of a Soviet intelligence officer, Konstantin Volkov, in Istanbul, which

Philby had stopped by telling his Soviet masters of Volkov's intentions. Volkov was duly executed. Insight splashed the story in the next issue, and Philby was sufficiently provoked to telegraph the paper offering to discuss terms for his memoirs. Though Hollis had retired, the success of the ploy of the Driberg book in quietening down the story no doubt suggested that it might be used in this case. Philby, of course, was quite capable of writing his own book, whereas Burgess, with his connection with Driberg, had naturally looked to Driberg to write a biographical study rather than expose his own soul in an autobiography. In addition much time had passed, and the ghosting of Gordon Lonsdale's book, a kind of writing which Philby had essayed before in ghosting a company history in 1957, together with the publication of *British Agent* had created a suitable literary genre that he could work within.

Philby sent out a request for someone to see him, much as Burgess had agreed to Driberg's presence more than a decade before. The journalist who went, Murray Sayle, duly returned both with a story and with the rights to Philby's book. It was published by MacGibbon and Kee as *My Silent War*, with a preface by Philby's old friend Graham Greene. A quotation from the preface was displayed on the cover of the paperback edition: "More gripping than any novel of espionage I can remember." A shrewd comment, for the book did indeed mark the point at which the real world of spies moved the fictional James Bond world from centre stage.

Although apparently an autobiography, and based on Philby's own first essays that he wrote when he was debriefed, the book was also as much a cold war text as Driberg's biography of Burgess. Philby was himself a KGB General, but he no doubt consulted closely with colleagues over his final text. When it arrived in England it was vetted by M15. According to his own account, Peter Wright was at least partly responsible for carrying this out. Wright's fanatically right-wing views would suggest that the vetting as far as he was concerned was thorough. At the same time his obvious political ignorance and naïvety, ruthlessly exposed when the spotlight fell on *Spycatcher*, meant that Philby's book remains as a significant text.

Eleanor Philby's *The Spy I Loved*, backed by the *Observer*, a personal document of intrinsic interest, came out in the same year. There also appeared a book by the veteran journalist E. H. Cookridge, *The Third Man*, which showed signs of the link-ups between M15 and outside publishers and authors that had been established with Driberg's book and, as will be seen, Bulloch's *M15*. The main reason for this conclusion was that its author had the benefit of letters and advice from Guy Liddell, Hollis's colleague and a shadowy figure who has been identified, most recently by John Costello, as a possible Soviet agent, on the basis of his friendship with Blunt and Burgess.

These books created an obvious resting place for the story which had already outrun all other comparable stories, and there was no shortage of people who would have been happy to see it finally die a natural death. Prominent among these must have been Anthony Blunt, who had been granted immunity from prosecution in 1963, in a deal organised by Hollis after final proof of Blunt's Soviet recruitment at Cambridge had come by chance through an American, Michael Straight, whom he had recruited before the war. When asked to serve as Chairman of the Advisory Council on the Arts, set up by President Kennedy, Straight decided to make a clean breast of his past rather than risk the position he would find himself in if the FBI did not discover it for themselves and he was subjected to pressures he might not be able to resist. This act of personal honesty which was conspicuously lacking in his opposite numbers in Britain—an echo of the moral standards of an earlier England—inevitably resulted in the facts about Blunt reaching M15. It took the greater part of the next decade for Blunt's story to rise to the surface and, while this slow process continued, a further, even greater scandal was being prepared in the real world inside M15—marked, in the first year of the new decade, by Hollis's recall from retirement to face a further grilling from the joint M15 and M16 committee, known as the Fluency Committee, to establish once and for all whether he was a Soviet agent himself.

The early seventies produced little that was new. Goronwy Rees published a volume of autobiography, *A Bundle of Sensations*, which gave his side of the affair that had ruined his academic life, mentioning Blunt again, indirectly. In 1973 a good restatement of the

Philby story was published by two journalists, Patrick Seale and Maureen McConville, as *The Long Road to Moscow*. That same year Hollis died; this had the effect of opening up the Blunt case completely, although it was to be the end of the decade before the final unmasking took place. In 1974 Malcolm Muggeridge added his autobiography to the growing number of accounts by contemporaries who had an interest in the affair or knew those involved. Muggeridge's interest had been shown as very much alive when he wrote the preface to Nicholson's book, though his observations added nothing of moment to the main story. In 1977 another journalist, John Fisher, wrote a resumé of all that was known so far, using the ubiquitous title *Burgess and Maclean* but with the subtitle "A New Look at the Foreign Office Spies." In resurrecting the Maurice Webb story and a number of others he provided the first clues towards the revelations about Burgess and his activities in the JBC and BBC which became known a decade later in *Truth Betrayed;* however, he missed the Blunt story which was about to break.

Sir Anthony Blunt, as he then was, had by the time of his exposure risen to great eminence. He was of course Surveyor of the Queen's Pictures, but it was his position as head of the Courtauld Institute, known in society simply as "The Courtauld," which gave him the greatest status. The cachet attached to the Institute was almost unrivalled, and gave access to many of the most sought-after posts in what has come to be called the arts establishment. When he retired in 1974 the praise heaped on him reached new heights. Blunt's biographers, the *Sunday Times* journalists Barrie Penrose and Simon Freeman, remarked:

> In September 1974 the *Burlington* magazine ran a lengthy article that verged on sycophancy. The magazine was edited by Blunt's close friend Benedict Nicolson, son of Harold Nicolson and deputy surveyor at the Palace from 1939 until he joined the *Burlington* in 1947 . . . with its emphasis on Blunt's integrity and devotion to truth it seemed, after 1979, heavy with irony . . .

In fact a large group of influential people in the art world had sprung up around Blunt as he grew older who owed a great deal to him. They could well be seen as members of a coterie who would carry on his views, which were not at all different from those which had led him to Marxism, as former students testified who remembered his lectures on Picasso's "Guernica." But keeping track of this exalted group, if the security services had been so minded, would have become an expensive and embarrassing business. Possibly for this reason, or because it was considered a growing scandal that Blunt should remain in the social position he had acquired, particularly after his retirement when he had far more ample leisure in which to cultivate his circle, leaks about him began to emanate from within the security services. There was no shortage of journalists willing to follow the story, but two were particularly determined, Richard Deacon and Andrew Boyle. Richard Deacon's *The British Connection* went a long way towards identifying Blunt as a Soviet agent and establishing the truth about his immunity. However, he experienced one of those catastrophes that authors dread: he identified as a possible Soviet agent a scientist who was still alive. The accusation was untrue and the person concerned was as alive as his solicitors, both to the libel and to its consequences. The book was pulped. It remained for Andrew Boyle in *The Climate of Treason* to give the account that resulted directly in the unmasking of Blunt, an event which took place in the House of Commons itself, when Margaret Thatcher, speaking from the same place as Macmillan when he had cleared Philby, branded Blunt and gave a full account of the immunity granted to him. The withdrawal of his knighthood followed immediately.

Surely, at last, this was to be the end of the saga. But, as we now know, even as Blunt was giving his famous press conference at the *Times* offices, a somewhat calmer and more distinguished example of the genre than the conference given by Philby, the most detailed and complex series of revelations of all had become detached from the rock of M15's most secret archives and begun a slow ascent to the light which would take almost as long as the unmasking of Blunt. Here again it was the press that provided the impetus.

The *Daily Express* had made much of the running on the spy

story from their first disclosure, and it was, in a Fleet Street sense, their story. Lord Beaverbrook himself was rumoured to have supplied some of the leads at an early stage, identifying, for example, the means by which funds had been channelled to Maclean's deserted family. It was therefore entirely appropriate that the next stage should be ushered in by Chapman Pincher, a veteran *Express* reporter from those days who was now a freelance author with many books to his credit. It was also appropriate that the Prime Minister of the day, Margaret Thatcher, should first have been alerted to the new developments by a letter from Jonathan Aitken, a scion of the Beaverbrook clan. The letter began ominously:

> I am writing to you in your capacity as Head of the Security Services to alert you to certain developments and possible new disclosures arising out of the Blunt affair. As you are aware a great deal of information about this subject is still circulating on both sides of the Atlantic. Some of it has already been published, but the most dramatic disclosures may yet be forthcoming . . .

After the allegations and suspicions that had gone before it might well have been asked what more could possibly be left to be told. The answer was indeed shocking, that both the head of M15, Roger Hollis, and his deputy, Graham Mitchell, had been suspected by their colleagues of being Soviet agents and had been the subject of full-scale enquiries into their actions and motives over their entire career by a committee of their peers drawn from M15 and M16. Although rumours were circulating among London journalists based on remarks by a friend of Blunt's that there had been a fifth man who had died "covered in honours" more important than Blunt or any of the other spies, anyone reading Aitken's letter in full would have realised that the allegations had originated from within M15 itself and not from any leak on which a journalist had made an informed guess. This alone should have alerted the authorities to expect something more than another "revelation." It should have given a clear warning that they were dealing with a political phenomenon. It was as a direct result of the neglect of this warning that the disgrace of the equity court trial in Australia involving *Spycatcher* and its author Peter Wright, head of the Fluency Committee, occurred.

Chapman Pincher has revealed that Aitken's information came to him from James Angleton, "the former Chief of Counter Intelligence in the CIA," who had then put him in contact with two former intelligence officers in Britain, one from M15 and one from M16. Both knew of the Fluency Committee from their own personal involvement in its proceedings, and it was their information which prompted Aitken's letter. Confusion was caused in the unravelling of subsequent events by the fact that Pincher, who had first heard of the story through these sources, did not in fact rely on them when he wrote his first book on Hollis, *Their Trade is Treachery*, but on an entirely different source, Peter Wright himself.

In due course Pincher visited Wright in Tasmania. Rarely can a journalist have found himself in possession of such material. Had Pincher relied on the original Aitken sources alone, as some other authors were to do, he would no doubt have come up with most of the story. But having Wright as a source, the very man who had debriefed Blunt over hundreds of hours, he could recreate the entire Fluency Committee saga in all its aspects. Leslie Nicholson, having once broken silence in *British Agent*, found that his knowledge of Philby's treachery proved too much for him to contain when he was confronted by a determined journalist who already knew a good part of the story. Peter Wright's knowledge was on an altogether different scale, but the same truth applied, for, like Nicholson, he had ended his service at odds with his employers, in his case M15. Malcolm Turnbull, Wright's lawyer in Australia, provided a graphic description of the scene of his first meeting with Wright which has echoes of Knightley's first meeting with Nicholson:

> . . . Peter had chosen to live as far away from England as he could without travelling to Antarctica. I asked for directions . . . and was confronted with a vision of rural poverty rarely seen in Australia . . . the whole place was in disrepair, and the house was a two roomed hovel which compared unfavourably

with some swagman's shacks I had seen in the bush . . . When Wright left M15 in 1976 he was a bitter man. On a personal level he was bitter that his pension was as low as it was . . .

As Turnbull went on to explain in his book on the *Spycatcher* trial, a far more important motive for Wright's actions had been his chagrin at having to leave the service without being able to prove his central thesis that Hollis had been a Soviet agent. Further "he believed that the British establishment had joined ranks to protect Hollis both before and after his death." Here was an echo of George Orwell's old charge that Britain was like a family with the wrong members in control, to which Nicholson and Wright would no doubt have added, "And who don't look after their own."

In going to live in Tasmania Wright's purpose had been to be near a member of his family, where he could run a small stud farm breeding Persian horses—ill-advisedly as it happens, because, apart from odd freak transactions, this was known as a hobby only the rich could afford. But as soon as he spoke to Pincher his position was transformed. It came to resemble nothing so much as that of Philby himself in Moscow, or of any other defector. Pincher's visit to Tasmania parallels Knightley's visit to Philby in Moscow, for whereas Philby was undoubtedly a defector, Wright's predicament and the moves of the British Government's advisers, unaware that they were in a wilderness of mirrors where their actions would have political repercussions of an unpredictable kind, made Wright's move to Tasmania seem like a defection itself. It needed no announcement from the Metropolitan Police, as had been made in Burgess's case, to make Wright aware that the Official Secrets Act would be brought into operation with full force if he ever returned to Britain. And if a young clerk like Sarah Tisdall could be awarded a prison sentence for leaking a single photocopy, the chances of Wright's spending the rest of his frail life in a British jail were high.

It was perhaps inevitable that, if the story of the defectors ran for long enough, those pursuing it would themselves become part of it. When Pincher began his long debriefing of Wright in Australia he entered the story as a participant; a rubicon had been crossed. Just as the publication of Philby's book had marked the eclipse of spy fiction by the life of the spies themselves, so Chapman Pincher's books based on what Wright told him—often more reliable than the later version put out under Wright's name—marked the emergence into the light of day of the struggles which had been going on within the security services as they reflected the political contradictions of the twentieth century. Burgess, Maclean and Philby could be seen as people who, in Lenin's phrase, had voted with their feet, but they could also be seen as figures from an earlier century, recusants fleeing to the continent from persecution in Britain, or Protestants fleeing the inquisition and finding refuge in Switzerland. In the introduction to his book on Petrov Michael Bialoguski wrote:

> . . . in any country with a totalitarian form of Government the secret service plays a far greater part in the framing of policy than in the Western Parliamentary democracies.

Although Britain was throughout the war a parliamentary democracy there was more than a hint of truth in Burgess's description of its form of government as administrative totalitarianism. And there was a tendency for Bialoguski's tenet to be exemplified within the security service during those years. There was of course little way in which they could openly affect policy except as agents of influence, and perhaps Burgess, only an agent, was in a better position to play that role than full-time officers such as Blunt, Fulford or Hollis. On this view when Wright denounced Hollis and brought the whole conflict within MI5 into the open he was doing no more than exposing the political history of the twentieth century as it had been reflected in the beliefs of MI5's members. It was this political aspect that was ignored or misunderstood by the Thatcher administration right through to the *Spycatcher* case itself.

Sir Roger Hollis, Director General of MI5.   (National Portrait Gallery)

D.N. Pritt on the platform during "The Revolution That Never Was" in London, January 1941. Pritt played a central role at this time in the organization of revolutionary activity aimed at creating a People's Government and stopping the war at any cost. He was to be involved in Stalin's last desperate attempts to strike a deal with Britain to avert the German invasion of Russia in 1941. (BBC Hulton Picture Library)

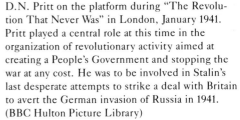

D. N. PRITT, K.C., M.P.

FORWARD
to a
PEOPLE'S
GOVERNMENT

PUBLISHED by the
PEOPLE'S CONVENTION COMMITTEE **1**D.

The Manifesto of "The Revolution That Never Was," written by Pritt. Despite its wide circulation it did not appear in the printed British Library catalogue. (Private collection)

Celebrities on the platform with D.N. Pritt: Beatrix Lehmann, who wrote the manifesto on Art and Education, and J.B.S. Haldane, who coordinated the "deep shelter" movement in which Nunn May was also closely involved. (BBC Hulton Picture Library)

A general view of the delegates, said to represent over a million people. Scotland was well represented, as were the Welsh, with Arthur Horner the South Wales Miners' leader coordinating the convention. (BBC Hulton Picture Library)

Krishna Menon and Indira Gandhi.
(BBC Hulton Picture Library)

WHERE FRANCE BEGINS

WHAT I SAW IN ALGIERS

BY

FRANK PITCAIRN

With a Foreword by the Editor
of the Daily Worker

PRICE TWOPENCE

This pamphlet by Cockburn gives a highly misleading account of his journey to Algiers in 1943. Banned from going by the War Office and the authorities, he finally got there through the connivance of Hollis at MI5. Files in the Public Record Office have enabled the actual story to be established here. The title is a reference to the attempts by the Communist Party to set up a Revolutionary Government for the whole of France based in Algiers. (Private collection)

A Soviet radio communication center in 1936. Messages were even sent at high speed on tapes: the reels and machines used can be seen clearly here. This enabled wartime spies in Britain such as Sonia Kuczynski to send coded messages at a speed which could not be taken down by the monitors. The comrade here is shown playing wireless chess using Morse code, which caused considerable difficulties at first to spycatchers who were unaware what the signals were.   (Hutchinson)

Wartime *Realpolitik:* Anthony Eden with Ivan Maisky talking to Ernest Bevin at a reception at the Soviet Embassy in London. As Soviet Ambassador, Maisky hosted a large number of receptions which were a center point of the "open" Communist world in wartime London. Guy Burgess's colleagues remember that he never missed one of them.   (Popperfoto)

Lord Inverchapel, Archibald Clark Kerr, Maisky's opposite number in Moscow for much of the war. Like Hollis, Inverchapel was in China before the war and found that his loyalty to the Chinese fighting the Japanese led him to close friendship with Russia in her support of China. Inverchapel became a friend of Stalin, who gave him a tommy gun as a present when he returned to Britain! Guy Burgess arranged meetings between Inverchapel and Peter Smollett, a Soviet agent running the MOI Russian desk, when the former made brief return visits to London, thus establishing direct links with all involved. (Private Collection)

A meeting of the Executive Committee of the Communist Party of Great Britain. Behind Idris Cox, from left to right, are Phil Piratin MP, Bill Brooks, leader of the Young Communist League, and Professor George Thomson of Birmingham University.   (Popperfoto)

Tom Driberg and Guy Burgess in Moscow at the time of writing of Driberg's *Guy Burgess: Portrait with Background*. The entire project was coordinated by Hollis at MI5, with the full knowledge of the KGB, both of whom monitored the final text. In divulging details of his secret work to Driberg, Burgess provided the first actual evidence by which he could have been prosecuted under the Official Secrets Act if he returned to Britain.   (Popperfoto)

An informal portrait of Burgess taken just before his death in Moscow. His attempts to return to Britain had been blocked by Hollis despite clearance from the Home Secretary of the day: Hollis's reasons remained a mystery to the Fluency Committee as only the Russians had anything to lose by any re-defection. The Soviet authorities prevented Burgess from meeting Philby, who had recently returned to Moscow. Burgess therefore died without making any final communication of what he knew, and without seeing any of his close surviving friends.   (Popperfoto)

12
The Director General
of MI5 -
Spymaster or Spy?

I T was the intense conflict in MI5 between those who believed in Hollis's innocence and those who were convinced of his guilt that led, finally, to the court scenes in Australia. The cynical might view the whole episode as a supreme example of office politics carried to preposterous lengths after the leader of one faction had actually died and the others had long retired. Such a simple view is discounted by anyone examining the matter, which was one of the greatest seriousness in modern British political history. However, the official response was never one of formal denial of specific charges. Internal committees and enquiries, notably that of Sir Burke Trend, had reported to the Prime Minister, but in public the response was strangely reminiscent of an internal dispute. All reference to the allegations against Hollis were banned on principle. Anyone speaking about what had gone on within the security service whose knowledge was in any way based on inside information was automatically in breach of the Official Secrets Act, and any book written with such knowledge was to be banned. The case in Australia was thus seen, on the Government side, simply as a justified and determined attempt to prevent an ex-employee from breaking his duty of loyalty and confidentiality, which was held to be lifelong as part of the condition of his service. The case for

Hollis at this level is simply that the case against him should never have been put. At this level also it is clear that nothing more can be said on the subject within the United Kingdom, or in a book to be published in the United Kingdom, without infringing the terms of the Official Secrets Act.

Fortunately this is not the end of the matter. As was pointed out in Australia, *Spycatcher* in its published form had been stripped of any fact which had not previously been mentioned in his books by Chapman Pincher, notably in *Their Trade is Treachery* and *Too Secret Too Long*. Indeed Pincher frequently has a more accurate version of a story than appeared subsequently. The case against is therefore taken here as Chapman Pincher's case. Nor does the case "for" have to go by default in the absence of the Trend report, or any other official analysis. By an extraordinary series of connections and coincidences a competent defence was mounted by an academic living in Oxford, Anthony Glees. Neither of these cases, for or against, has any knowledge of the mass of new material which has been brought to light in the present book. However, the examination of them is an essential prerequisite for an understanding of the significance of what has now been discovered.

Their Trade is Treachery created a sensation when it was published, and established a benchmark for subsequent publications. A new plane had obviously been reached, since the book appeared to have been written with massive cooperation from persons within the security service itself. Apart from the "recognised" books on Burgess and MI5 published during Hollis's time, the book by E. H. Cookridge, which had the benefit of help from Guy Liddell, a colleague of Hollis's in MI5 who some have suggested might have been another mole, as we have noted, and a few other trivial cases, there had been hardly any comparable accounts. With its open description of the most traumatic events within the heart of the country's most secret services, it was astonishing that it had been published at all without an injunction being served both on the author and the publisher. The point was to be made repeatedly in Australia, but the real reason why publication had gone ahead was not known in detail until Chapman Pincher himself published his account of it. Pincher explained that the book had been shown to an intermediary, "the Arbiter," who had approached the authorities before publication to learn if there would be any objection. Both author and publisher expressed complete willingness to be bound by any decision made. But someone along the way appears to have over-dramatised the situation, and those in authority, up to Cabinet level it would seem, were under the delusion that the document they were reading had been come by illegally. They therefore could not apply for an injunction banning the book without revealing how they had obtained it, or so the story went. The book had been published causing a storm at least equal to any caused by the previous revelations and cover-ups, from the original defection of Burgess and Maclean to the exposure of Blunt. The existence of Wright was as yet unknown to the general public and was to remain so for some years. On the face of it the book might have been the wildest of any conceivable allegations, as indeed many ordinary people reading it must have thought it was. The security service knew differently, of course, but kept silent, leaving refutation to a formal statement by the Prime Minister clearing Hollis's name and referring to the Trend report.

The first actual evidence that might serve to refute the allegations in Pincher's book came the year after its publication, when *The Times* published a series of letters by Roger Hollis written before he joined MI5 which had been brought to the attention of Anthony Glees by Hollis's son, who happened to be his next-door neighbour in Oxford. They had been found among Hollis's mother's effects after her death, in circumstances that suggested that Hollis himself may not have realised that they had survived. Certainly he never alluded to them when he was being interrogated, and MI5's molehunters never looked at them.

It was thought at first from the excerpts published in *The Times* that any idea that Hollis had become involved in a Communist circle while in China as originally suggested by Pincher would have to be drastically modified, if not rejected altogether. The letters seemed to be those of a typical product of a distinguished public school living an arduous and interesting life in China. There was of course no "Raj" in China, although the privileges extended to companies in the treaty ports, known as those of extra-territoriality, were in some ways equivalent and the Hollis letters savoured of that world rather than of the internationally famous cosmopolitan atmosphere of Shanghai, as we have seen. The very fact that they had continued in an unending sequence suggested that Hollis had not gone off the rails, as he had at Oxford; rather the reverse. It seemed impossible that anyone sending such letters could, at the same time, be turning into a dyed-in-the-wool Communist activist. As Glees pointed out, Wright himself, in a television interview in 1984, seemed to have been impressed by these letters and to have shifted his emphasis from China to the next two years, the so-called two missing years, in his search for the most likely date for Hollis's recruitment to some Communist secret service which he was convinced must have taken place. Chapman Pincher stuck to his guns with a journalist's intuition that China was a long way from Britain and that letters home tend to fall into a special category with a tone and content of their own, a natural extension of letters written home from boarding school, though in an adult form. Certainly, as has been remarked, it is unlikely that Hollis would have included details of Comintern infiltration of the firm he worked for, let alone of the fact that large numbers of his fellow workers had been arrested.

In the same year that the letters appeared in *The Times* (1982) Glees's own book, *Exile Politics during the Second World War: The German Social Democrats in Britain*, was published. At first sight the book might seem to have little to do with Hollis and the allegations made against him. But, as Chapman Pincher immediately realised, it contained a great deal of information about German Communists in Britain during the war when they had been the bitter foes of the German Social Democrats, though, as we have seen, not above trying to get them into a variety of joint front exercises. Roger Hollis had been the officer in MI5 responsible for monitoring the activities of these people, and it was Glees's discovery of some MI5 reports in the Public Record Office signed by Hollis that had led to his interest in the Hollis case, and to his publication of the Hollis letters that had fallen into his lap. These documents in the PRO, together with others not known to Glees cited here, provided the key to much that had been unknown about Hollis's wartime activities. The molehunters of the Fluency Committee, coming on the scene a generation later, seemed to have misinterpreted great areas of Hollis's work and to have known little of it generally. Glees's book helped fill in some of the gaps and was one of the first books written by someone with an academic background in a field which had hitherto been the preserve of journalists.

In 1984 Pincher published a greatly extended and far more convincing, if circumstantial, account of the case against Hollis entitled *Too Secret Too Long*. On reading this work Glees felt that his own book had been misunderstood and that some remarks had been taken out of context or actually distorted. His own opinion about Hollis was that, far from ignoring Communists as Pincher appeared to suggest and actively protecting them, he "seemed to be the only person in MI5 actually doing his job." Glees had been working since the late seventies on British intelligence and Communist subversion. After the publication of Pincher's book he concentrated on the question of subversion, and the secrets of MI5 generally. In his next book, *The Secrets of the Service*, he focussed on the Hollis question in terms of a strict refutation of Pincher's case. This was extended to a general defence of Hollis against all those who used what he referred to as the "Pincher-Wright" approach, that of accumulated circumstantial evidence, contained in his last two substantial chapters.

At first sight this situation as it developed produced a very unusual encounter between a book fought for on the frontiers of journalism, *Too Secret Too Long*, and a scholarly covering of the same ground in *The Secrets of the Service* brought about in large part by the chance propinquity of Glees to Hollis's son. However, an examination of Glees's book and its sources, as revealed in his footnotes, establishes that he too had been drawn into the "wilderness of mirrors." Few of his references in the chapters refuting Pincher are to contemporary documents. Instead there are numerous references to other books on a par with Pincher's, or of lesser standing—Pincher is a reliable and thorough practitioner. The final chapters of *The Secrets of the Service* in particular contain a large number of references to potentially the most distorting mirrors of all, witnesses, some from MI5 and MI6, who had insisted on re-

maining anonymous. It is arguable whether they or defectors with
deliberate disinformation are the greater problem for anyone trying
to reach an understanding of espionage matters. The reader is
obliged to accept the judgment of the author in evaluating the
evidence and, even if he does, he has absolutely no way of testing
it against other evidence, since he has no idea of its background.
He may easily arrive at a totally erroneous conclusion, or at the
correct conclusion for entirely the wrong reasons. Indeed he is in
the "wilderness of mirrors."

Glees points to three main areas of suspicion in the case made
out by Pincher and Hollis's detractors generally. First, there was
the information provided by defectors, notably the GRU cipher
clerk Igor Gouzenko who defected in Ottawa in 1945, bringing
with him information which resulted in the arrest of Nunn May in
England and of many others in Canada, coupled with information
derived from the interception of coded wireless traffic known as
"Venona" and "Hasp." Secondly, there was the undoubted penetration of British security services and other institutions, with
resultant subversion. And lastly, "the most testing of all, there is
the question of motive and the assertion that Hollis was himself a
secret Communist."

The evidence of defectors, which Glees examines in detail,
might seem to the layman to be of the first importance: after all, if
a Soviet spymaster, or someone with inside knowledge—such as a
cipher clerk who while doing his job has inevitably had access to
information going to and from spies—comes over and talks freely,
surely he must be able to give vital clues? Things are not that
simple. Soviet spycraft, based on the deep wisdom of Czarist pre-
decessors, made absolutely sure that secure sources stayed secure
and that they had code names known only to the man running
them. Gouzenko was thus only able to identify a spy called "Elli"
in London. Volkov, the intending defector in Istanbul whom
Philby had removed just in time by informing his Russian masters,
identified only someone in "Five of MI [Military Intelligence]."
This example became notorious, because it could mean either MI5
or department 5 of MI6! The latter would have been Philby, the
former *might* have been Hollis. In fact this area is the classic ex-

ample of the wilderness of mirrors: endless speculation on data that anyway were so thin that a true explanation was impossible even for those who got the clues first-hand. Pincher deals with the allegations at third-hand, and Glees's refutation is at one remove again.

Intercepted wireless traffic is another matter entirely. It was the breaking of coded messages taken down during the war and only decoded years later that identified a spy in the British Embassy in Washington known as "Homer" who turned out to be Maclean. This recorded radio traffic was known as "Venona," and for many years its existence was a closely guarded secret. It did not become at all widely known until the 1970s. There was a further quantity of recorded traffic found in Sweden mentioned by Peter Wright, who gave it the name "Hasp." The fact that Soviet agents have to communicate with their controllers in Moscow by radio, and the presence or absence of traffic, are central elements in Pincher's thesis in *Too Secret Too Long.* As Glees remarks, "Chapman Pincher has, of course, used 'Sonia' [Kuczynski] as the fuse for his massive work . . ." Pincher suggests that Sonia was running agents from her house in Oxford during the time that Hollis was living in Oxford and leading the counter-espionage section of MI5, located for the duration of the war at Blenheim Palace. Drawing on her autobiography, published in East Germany, Pincher makes a case for saying that Sonia had Hollis himself in her stable of agents, while confirming that the main agent she dealt with was Klaus Fuchs. Pincher adds to his case by pointing out a number of remarkable coincidences, not least the fact that Sonia had been in China at the same time as Hollis and that they had mutual friends including, allegedly, Agnes Smedley and Arthur Ewert, although he knew nothing of the one person who certainly knew both Hollis and Sonia, Claud Cockburn.

Glees's first attack against Pincher's case is on both these points. He first makes a substantial assault on the reliability of an account put out behind the Iron Curtain which, like Philby's autobiography, would of its nature be self-serving and liable to contain the most sophisticated kind of disinformation. But all literature in this field automatically has that charge against it; this is a basic element in the wilderness of mirrors which journalists have to live with all their lives. What is done is to remove a substratum of facts common to all accounts and then look around for any information which confirms or controverts the most obvious provisional conclusions. As in strict scientific method one looks at the facts, forms a hypothesis, makes predictions on the basis of that hypothesis and then looks for confirmation or otherwise of these predictions. If none is found the question remains open; if contradictory material emerges the hypothesis fails; if the predicted fact is found, this constitutes new evidence for the theory, a new hypothesis is set in place of the old one and the process is begun again. Pincher (a trained scientist) is better at this than Glees who unfortunately for him mounts a central attack, on the credibility of Sonia's evidence that she ran a wireless station in Oxford, that is immediately refutable on scientific evidence well known at the time.

His attack is based on the fact that a lookout was being kept for illegal wireless transmissions during the war. "Someone," he says, "sending wireless traffic from an illegal source would have been picked up before they cleared their throats." This was far from being the case. Morse transmissions during the war were monitored by a team of about 1500 amateurs who were very efficient; but for much of the time they were tracking consistent known sources. Illegal traffic originating within the United Kingdom had been zealously sought out, both when war broke out and at the time of threatened invasion when Germany dropped some parachutists, each with a radio, and even then when nothing was found attention for this kind of source waned. But the main reason why Sonia Kuczynski could have been transmitting without being detected, even if someone had been listening, is that the volunteers were entirely without recording equipment, in the days before tape recording, and took down all their morse by hand. The Soviets were able to defeat any attempt at monitoring by the simple process of transmitting morse with a tape machine run at a speed which prevented its being taken down manually. There is no doubt whatever that the Russians used such machines, since there is an illustration in Peter Smollett's *Forty Thousand Against the Arctic* which actually shows (see photo) the interior of a transmitting station showing tape machines and describing their use. It also

shows, incidentally, a comrade playing radio chess, a favourite pas-
time which must have wasted many hours of the codebreakers'
time before they realised what it was.

The problem of how to detect high-speed transmissions was still
unsolved decades later when the Krogers were able to transmit
Gordon Lonsdale's messages from their suburban house in London
by the same means without being detected, despite the much more
sophisticated equipment then available for the job. It is quite clear
that Glees is wrong and that it would have been perfectly possible
for Sonia to be running the GRU agents she claimed. Glees makes
a subsidiary point that, if Hollis had been one of her agents, he
would have advised her to use the London Embassy transmitters
which, Glees says, were transmitting freely, no attempt being made
to decipher their traffic as a result of an order given when Russia
came into the war that all such deciphering was to cease. But the
reverse would have been the case. It was the ordinary coded traffic
from the Embassy that *was* being taken down, even if it was not
being deciphered, and the rapid advances of the ENIGMA machine and those using it at Bletchley would have made it perfectly
obvious that, if there had been any further change of allegiance, or
a decision to start deciphering again, it would be very probable that
the Embassy messages would be read and Sonia's traffic quickly
understood. Hollis would have had to tell her that she was much
better off using high-speed transmissions of her own at irregular
times which were highly unlikely to be taken down, let alone
decoded. It is not known whether the Soviet Embassy in London
used high-speed machines during the war, but if they did they
would be the ones most likely to be recorded using the primitive
disc methods of the time.

Going beyond the technical details of whether Sonia did or did
not transmit Fuchs's and other traffic from Oxford, Glees makes a
full-scale assault on the question of Hollis's putative responsibility
for the clearance of Fuchs, the most damaging of the atom spies, as
suggested by Chapman Pincher. As his first line of evidence,
Pincher relies on the minutes of a talk given by Hollis to a Tripartite Conference on Security Standards at Washington in June 1950.

The opening paragraph of the official record of Hollis's contribution makes the position quite clear:

> Mr. Hollis began by pointing out that he had not been briefed
> in detail for this discussion and was speaking "off the record,"
> but he had, throughout, been concerned with all the security
> *clearance* aspects of the case *and was confident that the facts as he*
> *would report them were substantially correct and represented all that*
> *was known at the times in question.*

The words printed here in italics are unaccountably omitted by Glees, without any indication of their omission. The significance of this document (which is reprinted in full in Appendix 2 [i]) is that Hollis was without question the officer who was responsible for the vetting of Fuchs. In his remarks Hollis goes on to say that a mistake had indeed been made, but that there had been only two occasions when Fuchs had showed any possible Communist links. One was the report sent to the Bristol authorities in 1933 when Fuchs first arrived saying that he was an active Communist, but since the report came from the Gestapo it was thought proper to discount it. The other was when Fuchs was deported to Canada and spent time with what Hollis called "a well known Communist," though without identifying him as Hans Kahle. As we now know, this was incorrect and there were other links. Hollis probably did not identify the "well known Communist" because someone in his audience would have realised immediately that the statement was suspicious. Pincher, without the detailed information that has been assembled here, merely remarks in his book that from the circumstantial evidence Hollis had either been extraordinarily negligent or had actually allowed Fuchs through.

Glees's defence of Hollis on this question involves the account of the Fuchs affair given by Professor Margaret Gowing in her official history of the Nuclear Weapon and Atomic programmes in Britain, in which it was pointed out that the final responsibility for employing Fuchs was Sir Edward Appleton's. Glees is very conscious of the importance of the matter for Hollis:

> In short, what this issue hinges on is whether Sir Edward did
> ultimately clear Fuchs, as Professor Gowing has alleged, or

whether Hollis provided the full version of events in America [where he made no mention of Appleton]. If it was the latter things look very bad for Hollis, but if it was the former, it suggests not only that Hollis had behaved responsibly and properly, but that he was so totally unaware that anyone might adduce sinister motives that he missed out a vital piece of evidence in the jigsaw.

However, Glees's restatement of Professor Gowing's remarks in his defence is selective, both on the Fuchs question and on the related case of Niels Bohr, the famous father of nuclear research, in the field that led to the making of the bomb. The details of the Bohr case cast light on that of Fuchs, and on Hollis's response to it. I shall deal with it here first before proceeding to the specific defence which attempts to shift blame onto the shoulders of Sir Edward Appleton.

Niels Bohr was a far more important figure in 1944 than Fuchs. It is therefore of great significance that he was warned most severely against betraying nuclear secrets to the Russians and the MI5 and Hollis were fully aware of this warning. Glees remarks:

> In April 1944 Bohr returned to London from America and found waiting for him a letter from a Russian scientist who had been part of the Cambridge Cavendish Laboratory team in 1934. Bohr formed a "strong impression" that the Russian knew about the Tube Alloys project [the atom bomb cover name] and Bohr was invited to visit Russia to discuss his work in detail. Bohr replied in a non-committal letter *which had the full agreement of MI5* [my italics].

What Glees does not say is that it is clearly stated in Professor Gowing's account that the letter was waiting for Bohr at the Soviet Embassy and that the scientist writing was Peter Kapitza who, it seems from the letter, was running the Soviet bomb programme and was trusted by Stalin. Bohr knew Kapitza well. He had been corresponding with him and, though his previous correspondence was apparently clandestine, conducted through the Soviet Embassy, he showed his reply in this case to MI5. On the Russian side it is crystal clear that they were using the most secure method of communication they had, letting the letter rest for six months in their London Embassy rather than risk getting it to Bohr in America. *After* seeing MI5, according to Professor Gowing, Bohr tried to convince Churchill that the bomb should be given to the Russians. As we have remarked Churchill was so angry that he threatened Bohr with internment, saying that it would have to be made clear to him that he was on the edge of "mortal crimes."

Two things are obvious from these events. The first is that Hollis must have been absolutely clear in 1944 that the atomic bomb project was of the greatest seriousness, and not merely another wartime scientific project. The second, even more important, was that he knew that Churchill regarded any possible leak to the Russians as a capital offence and was prepared to threaten even a relatively apolitical and highly respected figure such as Bohr with internment on the question. Yet Hollis went on clearing Fuchs, by his own account no less than six times, knowing that Fuchs not only had the contacts with the Communists he described in America in 1950, without naming Kahle, but that Kahle had further directly involved Fuchs in Communist affairs in Birmingham in November 1943 in setting up that branch of the Communist Free Germany Committee. He must also have been aware that any assurances given by Birmingham police or Special Branch that Fuchs had not been involved openly with the CPGB in Birmingham were worthless, since there was an actual committee member of the CPGB in the university, the Professor of Greek, George Thomson, making open contact with the local CPGB branch not only unnecessary but infra dig.

The specific defence that Glees takes from Professor Gowing is that initially MI5 did express reluctance to clear Fuchs, citing the earlier report made in Bristol and his time in internment with Kahle. However, the Secretary of the DSIR (Department of Scientific and Industrial Research) running the project, Sir Edward Appleton, had urgently needed Fuchs for highly specialised work. He had made the final decision over MI5's caveat, and of course relying on the reports Hollis showed him. This is the ploy we have seen used over Cockburn's request to go to Algiers where the ball was put back in the Foreign Office's court by the very people who were supposed to be advising them. When the ball is put in the other man's court in this way he is given the illusion that he is making the decision, when in fact there is only one stroke he can play and all the rules, the entire game, has been set up by the person affording him the stroke. Hollis knew perfectly well that the Communists with whom Fuchs had been associating were not merely Communists but the leading Communists from Germany in Britain whom he himself had placed on a list of dangerous Germans in Britain which he had forwarded to America at the time. Later, at the actual moment of the Bohr incident, when he was clearing Fuchs afresh for the Americans before Fuchs's departure for the final stages of the project over there, he again knew perfectly well that Fuchs was part of the Free Germany Committee movement which was effectively run by Kahle and whose chairman was Robert Kuczynski, Sonia's father.

Glees finally suggests that Hollis omitted Sir Edward Appleton's role in the account he gave in America simply through forgetfulness, as he was speaking without notes and off the record. Others have suggested that he did not mention Sir Edward for good reason: as it might have led to an investigation which would have thrown too much light on his own role in the matter. Glees dismisses this idea out of hand, although it seems plausible, particularly as, though Glees does not mention it, Sir Michael Perrin, who had debriefed Fuchs after his confession of guilt, was sitting next to Hollis when he gave his talk and would have noticed any attempt to shift blame onto Appleton.

Appleton's decision was made under the stress of wartime administrative responsibilities, and once made it was not reconsidered. Hollis's clearances were indeed made on six different occasions, several of which were after it had become as clear as daylight that the atomic project was of absolute importance, and that the Prime Minister himself had shown that any danger of a possible leak to Russia, which had been openly discussed by Niels Bohr with MI5, must be treated as an offence of a capital nature—in fact, in a British subject, as treason. It has always been possible to suggest, though Glees does not do so, that Hollis may simply have been unaware that he had made a mistake, or that someone in his department had, and that in America he felt he should accept the blame while toning down what had happened and avoiding names. But bearing in mind his detailed account, the Niels Bohr affair, which made the position absolutely clear on nuclear espionage to MI5 as early as 1944, and the repeated clearances despite it by Hollis over the years, this seems the least likely hypothesis of all.

Mention of the Kuczynskis in this context is made by Chapman Pincher and taken up by Anthony Glees in a way which shows even further the fragile basis for his defence. Pincher was the discoverer of the report on dangerous Communists mentioned above which was sent to America. He points out in *Too Secret Too Long* that the Kuczynskis are absent from the list, which seems unaccountable, and suggests that this was because Hollis, responsible for the list, was protecting them. He goes on to cite Glees's own book on German politics in exile as a source of the statement that MI5 reports *never* mentioned the Kuczynskis. As Glees correctly points out, he makes no such statement. Although there is only one reference to Kuczynski *père* in the index to the book this index is very seriously defective and he does in fact make reference to the Free German Committee and directly mentions Robert Kuczynski, with other allusions. However, Glees admits that he has found no reference to Sonia Kuczynski in MI5 reports, all of which, he implies incidentally, were by Hollis, although in fact many of the reports cited by him as mentioning the Kuczynskis were not prepared by Hollis at all but, for example, by Capt. Brooke-Booth, who compiled the report of the first meeting of the Free Germany committee at which Robert Kuczynski had taken the chair. Glees suggests that Hollis may not have mentioned Sonia because "he probably did not know about her." To those who have read many reports by MI5 on exile politicians, particularly on leading Communists such as the Kuczynskis, the likelihood of a close family member such as Sonia escaping notice would be remote; but there is a particular reason why it was most unlikely that Hollis would not have known of her when she was in Oxford. This is worth examining.

The house that Sonia took when she came to live in Oxford was in fact the coach house of a large residence in North Oxford which was occupied throughout the war by Neville Laski, a judge and the brother of the Chairman of the Labour Party, Harold Laski. Besides his formal duties Neville Laski had been for many years engaged in highly dangerous and indeed courageous work which had made him well-known to the authorities, including the police, Special Branch and MI5 itself. This work consisted of conveying to those concerned the results of surveillance of the British Union of Fascists and other right-wing anti-Jewish organisations. He came by some of this information through his position as secretary of the Chamber of Deputies of British Jews, but a great deal of it he acquired himself. His numerous reports in files in the Public Record Office dealing with Sir Oswald Mosley and his followers establish that he would himself attend meetings and make a full report of what was said to whoever he thought was the proper person to receive it. It is clear that he was one of the best informants on such matters. It would be almost impossible for Hollis not to have been aware that he was living in Oxford less than a mile away from him. Had he been an agent of the kind run by Maxwell Knight there might have been some doubt, but Laski acted on his own. The MI5 man said to have been responsible directly for monitoring Fascist movements in Britain was Graham Mitchell, but Hollis was his superior for a considerable part of the relevant period, and this eminent and courageous anti-Fascist must have been known to him. Further, there would have been particular reason for Hollis to know of him personally, for both were keen members of the Old Cliftonians, Laski having attended the Jewish House at Clifton. It seems unlikely, to say the least, that over the years the presence of Sonia Kuczynski in his coach house would not have become known both to MI5 and to Hollis himself as she often visited the house. Neville Laski may well have vouched for her, and this might in itself have been reason for her to be deleted from reports altogether. Nor did Sonia keep her interest in wireless particularly secret, since one of Laski's daughters has recounted that Sonia used to put her aerial up across the garden, though naturally this would have been thought to be for better reception rather than transmission.

This failure to identify Sonia Kuczynski, whose role is seen in retrospect to have been so important, does cast doubt on Hollis's abilities and the extent to which he kept watch on German exiles in Britain, if nothing else. Glees is aware of this and to counter it makes a detailed case for the fact that MI5 and by implication Hollis, far from being negligent on the question of Communist subversion, were acutely conscious of it to the point of being ridiculed by the Foreign Office. While such feelings may have been common generally in MI5 in the years between the wars, they are so out of keeping with what is known about MI5 during the war years that Glees's statement requires careful scrutiny. Glees bases his case on a quotation from Foreign Office papers relating to the granting of a licence for a Social Democratic newspaper. It is manifestly a selective quotation:

> MI5 exaggerates the danger . . . of Communist influence . . . and suffers from so many delusions . . . that the Foreign Office will have to educate them.

The first two phrases are not to be found in the minute cited by Glees but in an earlier one by a different author; the latter part of this quotation actually reads, in the original minute by a Foreign Office official, A. W. Harrison:

> Mr. Robson-Scott and Mr. Thwaites seem to be suffering from so many delusions both about the German and Austrian emigrants that I fear that Mr. Allen and I will have to ask them around for a talk in order to educate them.

Robson-Scott was the MI5 officer dealing with the matter, and Thwaites was his opposite number in the Ministry of Information. It was Thwaites who was particularly worried that all the newspapers being put out by the exiled German groups would be dominated by the Communists of the Free Germany Committee. After they called round to the Foreign Office A. W. Harrison added a note to his original entry reading: "As a result of our talk I think the delusions [of Communist influence] are all Mr. Thwaites'." This completely destroys the force of Glees's argument, since it is quite clear that it was the MOI officer that was taking an alarmist, but in fact correct, view of Communist activity, not MI5.

The view expressed by MI5 was clearly the reverse of what Glees said it was, and in any case was not given by Hollis, as is implied, but by another MI5 officer entirely, Robson-Scott. About one document that Hollis did sign which Glees cites, written in September 1945 warning of Soviet aims in Germany, Pincher has remarked: "It has been suggested that this is *prima facie* evidence that he was loyal but there was little else he could have said at the time because it was self-evident." This is quite true and applies also to the MI5 documents cited by Glees from Brooke-Booth and Robson-Scott for which Hollis would have had general responsibility as head of the department. The days when Hollis was dealing personally with such matters as the *Daily Worker* suppression, with the files on this and Cockburn his sole domain, were gone. His position was already a senior one and, like Philby, his opposite number in MI6, he would be spending a lot of his time at Joint Intelligence Committee meetings where direct intervention, if he was a spy, would have to be very sparing and discreet.

The second major group of allegations by Pincher are those relating to the undeniable failure to spot the so-called "moles" in the Foreign Office, the security service and elsewhere: that is, Soviet agents acting under cover, either outright "spies" taking out information as fast and as safely as they could, or agents of influence who would unobtrusively steer policy in a way that could benefit the Soviet Government, as Burgess did over China, or frustrate operations, as Philby did over plans for revolt in Albania. Pincher's attack, not surprisingly, is all-embracing. He has after all lived through a period of forty and more years when time after time statements by senior civil servants to the press in briefing after briefing have been found to be nothing more than a stream of disinformation and lies. Pincher says:

> The confusion and shame [of the Burgess and Maclean defection] were so great that a new attitude to information about the event, and others like it that might arise, was quickly gener-

ated in the Foreign Office, Cabinet Office and in the secret services. The truth had to be kept from the public by every means, from misinformation when total silence could no longer be maintained to blatant lies. The policy of cover-up concerning disasters which are embarrassing to politicians and their senior servants has continued to the present time.

And naturally the core of his case is that Hollis, in his position of anti-Communist expert and then leader of the security service itself, was largely responsible for many of the worst disgraces. Glees, for his part, and other defenders of Hollis, are eager to show that nothing could have been done and that, as in the Fuchs case, mistakes were made; but they were understandable. Each side suffers from incomplete information, largely brought about, it is true, by the kind of disinformation Pincher describes. But this could work both ways. The mole-hunters at the time of the Nunn May prosecution may have been far more effective than we know. Many people were prosecuted in Canada who in Britain were simply dismissed or moved to other jobs in the general cover-up policy that was adopted instead of one of "McCarthyism"; they found the moles but let them off. On the other hand, it is absolutely obvious that nothing was done to detect the Cambridge moles, and others, from Burgess and Maclean onwards, and Glees never really faces the fact that Hollis not only did nothing about them but was a close personal friend of them all, almost without exception.

As with the German Communists in Britain, Glees begins by citing a number of cases where Hollis had apparently been at work in tracking Communist spies down. He cites the case of Ormond Uren in SOE who, as we have seen, was found to be conveying information to D. F. Springhall. But it is clear that Springhall was being followed on a routine basis by Special Branch officers, and it would have taken a particularly bold "mole" within MI5 to try to suppress the appropriate action when what Uren was doing was discovered. On the other hand tracking moles in SOE would have been extremely difficult for a reason which illustrates perfectly the reality of life in wartime Britain when Russia was an ally. This is that there were three KGB officers actually within SOE in London working on joint KGB-SOE exercises. The principal operation seems to have been one involving an attempt, before the invasion of Europe, to draw away Gestapo units from France by spreading doubt about the loyalty of the Russian troops serving with the German Army under General Vlasov. It was hoped that the Gestapo would be so worried by this that they would move their men over to the eastern front to deal with the situation. Clearly the presence of these officers in SOE would have made it next to impossible to discover either whether a mole existed or whether the men themselves were not gathering more information than was necessary.

This applied generally. A close colleague of Guy Burgess's in the BBC who worked with the MI5 vetting system showed exactly how difficult things were by commenting to me on the distinction drawn by the vetting authorities between Communists who were "safe" and others who were "dangerous." Christopher Hill, for example, was known to the BBC to be a Communist because MI5 said so; but he was also a reliable Foreign Office official who was known to be "quite safe" and actually on the Russian Desk, and has never been suspected before or since of being a mole. On the other hand, E. H. Carr, despite his position on *The Times* and his occasional appearances at the microphone, was known to be "dangerous." As the political battles that were to shape post-war Europe began to emerge, as we have seen in Chapter 9, the detection of "moles" must have been impossibly difficult, especially as what was being looked at was essentially changeable political loyalty, and only far beneath that the fixed determination of a Philby or a Blunt who had joined the Party and stayed loyal through thick and thin.

Apart from the cases already noticed, the only people whom Glees defends specifically from a charge that Hollis might have protected them are the central figures of Philby, Blunt, Burgess and Maclean. As has been mentioned, Philby and Hollis were opposite numbers in MI5 and MI6 for a considerable period. Even allowing for the alleged feud between the two services, it is clear that it would be against the most basic tenets of human nature for two people in such a position to be spying on each other, with Hollis "checking out" Philby, the man who sat next to him on weekly committee meetings, as the joint expert on Communist matters. Glees sees these difficulties in the technical terms of vetting, remarking: "One former MI5 officer has provided an answer: there was no proper vetting. It was therefore largely a matter of chance as to whether MI5 would know who might be a hazard." And talking specifically about Philby later, he remarks: "A former MI5 officer emphasised to me very forcefully indeed that MI5 had not known about Philby in 1939, although during the war, possibly in 1944, Philby had been more thoroughly looked at." It is obvious that this 1944 check was the one conducted after Churchill's urgent instruction to vet people in the security services, a job done by Valentine Vivian in MI6, although apparently hardly at all in MI5, since there were so many Communists there that survived, as we have seen. Glees ends his rather weak case by stating finally:

> In other words, when we add to the haphazard vetting possible misinformation and the fact that alleged "Communist" sympathies unsupported by hard evidence may not always have been an automatic disqualification from high office, it is possible to argue that MI5's mistakes were the result of perfectly straightforward errors. If that is the case, it was nevertheless a remarkable coincidence that moles such as Blunt, Burgess and Philby got through despite their past.

Which is very close indeed to saying that Chapman Pincher had got a point.

On the question of the actual defection in 1951, which now bids fair to be an historical event in its own right, a symbolic representation both of Britain's lost status in the world and of the inevitable result of nearly half a century of unnecessary secrecy and suppressed political debate in a changing world, Pincher and Glees take their stand on their several grounds. Pincher believes that Philby couldn't have alerted Maclean and Burgess within the time-scale necessary. Glees cites diplomats who were there at the time, such as Sir Patrick Reilly, to establish that Hollis was a most unlikely person to be the famous "third man" who was thought to have tipped off Maclean and got Burgess in readiness, as has been suggested by Pincher. The publication of Robert Cecil's biography of Maclean has established that Philby is indeed the most likely person to have been the third man, and that objections on grounds of timing were based on an erroneous understanding of the sequence of events that led up to the signing of the order for Maclean's interrogation by Herbert Morrison, as has been suggested in Chapter 10. There are yet more possible interpretations of the exact sequence of events if they are looked for, and the fact that Hollis was not necessary to the timetable does not mean that he was not aware that the defection was taking place.

In contrasting the various cases made by Pincher and denied by Glees, as far as possible, it has been necessary to look at the areas where both make comment. In fact Pincher's case, though circumstantial, is far more extensive than is indicated here. In particular Glees has ignored large parts of Pincher's book which deal with matters after 1945. This may well be due to legal implications in dealing, even at second hand, with material that has unquestionably come from "insiders." Certainly, as was made clear in the preface, discussion of purely operational failures, and the persons responsible for them, is the stuff of office politics—even more in an area such as the security of the state. The *only* discussion of these areas possible for outsiders takes the reader immediately into the hall of mirrors. All that can be said is that the confusion caused is such that there is an unanswerable case for an official history of MI5. Indeed the shift of secret work from matters of a technical nature, such as the theft of a military secret, to active involvement in politics makes such a history as inevitable as the notorious court case in Australia, which resulted solely from the frame of mind which has no understanding of this simple truth.

The final question raised by Pincher and Wright, and examined by Glees in his analysis, is the question of Hollis's motives. This question will now be considered in terms of the new discoveries that have been brought to light here and as a result of the appearance of an eyewitness who destroyed completely a central plank in Hollis's defence—that he had not known Cockburn since his university days.

13
Behind the Mask

IN strictly modern terms it is obvious now that Sir Roger Hollis belonged to an older generation when it came to anything of the nature of a "positive vet." The fact that he was, in Evelyn Waugh's phrase, a "good bottle man" might not have disqualified him in an age when more wine was drunk than now among undergraduates. But his close friendship with an undergraduate Communist, that *rara avis* in those days a card-carrying member of the Communist Party of Great Britain, would have meant inevitable rejection if there had been no good countervailing evidence and clearly there was none. Even at the time when Wright was grilling Blunt through hundreds of hours, such a connection when revealed by Blunt was sufficient to have those involved removed from sensitive work, even if nothing more was alleged and no other connection was proved since their university days. One wonders what went through Hollis's mind as he initialled action on such people—and there were many of them—which effectively finished their careers.

The case of Blunt, so long covered up by the authorities, until Andrew Boyle's investigations discovered him, brought Hollis's position home to him uncomfortably, even though he was himself by then the actual Director General of MI5. The situation can best be seen in a story told by Philby to Philip Knightley just before he died:

> I remember one day Blunt and I were in Hollis's office. Hollis and I were chatting and Blunt was idly turning the pages of some report or other. There was a break in the conversation and suddenly, without warning, Hollis turned towards Blunt and called out "Oh Elli." Blunt didn't bat an eyelid. He just went on turning the pages as if nothing had happened. And Hollis for his part, resumed the conversation as if it hadn't been interrupted.

If all the allegations about Hollis are true, this anecdote of a test of Blunt to see if he was the mole "Elli" is about a meeting, clearly a regular occurrence, of three of the most accomplished spies in British history. After Philby defected Hollis must have discussed the matter with Blunt in an entirely new light, if Hollis was unaware of Philby's dual role. Again, after Blunt's confession Hollis if he was innocent must have realised that he was the only member of that particular triumvirate who had not been in the know. The question obviously arises: did Hollis tell anyone that he was in this position, or even that the three of them were in the habit of meeting regularly? As long as Blunt remained free, and he was not disgraced until after Hollis's death, the situation between them must have been ambiguous to a degree. Did Hollis ever offer his resignation or go over the position with anyone? The activities of the Fluency Committee suggest that he did not. If Hollis and Blunt were collaborators we are faced with the possibility that Wright's tapes of hundreds of hours of discussion with Blunt were listened to by Hollis and Blunt later, or in any event their content gone over, no doubt with amusement.

If the three in this anecdote were all spies, they are the obvious candidates for the famous ring of three spies known by their code-names in the intercepted radio traffic to Moscow concerning them: Johnson, Hicks and Stanley. All three knew each other, and they were regarded by the Russians as their most important sources. The suggestion that one of them was Burgess, an eccentric given to independent action, has never been proved and now seems a less likely alternative. As was suggested in the introduction, the English "spies" who knew each other, in defiance of normal Russian spycraft, must be considered as a group who existed autonomously with their own ideas, although looking towards Moscow as the central focus of their loyalties. Before considering Hollis's position and possible motives in detail, it is perhaps worth looking at Philby and Blunt to see why they should have decided to dedicate their lives to a Soviet, or more correctly, a Marxist-Leninist philosophy.

Philby's dedication to Communism plainly began as a result of his own thinking at university, as he has stated in his autobiography *My Silent War*. Other factors were no doubt the romance of people such as his exact contemporary Peter Smollett and the part he himself played in the battle in Vienna between the Austrian left and the forces of reaction who did not stop at shelling the famous blocks of workers' flats. We do not know whether Philby was shot at in this fight, as he undoubtedly was in the Spanish Civil War; but he certainly saved the lives of some of his comrades by providing clothes as a substitute for their uniforms when they were trapped in the vast sewers in Vienna, later seen as the backdrop for the final scenes of Graham Greene's *The Third Man*. Although a British subject, Philby was born in India and spent his early days there, being bilingual in Punjabi as a child. Though he was educated in England his father became an Arabist and remained one to the last, converting to Islam and spending most of his days in the Middle East, where he became famous through his connection with Ibn Saud.

Kim Philby's roots in England at that time cannot have been as strong as those around him who were native-born. Some with such a colonial background strive to be almost more English than the English. A classic example is George Orwell, who was also born in India. Others, like Claud Cockburn, born in China, remain cosmopolitan in outlook, or simply "colonial." Although Philby settled down in England and had a family, the tie with England seems never to have been complete. This is seen, for example, by his decision while in Beirut, shortly before he defected, to try to become an Indian citizen. This move at such a crucial and testing time for him is all the more interesting as it was clearly not made

at the request of his Russian controller, who would have known of
the legal difficulties in the way of such a request, and no doubt
would also have been able to find a way around them. Clearly
Philby was acting in response to a deep-seated need to return to his
earliest roots and the place where he had been, perhaps, most
happy. After his defection the special relationship between Russia
and India would have removed any barriers to a yearly visit to India
once he had settled down in Moscow. The picture is of someone
essentially international in outlook whose loyalty could have been
won by the possibility of joining what he himself called an "elite
force," the KGB, working for something which he not only believed in, but for which comrades of his had died.

Anthony Blunt had a far more stable background and was an
extremely powerful and unusual intellect. It is significant that neither of the two biographies of him which have recently been published, one by two journalists, Freeman and Penrose, *Conspiracy of
Silence*, and the other by John Costello, *The Mask of Treachery*, mention his voluminous writings on the history of art in any detail, if at
all. This is extraordinary, particularly in Costello's book, which is
described as "fully documented." This phrase, if it means anything, should imply at least a bibliography of Blunt's work which
was, after all, the central feature of his life from university days.
This aspect may have been of little interest to Costello in view of
Blunt's other activities, but to try to understand a man's mind
without considering at all the greater part of his life's work is clearly
impossible. Considerable though Costello's work is, it leaves open
the fundamental questions of Blunt's motives.

Not the least contradiction in Blunt's life was his avowal of the
dogmas of Marxism and in contrast his continued interest in religious themes in works of art. Shortly before he died Blunt dis-
persed part of his library at Christie's. It was found that he was an
extensive collector of early religious emblem books. His library also
contained numerous pre-war works on religious works of art and art
criticism, many in German, which he annotated copiously, usually
on slips of paper loosely inserted between pages rather than on the
book itself. At this time he did broadcasts for Burgess, one on the
Sistine Chapel, but another on the fate of works of art in Spain

during the Civil War, which showed an astonishingly naïve view: that of an art historian first, and of a political theorist a long way behind. Talking of the removal of pictures from the Prado, in what could well have been described as looting by the Communist forces, he remarked:

> The pictures in the Prado are now on their last journey to safety . . . I think we can imagine the ghost of Goya watching with approval the saving of his work—these two works [Goya's paintings the 2nd and 3rd of May] perhaps above all others from the dangers that now threaten them.

The mostly likely explanation for his Marxist loyalty is the influence of Guy Burgess and other Marxist thinkers such as Alister Watson. This then became converted through his personal loyalty, and adherence to the elitist attitudes of those he found himself surrounded by at Cambridge, into a passionate and unyielding conviction. Costello demonstrates convincingly that the person who recruited the Cambridge spies was an ex-priest, Theodore Maly, a man of great charm and sophistication whose view of the world might have appealed particularly to Blunt, whose youth had been spent in an ecclesiastical atmosphere in Paris, where his father was Chaplain of the British Embassy Church. By the time Blunt went to university the family were back in England and his father the incumbent of a conventional, undistinguished London parish, a sharp transformation that echoes the experience of Hollis, also of course a child of the manse, when his family had briefly gone to Leeds from Wells.

We have mentioned earlier an Anglican parson who followed much the same path as the Catholic Maly, though without abandoning the cloth: Conrad Noel. An excerpt from one of Noel's manifestos points to the close links with grass-roots Communist feeling:

> If you would destroy the kept press and fight for freedom of expression; if you would destroy the Capitalist Parliament and build a people's republic; if you would abolish classes, artificial

distinctions, snobbery; if, while you know that the most deadly tyrants are not kings but financiers, speculators, captains of industry, you would also, with St. Thomas of Canterbury, destroy that nest of flunkies, the court; if, while you measure swords with the New Plutocracy, you are ashamed of that Ancient Fraud which calls itself the Old Aristocracy; if you are striving for such transformation as shall make it possible to substitute "Oh Lord save the Commonwealth" for "Oh Lord save the King." Help the Crusade! We offer you nothing— nothing but adventure, risks, battle, perhaps ruin; with the love and loyalty of comrades and the Peace of God which passeth understanding.

Noel's banners carried the slogan "Crusade for God and the Worker's Commonwealth." While such outpourings would merely have been an embarrassment to the sophisticated Blunt, they undoubtedly formed the background to the conviction of many in the Church of England and would have been well-known to Hollis, if not through gossip at Wells then through talk of meetings on the downs at Clifton, where Noel's emblem of a cross with hammer and sickle on it was often seen in the twenties. The movement did not outlast the inter-war period, but there were many, such as Tom Driberg, Joseph Needham and the well-known East End vicar John Grosser, who were to acknowledge its influence on them. It is in this context that the otherwise extraordinarily high proportion of Communists, both open and secret, who came from clerical households can be understood. Blunt was the son of a clergyman. Hollis's father, as we have seen, was Bishop of Taunton. But there were many others. Dona Torr, one of the foremost theoreticians of the CPGB before and during the war, was the daughter of the Rev. William Torr, Vicar of Eastham and Canon of Chester. His successor as Canon was the Rev. Hewlett Johnson, famous as the "Red Dean," in fact the Dean of Canterbury and a member of the board of the *Daily Worker*, sitting alongside J. B. S. Haldane, throughout the crucial period leading up to its suppression, as we have seen in Chapter 5. At the People's Convention itself numbers of clergymen were present and even spoke from the platform. The intermediary used by the GRU at the time of the Profumo affair,

Stephen Ward, was the son of the Canon of Rochester. It may well be, when family diaries and papers of the period become available and the political history of modern Britain comes to be written, that these associations will be seen in the same light as, for example, those around Frederick Dennison Maurice and the Workers Educational Association, and similar movements in the previous century. Until the papers of the families involved reach the public domain, and the courage of later generations is equal to the publishing of them, the truth of these matters must remain a mystery. Meanwhile it is obvious that they formed a constant background to Hollis's career, and it is worth remembering that while his brother Christopher went over to Rome, Roger himself did not, and his son has remarked that he was not a Catholic of any kind.

Turning to the details of Hollis's career as they have become known through the new facts established here, it is possible to get closer to the real Roger Hollis and to the truth about some of the matters which have caused such difficulty and furore. It is obvious from what we now know about Hollis's time in China that he had considerable knowledge of Communist activity there before the Comintern was found to have infiltrated his own firm. Working as a journalist in Hong Kong while the conflict between Russia and China was at its height would have made him aware from the start of Communism as a living force. When he joined BAT he kept up his journalist connections, meeting people like Agnes Smedley and Arthur Ewert, if the evidence said to have come from Tony Stables and from Hollis's own interrogation is accepted. Certainly discussing Comintern activity with Peter Fleming he would have been in a position to know much more about such things than any normal BAT employee, which he certainly was not. BAT staff are sure that freelance journalism of this kind would have been unheard of among ordinary covenanted staff recruited in Britain in the normal way.

Hollis's general awareness of the Comintern would have been brought into sharp focus by the arrest of his fellow workers, many of whom he knew personally and worked with in Mukden. When the arrests actually took place he was in Shanghai, and he would have heard what had happened from the two men who escaped the arrests and came straight to BAT's Shanghai base. How did he react to this event? According to Glees, who did not know of any of the facts revealed here, his letters home did not mention the word "Comintern" at all. Not surprisingly, therefore, he seems to have kept it from his family. His allegiance to the Chinese cause, and his forceful statement of it in his talk in 1937, suggests that he took the view that the Japanese were to blame for everything, rather than the Comintern infiltration itself. This would have placed him in the same camp as Clark Kerr and others on the left. On his return to Britain his position would have been difficult to understand for those not intimately aware of what was going on in China. But his hatred of the Japanese and sympathy for the Chinese would have aligned him with the standard far-left view espoused by people such as Stephen Spender who were ardent advocates of the boycott of Japanese goods. Christopher Hollis wrote his biography of Lenin at this time, seeing things from his Catholic standpoint, although the fact that he wrote on Lenin at all showed that a serious debate was going on. Roger Hollis would have found himself somewhere between these two positions. Though there are no surviving letters between the brothers from this period, it seems inconceivable that they did not discuss the book and its contents as they bore so directly on Roger's experience in China of Lenin's teachings as they were then being played out in practice. In this context there is a passage in the book which is significant:

> All the activities of the secret societies in Russia always seem to have been perfectly well known to the Police. That is why the secret societies almost always failed in their coups; when they succeeded, they succeeded not because they had escaped the notice of the Police but because the policemen whose duty it was to prevent them were themselves members of the secret society.

When Roger Hollis discussed his possible career in MI5 with his elder brother, as he surely must have, it would have been obvious to him that he might get involved in this kind of work. Indeed it was a method used by Maxwell Knight at MI5 to infiltrate the

Communist party at Oxford through Tom Driberg. If the theory of Hollis's being a Soviet agent—and most likely under GRU control—is correct, then he himself would be the man fulfilling all the conditions of those infiltrators first used by the Czarist police, but now with the intention of bringing about revolution rather than stopping it!

There can have been very few people outside his family that Hollis would have discussed his MI5 prospects with, and MI5 would certainly have warned him to keep his application strictly secret. But the connection between Claud Cockburn and Hollis is so important that the possibility that he discussed the matter with him has to be considered seriously. We have mentioned Sir Vernon Kell's background in China; Cockburn's father "Chinese Harry" was actually there at the same time. The expatriate community was very much smaller in China than in India or anywhere else in the Empire, and the likelihood of their knowing each other, particularly as Cockburn's father held a diplomatic post, must be high. Kell's later career would have been known to him, and Claud would have known of it both from his father and from his Comintern controllers. All would have regarded the placing of a contact of theirs inside MI5 as a great coup of inestimable value to them. The possibility that Hollis discussed the question with him, perhaps without full understanding of the situation, is a tantalising one.

It will be proved shortly that Hollis was communicating with Cockburn right through the wartime period, and that Cockburn looked upon him as a "contact" within MI5 whom he could get in touch with when he needed to. The question is, when did this state of affairs come into being—before Hollis joined MI5 or after? If it was before then, there is every possibility that Hollis was in MI5 as a mole under the control of Cockburn, or his controllers, or at least that his position there was so compromised that they could see him in that light. If it was after then, unless Hollis was deliberately cultivating Cockburn as his own agent within the Communist Party and initiated the connection, he should have realised that his position was one of extreme danger. The fact that Hollis was later able to conceal his knowing Cockburn with complete self-assurance implies that the contact was clandestine throughout the wartime period, and that he was confident no one would be able to connect them. Whatever the truth of the matter, the situation would have been deeply worrying to Hollis's superiors in the service had they found out about it.

In later life Sir Roger Fulford discussed his old university friend Hollis with a number of people. He had worked with Hollis during the war and, indeed, owed his job in MI5 partly to Hollis's influence. He disclosed that Hollis had been known as a Communist expert from early on: "I believe he passed on some news of Soviet espionage activities in China and actually named one of their agents," he told one colleague. Fulford knew nothing of the BAT infiltration described here, or of Kell's interest in such matters, but the anecdote shows how Hollis came to get his reputation so soon. Hollis's skill in analysing Communist affairs must have been most obvious at the time of the signing of the Nazi-Soviet pact. This threw most analysts completely, but Hollis had seen the same *realpolitik* before, when Mao Tse Tung and Chiang Kai Shek had joined forces. Even earlier Stalin had happily backed Chiang Kai Shek in order to protect his Japanese flank, though Chiang Kai Shek was slaughtering Chinese Communists wherever they could be found. This perspective would have enabled Hollis to see the Communist Party as potential allies, as Kingsley Martin's mysterious informer did, even when they had joined Hitler in raping Poland. When the security executive was established in May 1940 Hollis's line would have been seen as "left," if not actively Communist. Whether he dissembled this or openly avowed it we shall never know, but we have seen him acting to protect the *Daily Worker* and *The Week*. It could be claimed that, rather than acting out of Communist sympathy here, or as an agent of influence, he may simply have been protecting his old friend Cockburn. He was of course doing that, but the only reason we have heard about the Cockburn case, rather than others that may have existed, is the high profile adopted by Cockburn, which ensured that some at least of the files relating to him were preserved. The particular case that suggests that the second view is correct, and that there were other moves of Hollis's which protected Communists per se, is the case of the atom spies, which we have looked at already in detail.

When Hollis accepted blame in America in 1950 he did so at an occasion which he thought would never be made public and so his admission is the more to be believed. If he was acting on Soviet instruction when he let through Fuchs and Nunn May, he could not have acted otherwise than he did, having full knowledge not only of their Communist connections but of the importance of their work.

Even Hollis's staunch defender Glees has remarked that things would look "black" for Hollis if Fuchs's clearance could be laid at his door, and without question it now can be. As Hollis supported anything that would oppose the Japanese, there may even be a general motive for his actions: for it had become known through the censorship authorities that the Japanese were using radioactive invisible ink in order to evade censorship, implying that they too were involved in nuclear research. Hollis had early remarked on the fact that the Japanese could use poison gas against the Chinese because the Chinese had no equivalent technology to throw back at them. Here perhaps was an opportunity to give the Communists in China, via their Soviet colleagues, an equal opportunity. We have, of course, here entered the wilderness of mirrors, and no evidence of any kind is likely to emerge; but some logic for Hollis's undoubted actions needs to be found.

With the end of the war the situation in Britain, as far as MI5 was concerned, changed rapidly. The German Communist expatriates and their problems soon dwindled as postwar Germany established itself in the apparently unstable split state which has miraculously survived to the present day, although the opening of the Berlin Wall and Gorbachev's policy of *glasnost* seem to have precipitated the move to reunification. Most German Communists went rapidly to East Germany and remained there, including zu Putlitz himself. The cold war, on the other hand, quickly developed, and the hallmark of those on the left in Britain was a rabid anti-Americanism. Hollis seems to have shared this feeling. So much so that when he went over to Canada to interview the defector Gouzenko his superior warned his opposite number in New York that Hollis was very anti-American. Accordingly he was steered straight on up to Canada. Hollis's address in America in 1950, which we have already referred to, might suggest that he had mellowed towards America, but this was not so. In fact his actual view of the occasion is seen in Glees's comment on the talk, which he refers to as a "performance":

> Indeed, we know that Hollis's performance which obviously impressed the Americans was a source of great pride to British circles generally. When Malcolm Macdonald reported this incident to Roger Hollis's brother, the Bishop in Madras, he told him that Roger had been able to squash American suspicions about MI5 by "making rings around them."

This anti-Americanism has first been noticed in Cockburn's paper *The Week* as a policy line, and it seems to have been the one unmistakable strand in the thinking of all those now known to be Soviet agents. When Hollis gave his talk Philby and Burgess were in Washington causing social outrage by their blatant anti-American attitudes. On one occasion they even insulted American guests in Philby's home. All this was in the context of Britain's complete failure to back America in her stand on China. The indications are that Hollis held to his original views on China, as we shall see; and his own aim in "running rings" around his hosts was to ensure that his actions in clearing Fuchs and Nunn May were not properly understood.

The most obvious facet of anti-Americanism as it affected MI5 was the outcry against McCarthyism. Just as the liberal voice protesting against the suppression of the *Daily Worker* was greater than the Communist voice, so the outcry against McCarthyism was sufficiently widespread to make the avowal of it by the security services, and Hollis in particular, seem normal. In John Bulloch's book *MI5*, passed in every detail by Hollis personally, we find the following description of MI5's activities at this time:

> A few years ago, at the height of the McCarthy witch-hunt in America, when the effect of that unhappy chapter was being felt in this country, some 5000 people each year were being investigated by MI5 and the security services . . .

And this no doubt echoed Hollis's view of the matter. But Britain's cover-up was not due to McCarthyism in America. It was due to the trials after Gouzenko's defection in Canada. Hollis's apologia, his "running rings around the Americans," was simply a faux-naïf admission of a mistake while concealing the cover-up that had taken place at *that* level, let alone the original passing of Fuchs. In other words the disdain of McCarthy's methods presumed that the things he revealed could not have been happening in Britain. The truth of the matter was to be brought home with a vengeance when the decoded "Venona" traffic identified Maclean and precipitated the defection of him and Burgess. The cover-up that followed made its counterpart after the Nunn May and Fuchs cases seem like a frank and total admission of guilt.

With the defection Hollis was for the first time put in an acutely embarrassing position. Whatever lies the press were told about Burgess, Hollis knew precisely what his opinions were. He knew also that Philby and Blunt were intimate friends of Burgess's. Indeed he knew them all himself. To establish guilt by association is always dangerous, but the situation here was one in which even the simplest "vet" would have suggested extreme caution in the future deployment of those involved. Thus the American authorities insisted on the immediate withdrawal of Philby and voiced suspicion of Blunt. Precisely how much Hollis told of what he knew to his superiors or political masters is not clear; probably we shall never know. The Labour Government at the time were in difficulty, with a reduced majority, and would not have wanted any revelations that might damage their electoral prospects, which many MPs from Maurice Webb downwards would have assured them was inevitable if the defection case were pursued. The election of a Conservative administration in 1951 must have been a blessing for Hollis and his colleagues, as the security services were able to conceal the most damaging facts from the incoming administration. In fact not only did Hollis fail to establish a rapport with Macmillan, he played a significant part in the downfall of his administration, as we shall see, through his handling or "running" of the Profumo affair. When Philby returned to London he was given an internal "trial" at which he managed to avoid giving himself away. Philby must have made some contact with Blunt at this point, and if Hollis was innocent of any knowledge of what had been happening he was the only one of the three who was.

Burgess and Maclean's reappearance caused a sensation, but if it had been said in the papers that the deputy head of MI5 was actually a close associate of the men who were now seen for the first time to be in Moscow the sensation would have been unlimited. Even the most obtuse man in Hollis's shoes would have realised the danger of his position. Hollis seems to have done nothing. A game was apparently begun at his expense, played by Burgess, zu Putlitz, Driberg and the others. The events which followed the reappearance of Burgess and Maclean in Moscow were astonishing, though when they were first revealed by Chapman Pincher their significance was not fully understood in the stream of the new facts that emerged as the *Spycatcher* saga evolved. Pincher was approached by Hollis with a story that was to be disclosed in the press to guard against a whole series of revelations that Hollis suggested were now being planned by Moscow which would be used to discredit Britain and America:

> [Admiral] Thomson told me that Hill [Bernard Hill, chief legal advisor of MI5] had been asked to see me at the request of Roger Hollis, then still Deputy Director-General . . . [Hill] said that he and his colleagues had concluded that the theatrical production of Maclean and Burgess was just the prelude to further statements calculated to sow the maximum distrust between Britain and America. The meeting ended with a request that the *Daily Express* for which I was then defence correspondent should publish a prominent article warning the public that whatever Maclean and Burgess might say in the future would be a KGB exercise and was not to be believed.

Pincher duly ran a story given him in detail from Hollis. This included the suggestion that Burgess might even appear on Moscow radio (an echo no doubt of his BBC days) providing information about British diplomats negotiating with the USA which might embarrass them severely. In fact, as Pincher pointed out, no such stories or broadcasts appeared. In the light of what has been described here about Burgess's knowledge of the situation in China and Britain's position vis-à-vis the USA, Hollis clearly had more to worry about than defamation of a diplomat: what was to be feared on the home front was even greater. The whole exercise has strong echoes of the kind of activity Hollis was involved in before the war with Peter Fleming in China. That the concern, and the steering hand, was Hollis's became absolutely clear with the next stage, the dispatch of Tom Driberg to Moscow to talk to Burgess. This journey has been touched on earlier. Chapman Pincher has given a largely accurate account of the background and of the result, clearly to be foreseen, that Driberg ended up as a double agent or simply a liaison man working for Hollis and the KGB for much of the rest of his life. New information has come to light, however, from an old friend of Burgess's who knew him well in the years before the war and also knew Driberg. At the time of the visit Driberg was warned by the Russians that he would not be happy when he saw Burgess and would be shocked by the change that had come over him, as indeed he was. The insistence on the visit came from the British side. Driberg made a point of looking up Burgess's friend, and asked particularly whether he had any communication from him. Driberg was clearly trying to find out whether anyone outside his left-wing circle, or any person such as Harold Nicolson, was in communication with Burgess. What was feared, equally by Hollis, who monitored the journey from the beginning, and by Moscow, was that Burgess would find an outlet for what he knew that was outside the control of either side.

The reason Hollis had wanted Driberg to go to Moscow became obvious with the first important sequel to the visit before publication of the book itself. When Driberg produced the first manuscript it contained many references to Burgess's JBC days, and to other secret matters given to him by Burgess in breach of the Official Secrets Act. These were deleted, of course, when MI5 rewrote the book in line with their—that is, Hollis's—interests; but the offence had been committed and there was documentary evidence in the form of the original manuscript. There were now grounds for prosecuting Burgess. This, according to the line given to Pincher, had been the main purpose of the visit.

That the possibility of Burgess's return to Britain was the basis of Hollis's need to get actual evidence against him was obvious to those behind the Iron Curtain. This became even clearer when zu Putlitz published his memoirs, *The Putlitz Dossier*. After naming Blunt as one of his close friends in the prominently placed preface, as a reminder to Hollis and others in the know that the Blunt affair was still alive as far as the East was concerned, his most interesting indiscretion was a paean of praise for Burgess which ended with a moving plea that could have been dictated by Burgess himself:

> I sincerely hope that the day will come when he will be able to set foot again in his beloved England and prove to himself as well as to his countrymen, that he did everything in his power to serve his country well and honestly.

If this was another move in the game being played at Hollis's expense—and, of course, at Blunt's—it worked admirably. Hollis became more than ever determined that Burgess should not return, until in one famous case a rumour that the return was about to take place caused the actual issuing of arrest warrants to be served on Burgess the moment he landed. This was the news that broke in the *Evening Standard*. In a frequently described incident, television crews and journalists waited at the airports for the expected arrival. Like the broadcasts by Burgess promised earlier, Burgess and Maclean did not materialise. The single-minded determination not to allow Burgess to return, even when it was rumoured that he wished to visit his mother before she died, aroused interest at all levels, even the highest. R. A. Butler as Home Secretary in charge of MI5, to whom Hollis presumably must have been reporting on the matter, was said by Stephen Spender to have expressed bewilderment:

> Please tell him [Burgess] that, as far as I am concerned, he's perfectly free to come and go as he pleases. I know of absolutely nothing to prevent that. Of course, if he does come back and the Home Secretary takes no action then I'll be criticised, the press will be after me, but I'm prepared to face that. As far

as I am concerned there is nothing against him. Of course, the fellows at MI5 may take a different view of the matter. I know nothing about that. Tell him I'll stand by what I say.

Driberg, working for Hollis and the KGB, was foremost among those who warned Spender that on no account should he convey this news to Burgess. In the end he did not, though he cannot have known of the close connection between Driberg and Hollis. Hollis's likely answer to Butler's offer when it reached him can be seen in the charade of the arrest warrants.

Pincher remarks that the Fluency Committee could not understand why Hollis should want to prevent Burgess from returning, since he would clearly be a most valuable source of information even if the KGB's blessing on his exit from Russia would imply that he would not know much of great secrecy. This seems to suggest that the Fluency Committee, despite the defection of Philby and the confession of Blunt, which had taken place by the time they were sitting, still had no idea of the Burgess China scandal, or of any of the wartime events described here and of Hollis's part in them. Nor, it seems, did they understand the liaison between Hollis, Driberg, Burgess and the KGB.

The years of Hollis's directorship of MI5 were not entirely without success. One of his triumphs was the trial of Gordon Lonsdale, followed by the slightly more embarrassing Vassal case. John Bulloch had followed both cases and had written a book about the Lonsdale affair, *Spy Ring*. As a result of his interest he was called to give evidence at the Vassal Tribunal, and his publishers submitted as written evidence a proof copy of his book *MI5*. The book came as a complete surprise to Hollis and it was returned to the publishers by the secretary of the D-Notice Committee marked with massive emendations, from the rates of pay of serving officers to matters of detail concerning Kell's dismissal from the Service.

MI5 realised immediately that the book depended on help from someone who knew a great deal about the service. The inference was quickly drawn that this was Lady Kell, Sir Vernon's widow. She had written an account of MI5 and her husband's part in it a few years after his death. Publication had been prevented at that time. With the passage of years she had tried once more, through the efforts of her son, to find a publisher. MI5 had again acted to restrain publication. At this point Kell's son, perhaps attracted by the success and ability evinced by *Spy Ring,* approached Bulloch with the suggestion that he build a book around the original manuscript. *MI5,* the first published history of the service, was the result. After the initial approach to the D-Notice Committee a long drawn-out confrontation took place between the Government, in the shape of MI5, the Home Secretary and the official solicitor on one side, and John Bulloch, the publishers and their lawyers on the other. But the first move, made perhaps in panic, was Hollis's.

Although *MI5* was published in 1963, it had been written before Philby's defection. Hollis may have thought that the book was the beginning of a similar situation to that involving Burgess and Driberg or that Bulloch might have come across evidence of MI5's involvement in the Profumo affair, which was just about to enter its final phase. Whatever the reason, he began by visiting Bulloch in person, not on official premises, giving a false name to Bulloch's receptionist. He was entirely alone and the interview was conducted without witnesses, and without any monitoring (unless Hollis was wearing a portable microphone and transmitter; highly unlikely in 1963). After apologising for the false name, which he referred to as "this Boy Scout business," Hollis discussed the book in general terms and left after a short while. Further meetings then followed, but with others present. The conclusion to be drawn from this highly unusual encounter—Bulloch was then a young man at the beginning of his career, Hollis the most senior officer in the most secret Government organisation—was that Hollis wanted to be absolutely sure of knowing for himself from the first what Bulloch intended in his book, and why it was being written. In fact Bulloch knew nothing of Philby or the Profumo case, and his book's appearance at this time was simply a coincidence.

The sequel to this strange beginning was that the book, which had by then been bound, was disbound at MI5's expense. Twelve or more pages were removed, a fresh text was substituted of exactly the right length for the deleted passages, and the whole was rebound and sent out as if nothing had happened. This procedure, besides being immensely expensive, seemed to show either that MI5 was unaware that such a procedure was uncommon—normally a book would be pulped and reprinted at less cost—or that they wished to ensure that no copies at all of the unexpurgated book existed. Hollis's personal concern, which he carried to the length of bringing about a meeting of the author with the Home Secretary, would suggest the latter.

The defection of Philby placed Blunt in great difficulty. He was already being interrogated by MI5, and Hollis was seeing the transcripts. It would appear very unlikely that Hollis was not also in contact with Blunt himself in some way. If he and Blunt were waiting for some contact from Philby after his defection they appear to have waited in vain. Finally, in March, Blunt went to Beirut, supposedly en route to a talk he was to give at the Weizman Institute, staying there with an old friend. It can hardly be a coincidence that Yuri Modin, Blunt's controller from his wartime years, had been in Beirut at the time of Philby's defection two months before. Costello has suggested that Blunt met Modin there and was told that Philby had been offered an immunity deal and that this was the way things would probably go for him. There can of course be no evidence for this, but it seems highly plausible. In fact only a few more months were to pass before evidence appeared which identified Blunt, as it had Philby, in the form of a face from the past whose conscience overcame him in his middle years. In Blunt's case it was Michael Straight.

Hollis of course dealt with the matter from the start, and an immunity deal was offered to Blunt, just as it had been to Philby. Blunt's career in the art world had been crowned by the coming to fruition of one of the ideas he had backed, the public opening of the Queen's picture gallery in the Royal Mews. Exposure was unthinkable and, as presumably no convenient reason for his removal could be found, it was decided to let him remain in his post until retirement. We cannot know what Hollis's motives in this were, other than the obvious ones of protecting the monarch from embarrassment. Certainly he knew now, if he hadn't known before, that throughout his time in the war his two closest collaborators had been Soviet agents. He seems to have told no one. His position was made all the more difficult because at this time the "molehunters" had begun to take seriously the possibility that there still was a Soviet agent in MI5, and that he and his deputy Graham Mitchell were the most likely suspects.

Hollis had no option but to join in the check on Mitchell, which included full-scale surveillance. During these investigations he began to discuss political matters with Wright, presumably in an attempt to bring him round to some understanding of his perspective. While Wright's testimony in *Spycatcher*, as we have seen, is tainted, his account of what Hollis said is plausible, particularly as he himself had no knowledge of affairs in China.

> Occasionally, during the searches of Mitchell's office Hollis talked about his early years. He told me about his travels in China during the 1930's where he worked with British American Tobacco.
>
> "Dreadful business out there. Any damn fool could see what the Japanese were doing in Manchuria. It was perfectly obvious we'd lose China if we didn't act," he used to say.
>
> As with many elder MI5 officers, the roots of his dislike of the Americans lay prewar. He said the Americans could have helped out in the Far East, but refused to because they were gripped with isolationism. The French in the Far East were, he said, effete, and would rather have seen the whole place go down than help us. That left only the Russians.
>
> "They watched and waited," he told me, "and they got it in the end after the war, when Mao came."

This statement of his position is all the more convincing because quite clearly it was Hollis's own, echoing the position we have seen him take up in 1937. His view that the arrival of Mao was the equivalent of Russia's winning China chimed exactly with Burgess's line, that Mao was the leader of a Russian-style Communism on a strict Leninist analysis, only carrying it one stage further. And, most damaging, it is obvious that Hollis did not tell Wright anything about the activities of the Comintern in China, or about his experiences there involving Peter Fleming or his other contacts, which have been revealed in this book for the first time. Had

233

Wright shown some signs of sympathy in these talks with Hollis, or even of understanding, Hollis might have begun to give him the wider perspective in which he saw Chinese affairs. But he did not. Hollis's silence under the circumstances is extremely suspicious.

When the time came to brief the American security services on the enquiry into Mitchell, Hollis himself went over and made the necessary disclosures. Pincher and others have commented on this as suspicious, and it is another example of Hollis's acting on his own to ensure that he knew before anyone else exactly what was being said. Yet on such a serious matter it would only have been proper for him to go over in person, especially as MI5's previous track record on collaboration had been so chequered.

Some writers, notably Nigel West, maintain that Mitchell is still the most likely suspect; but Mitchell was cleared and there followed the investigation into Hollis himself which marked the nadir of internal self-confidence of MI5 and in the end precipitated the *Spycatcher* fiasco. Hollis clearly bore the various investigations with fortitude. Finally, if Wright is to be believed, shortly before his retirement Hollis called him into his office and asked him face to face why he thought he was a spy. Wright went through his arguments. They were largely circumstantial and evoked the classic reply which has been so frequently reprinted:

> "You have the manacles on me. All I can tell you is that I am
> not a spy."

Wright was not satisfied, of course, but the matter was left there while Hollis grappled with some of the most difficult problems to afflict MI5—principally the Profumo affair, which was so complex that it is dealt with in a separate chapter here.

Some while after Hollis had retired, the Fluency Committee reconvened, although not this time under Wright's chairmanship, and looked at Hollis's case again. A fresh look at the facts forced them to conclude that Hollis really was the most likely suspect for a number of unexplained leaks and failures in MI5. They determined to take the very serious step of calling Hollis back from retirement to answer a full statement of their suspicions. Hollis

agreed to this, rather surprisingly. Calling someone out of retirement is a thing not often done and in Hollis's case the effect on
morale would have been obviously so great that it is difficult to see
why, if he had anything to hide, however innocent, he did not go
to the then Director General with it and call a halt. Instead he
appeared for his interview by the committee, which took place over
two days.

In the published accounts of Hollis's interrogation there is one
significant passage, that involving Claud Cockburn. It was put to
Hollis that it was irregular not to mark Cockburn's file with the fact
that he had known him at University. At first Hollis said merely
that the rule requiring officers to note when they knew someone
was frequently ignored in prewar days. The committee noticed, as
Wright had, that Hollis had kept Cockburn's file by him during the
war years, but they seem not to have drawn any conclusion from
this; presumably Hollis had weeded the file so carefully that there
was no trace of the facts disclosed earlier here. On the second day
the committee again asked Hollis about Cockburn, and this time
Hollis produced what can now be proved to have been a well-
prepared fallback position that was completely untrue. He remarked with seeming frankness that, yes, he had deliberately
omitted to say that he knew Cockburn. He was aware that since
leaving university Cockburn had acquired a left-wing reputation
and he did not wish to prejudice his career by disclosing that he
knew him. So he decided to keep silent. This was accepted by the
committee as a candid admission, which apparently disposed of the
matter.

And there things might have stayed had not evidence emerged,
while this book was being written and from a totally unexpected
source, that Hollis was lying to the committee. Right up to the
present day Hollis's supporters have followed his lead in protesting
that he did not know Cockburn after his university days. In fact he
had been meeting him almost up to the time the Fluency Committee began to sit and had lunched with him at the height of the
Profumo affair, actually disclosing information about it. Cockburn
had arranged the lunch for this sole purpose, aiming to get a scoop
for the magazine he was editing at the time, *Private Eye*.

Claud Cockburn was not the regular editor of the magazine but had willingly accepted an invitation from Richard Ingrams to take over from him for a special issue to be devoted to the Profumo scandal. Cockburn set to work immediately, choosing as his assistant a fellow journalist Alan Brien, whom he had first met at the time of the People's Convention during the war. He announced to Brien that he was going to reactivate some of his old contacts to get to the bottom of things; the most important of these proved to be Hollis.

When Cockburn first mentioned the name Hollis, Brien thought that he must be referring to Roger's brother Christopher, who was then a well-known figure. On the day of the meeting Hollis arrived early and chanced on Cockburn standing outside *Private Eye*'s Soho offices talking to Brien, whom he did not know. Following strict security procedure Hollis walked straight past them without showing any sign of recognition. His efforts at anonymity were in vain, however, for Cockburn was so startled that he set off after him, calling his name as he did so to attract his attention.

Brien had seen immediately that the man who met Cockburn was not Christopher Hollis and assumed that he was simply someone with the same name who worked for MI5. He did not enquire further of Cockburn after he returned from his lunch and they settled down to write what became the 9 August 1963 issue of *Private Eye*. It was not until the *Spycatcher* story broke and Hollis's picture began to appear in the papers that Brien realised that it was Roger Hollis who had helped Cockburn. Nor did he understand anyway until he read the first draft of this book that such a meeting could have had any significance at all.

This discovery of a connection between Hollis and Cockburn is damning, as those who have followed the story will realise. Cockburn referred to Hollis as an "old contact." That description enables us to place their previous meetings with some precision, for Cockburn had only recently returned to Britain. After the war he had gone behind the Iron Curtain on a number of escapades, some of which came to the attention of the authorities at the Foreign Office, before going to live in Ireland. Their previous contacts must therefore have dated from the wartime period, and cannot have been further back than 1938, when Hollis joined MI5.

The conclusion is inescapable that the connections between the two men, examined in earlier chapters, are those that Cockburn was alluding to when he spoke to Brien, that Hollis was indeed Cockburn's man in MI5 who had tipped him off about the impending closure of *The Week* and who smoothed his path at the time of the Algiers incident and so on. Well might Hollis desperately try and pretend that he had not known Cockburn since those days at Oxford some forty years before. If it had been put to him that he had been meeting Cockburn in 1963, he would surely have been forced into a confession of some kind, although whether this would have included some recruitment to the GRU rather than simply a compromising friendship with Cockburn will never be known for sure. Some further indications of the truth about Hollis can be seen in the Profumo affair itself, in which Hollis played a vital role.

14
The Profumo Affair

BEFORE the war Claud Cockburn had scored one great propaganda success in his magazine *The Week*—the creation of the "Cliveden Set," supposedly a group of rich establishment people who favoured appeasement of Hitler and who gathered at Cliveden House on the Thames. In the early 1960s a new Cliveden Set came into existence, centred again on the great house occupied by Lord Astor but this time famous for the good life. Two regular visitors to the house were to dominate the Profumo affair—Profumo himself, then Secretary of State for War, and an osteopath who had a cottage on the estate and regularly went to the house both professionally and as a guest, Stephen Ward.

In stark contrast to the carefree life of opulence at Cliveden, the political world was going through a period of acute international tension. Russia was involved in a direct confrontation with the West that produced the Berlin crisis, the setting up of the Berlin Wall, and then the Cuban missile crisis that brought the world to the brink of nuclear war. So seriously did Russia view what was happening that she set in motion a series of direct measures of a highly secret kind that were run by her military intelligence organisation, the GRU. These operations in America have become well known, including discussions with the President's brother Robert

Kennedy, at the time of the Cuban missile crisis, designed to conceal the existence of missiles in the shipments of material being sent to Cuba. The object of all these moves was to conceal Russia's actual aims and to drive a wedge between Britain and America if at all possible—the same policy they had pursued over China after the war.

Just as the Russians had attempted to set up alternative means of communication with the British government before the German invasion during World War II, using D. N. Pritt and Walter Monkton as a means of gaining access to Anthony Eden, so, too, in the crises of the sixties they tried to set up unofficial links with Britain, having as their main target Profumo. The man chosen by the GRU to carry out this task was Eugene Ivanov, who had arrived in Britain on 27 March 1960, ostensibly as a junior naval attaché at the Russian Embassy in London.

As in chess, the first moves in the espionage game are often as intriguing as the last. Within a very short time the GRU's man Ivanov had met Profumo on a social basis and was on good terms with him. How had this been achieved? The key link had come through Stephen Ward, who had introduced Ivanov to Profumo one weekend early in July 1961 at a Cliveden House party. The question of how Ward himself had come to meet Ivanov is indeed intriguing. The introduction had been made by a patient of Ward's, the editor of the staunchly conservative paper the *Daily Telegraph*, Colin Coote. As with so many of his patients, Ward knew Coote socially and was one of his regular bridge partners. Another member of Coote's circle, a close friend and his principal golfing partner, was Roger Hollis.

Lord Denning did not mention Coote's knowing Hollis when he went into this important meeting in his report on the Profumo affair. He may not have known that there was any connection, but what he did say was that the meeting between Ivanov and Ward had been made at Ward's suggestion because he wished to go to Russia to sketch Khrushchev—Ward was a competent amateur portraitist—and wanted to meet someone who could help him get a visa. This was untrue. In fact the introduction was set up by Coote, and Ward had no intention of going to Russia. As he wrote in a memoir shortly before his death, "There is no truth in the suggestion that I befriended Ivanov because I wanted to draw Khrushchev." Almost all the recent commentators on the Profumo affair have assumed that the introduction was made at Hollis's direct instigation and this has been confirmed to the author by Chapman Pincher; however, none knew of the GRU connection. If Hollis did set up the introduction it would imply so much that the matter must be left open until actual evidence proves it beyond doubt. What is made clear, as was made plain to Denning by Hollis, is that MI5 knew Ivanov was a GRU officer from a very early stage. They kept him under the level of observation that this implied and which readers of Peter Wright's *Spycatcher* will know was intense, if not always completely effective.

Stephen Ward was an attractive personality to his hosts, as we have said, because of his unusual medical skills (Ward's degreee was American, one not recognised in Britain, and the claims of osteopathy were disputed by the medical establishment as indeed they still are), and because of his ability to produce flattering portraits. Even more fascinating was his habit of surrounding himself with attractive young girls who came to his Cliveden cottage regularly and spent time at the swimming pool belonging to the great house.

The weekend party at which Ivanov and Profumo met has become famous. This was also the weekend when Profumo became involved with one of Ward's girls after seeing her at the pool, an involvement that was to bring about his downfall. Their affair began shortly after that weekend. Hollis knew about it immediately by report from Ward, who had four weeks before been brought into MI5's net through a meeting with an MI5 officer to whom he reported anything of interest that came his way.

Ward's introduction to MI5 had some unusual features. He had first met Ivanov on 20 January 1961. Over the next months he got to know Ivanov very well indeed and was his almost constant companion. He was already broadly sympathetic to Russia, and Ivanov swung him around even more, but Ward did have certain doubts. On one occasion at his cottage during a discussion, he asked Ivanov if such meetings could have taken place in Russia without the

KGB's getting to hear of it and then becoming involved. Ivanov agreed that would happen but then said that the same thing applied in Britain and that Ward would soon find himself in touch with the KGB's equivalent MI5. Ward scoffed at this but within a week, according to Ward on 8 June 1961, he was contacted by the War Office and shortly afterwards an MI5 officer came to interview him.

It is not clear how Ivanov can have known of this approach—unless it was pure guesswork. It is possible that once Ward had raised security questions in a room quite likely bugged by Peter Wright's surveillance men he was considered "in play" and of possible security interest. Alternatively Ivanov, having made his remark, might then have let his GRU controllers know, who subsequently leaked the fact by whatever route back to MI5, or indeed Hollis himself. Lord Denning's report included the full statement made by the MI5 officer after he had spoken to Ward. It contained one passage that did not fit with the facts as now known:

> Ward, who has an attractive personality and talks well, was completely open about his association with Ivanov. Despite the fact that some of his political ideas are certainly peculiar and are exploitable by the Russians, I do not think he is of security interest but he is obviously not a person we can make any use of.

Ward *was* being used by MI5 but, more importantly, the fact that he was introduced to Ivanov in the way that he was establishes that if Hollis arranged it then he did not tell his junior officers in MI5. The man who interviewed Ward clearly thought he was looking at a completely fresh situation. In fact it was one that was just coming to fruition and one that was highly dangerous for all involved.

If Hollis was keeping his junior officers in the dark, the same applied *a fortiori* to the evidence he gave Lord Denning. Indeed, Lord Denning had as much chance of seeing daylight on the affair after talking to Hollis as a man locked in a windowless room in a sub-basement of MI5's Gower Street headquarters. Hollis's account to Denning of the next moves in the game took as a basic assumption, quite false, that MI5 knew nothing of Profumo's affair

241

with one of Ward's girls. Hollis merely said that MI5 had been informed by Ward of Ivanov's meeting with Profumo at Cliveden and that subsequently Ivanov had asked Ward if he could find out when Germany was to be armed with nuclear warheads for her missiles. On 31 July 1961 Hollis acted. He decided to approach Profumo and did this through the Secretary to the Cabinet at the time, Sir Norman Brook. He asked Brook to warn Profumo of the difficulty he might be getting into, implying that the warning concerned Profumo's links with Ward rather than with his mistress who shared Ward's flat, which he kept to himself. But then Hollis made one further astonishing suggestion, that Profumo be asked to approach Ivanov directly and get to know him better. His reason, as explained to Sir Norman Brook and reported to Lord Denning, was that ". . . perhaps, with Mr. Profumo's help, it might be possible to get Ivanov to defect. Mr. Profumo might be a 'lead-in' to Ivanov."

Even the best spymasters have occasionally lost their bearings, but this suggestion of Hollis's was far worse than some simple error. The crass folly of inducing a Minister of War to get on close terms with a known GRU officer was bad enough; to actually suggest that he might become involved in a scheme to get him to defect was the final absurdity. Lord Denning should never have believed that, any more than Sir Norman Brook, as he then was, should have listened to the suggestion in the first place, as he unfortunately did.

Profumo resisted the temptation placed in his way and deserves the greatest credit for doing so. Had he become involved with Ivanov, then the suggestions which were made through Ward at the time of the Berlin crisis and later the Cuban missile crisis would have had a far greater chance of being taken seriously. The most important suggestion was that a summit conference be held in London, as this would have made Britain an "honest broker" rather than America's ally. When Ward approached the Foreign Office through Lord Astor and carried letters to and from Ivanov at the Soviet Embassy, his efforts came to nothing as approaches of that kind often do. If it had been Profumo who was asking for a hearing for the proposals, there would have been a more considered response. Effectively "honey-trapped" by the situation at Stephen

Ward's, he might well not have been able to resist the seeming logic of Ivanov's ideas, especially as they came direct through Moscow rather than via the Embassy in London.

The straight refusal of Hollis's tempting offer should have ended the matter as far as Profumo was concerned, especially as he also dropped Ward and his girls immediately. Instead, a story rapidly built up that was to lead to Profumo's resignation and disgrace. Profumo resigned because he had lied to the House of Commons, declaring in a personal statement that there had been no "impropriety" in his relationship with Ward's flatmate who had taken his fancy at the Cliveden pool. But all realised that there were more serious security implications, and the official enquiry by Lord Denning was set up. Its terms of reference are worth repeating as an antidote to the smokescreen that has arisen around the affair, culminating in the appearance of the film *Scandal*, which concentrated entirely on Profumo's personal life. Lord Denning was instructed:

> . . . to examine, in the light of the circumstances leading to the resignation of the former Secretary of State for War, Mr. J. D. Profumo, the operation of the Security Service and the adequacy of their cooperation with the Police in matters of security . . .

It will have been realised, from references to this report already, that as one former MI5 officer is reported to have said, Denning "had the wool pulled over his eyes." The most important way this was done was to direct his attention away from the actual basis of the affair, Ivanov's proposals, and the attempt to fracture the special relationship between Britain and America at the time of the Cuban crisis, and to lead him to concentrate on the "Mata Hari" idea—that the risk to security came from Profumo and Ivanov's allegedly sharing a mistress who was supposed to have sought to prise secrets from Profumo and convey them to Ivanov in the best spy-book traditions. It says much for the atmosphere in Britain in the sixties that Lord Denning believed this, describing it as "one of the most critical points in my enquiry," despite the fact that the proposed Mata Hari was only seventeen years old and without any education or knowledge other than that which her native wit had given her. Hollis must have been more than glad to have this smokescreen to shelter behind. His supporters today must have been equally gladdened by the appearance of *Honeytrap* by Anthony Summer and Stephen Dorril, the book on which the film *Scandal* was based. This carried the Mata Hari idea to ludicrous heights, suggesting that the entire operation, from Coote's introduction of Ward to Ivanov, had been nothing less than an attempt by MI5 to "honey-trap" Ivanov using Ward's girls as bait. The spectacle of the Director General of MI5's getting the editor of the eminently respectable *Daily Telegraph* to introduce a Soviet GRU agent to a man for the purpose of getting him seventeen-year-old girlfriends, always assuming his interest ran that way, was less than edifying. But it was preferable to the other alternative—that Hollis had set up the entire operation, without the knowledge of his staff, for very different reasons.

Lord Denning's report cleared Hollis and MI5 as he was running it. Apart from the very damaging omissions and falsehoods already noticed, there were two final acts by Hollis that deserve mention. First, as soon as the balloon began to go up Hollis issued explicit instructions that MI5 should stand well clear:

> Until further notice no approach should be made to anyone in the Ward galère, or to any other outside contact in respect of it. If we are approached, we listen only. 1 February 1963.

Even more important, he decreed that no report be made to the Prime Minister or any of his Ministers or subordinates. A case officer in MI5 who had been working on the Profumo affair wrote a memorandum which Denning quoted. In part, it said:

> If in any subsequent inquiry we were found to have been in possession of this information about Profumo and to have taken no action on it we would, I am sure, be subject to much criticism for failing to bring it to light. I suggest that this information be passed to the Prime Minister . . . 4 February 1963.

Hollis minuted this shortly afterwards: "The allegations . . . referred to are known to Admiralty House [the temporary home of the Prime Minister while Downing Street was out of use]. No inquiries on this subject should be made by us." Denning commented on this: "The Head of the Security Service felt that the action which the officer was suggesting was leading them outside the proper function of the Security Service and he ought to pull him back a bit." He made no attempt to seek for a proper explanation of Hollis's outrageous recommendation.

Secondly, as the situation became clear to Profumo, and he learned that the newspapers had got hold of the story and some letters he had sent to his mistress, in themselves so neutral that he had written them on War Office notepaper, he asked to see Hollis in person. Hollis duly arrived, although the request for such a meeting was highly unusual, and he listened to Profumo's request for him to use his *de facto* powers under the D-Notice system to stop the reports from appearing. Hollis refused point-blank to cooperate and did not refer the matter to either the Home Secretary or the Prime Minister. This must have been a deliberate act of policy on Hollis's part. Ironically it was Ward who succeeded in holding the press back by warning them that Profumo's ex-mistress was not reliable. And indeed the story sounded incredible.

The only conclusion possible from all of this is that Hollis was personally responsible for the Profumo debacle from start to finish. That Denning cleared the situation, and cleared Hollis, surely says more about the mystique then attached to the spymaster and his trade than anything else. If Hollis was acting as a GRU agent, he couldn't have acted with greater effectiveness.

The real impact of the Profumo affair on international politics was for the most part insignificant; Britain's role in the Berlin and Cuban crises was that of a spectator. On national politics, however, the effect was massive. It was even said that the downfall of Profumo also led directly to the fall of Macmillan's government at the next general election, and there is more than a grain of truth in this. The actual sequence of events that ended in the final disgrace was often entirely random: a boyfriend of Profumo's ex-mistress took it into his head to attack her with a gun, and a court case resulted;

reporters built up lurid stories based on gossip wherever they could find it. But underlying these accidental happenings was a consistent push towards exposure both of what had happened and of the low morals current in high places, which has still not been explored.

For a scandal to have the devastating results seen in the Profumo affair, two essential ingredients are necessary. The facts must become widely known to the public—not an easy thing to bring about with the libel laws as they are in Britain—and questions must be asked in the House of Commons and the scandal brought home there. Both were provided by one man, the Conservative MP Henry Kerby. The first public knowledge of Profumo's role came from the small circulation news sheet *Westminster Confidential*, edited by a refugee from the McCarthyite purges in America. The source of his information was Kerby, who was also feeding his material to the Labour Party through George Wigg, Harold Wilson's advisor on security matters. This ensured that the matter was known to politicians and, having appeared in print, could be spoken of reasonably openly.

The sequence of events which led to Profumo's crucial statement in Parliament moved forward with the inexorable logic of fate. His ex-mistress had disappeared behind the Iron Curtain, it was thought (no doubt with the secrets she had got from Profumo), and Profumo was obliged to deny to the House that he knew of her whereabouts (in fact she was on a seemingly innocent holiday in Spain) or that he had been guilty of improper behaviour. There the matter might still have rested had not the political angle developed rapidly through questions by Harold Wilson, who was using a substantial dossier on Profumo prepared by Wigg. Wilson asked Macmillan for assurances that there had been no security angle and would not accept Macmillan's replies based on bland statements from Hollis. Macmillan went back to MI5 and discovered, no doubt for the first time, that Hollis had been holding back information from him, for example the attempt made by Ivanov to find out information about the missile warheads through Ward. Hollis's report to Macmillan was published by Denning. It concluded:

> I am advised that the evidence would not be likely to support a successful prosecution of Ward under the Official Secrets Act. He is not known to us to have been in touch with any Russian since Ivanov's departure. The security risk that Ward now represents seems to me to be slight.

The echo of the reason given by Hollis for not acting against Cockburn during the war years adds a touch of the surreal to his stonewalling of Macmillan, who by now had realised that there must surely be something afoot. He wrote to Wilson telling him that he had asked the Lord Chancellor Lord Dilhorn to look at all the relevant papers. Dilhorn began his enquiry on 30 May 1963. By the time he finished, the case had exploded.

Reassured by the stability that a formal enquiry ensured, although no doubt still worried, Profumo went off on holiday with his wife to Venice on Friday 31 May. But on the same day the fact that he had lied to the House was run in the press. The story appeared in the "Brutus" gossip column of a short-lived national newspaper, *The New Daily*. The column was written by Paul Minet, now the proprietor of an influential literary magazine, who confirmed to the author that his source was, once again, Henry Kerby. Events followed rapidly after this disclosure. Profumo returned immediately from Venice and placed his resignation in Macmillan's hands.

Henry Kerby remains a mysterious figure. Although a right-winger, he was greatly angered by activities such as those that went on at Cliveden; he readily leaked information on such matters not only to George Wigg without scruple, but also had links with MI5. Whether Hollis was involved in these final stages of the game will never be known. However it is worth putting forward one line of defence for Hollis, although it only covers his actions over the Profumo affair: like Kerby, he may have been acting from a political motive rather than a covert one. There was widespread disgust with the state of affairs in the ruling party. Hollis may have acted as he did, even using Kerby, to create a climate in which it was as certain as possible that a Labour administration came into power.

There is a pointer in this direction to be found in the only public statement ever attributed to Hollis's younger brother Marcus, who remarked that Roger had said to him, "The best Prime Minister I had to deal with was Harold Wilson." If this was so, then Hollis spent the last few years remaining to him as Britain's spymaster in a congenial atmosphere. That this should have resulted in any degree from his own actions suggests that Hollis could have left behind him a legacy that was at least as controversial as the actions of the Soviet agents themselves.

15
The Spymaster's Legacy and Harold Wilson

SPIONAGE is said to be the second oldest profession, but spying and even more spying on your fellow countrymen on an all-embracing scale are recent activities as far as the English-speaking nations of the world are concerned. In Britain, as in America and Canada, Australia and New Zealand and elsewhere, there is no great tradition of conspiratorial activity of the kind which flourished in Europe from Paris to Moscow, via Istanbul, nor even a political police worthy of the name. Not surprisingly, the kind of legacy which a spymaster who was also a spy at the head of one of the newly established security organisations such as MI5 might leave behind had been little thought about. This was particularly so in the case of Roger Hollis, the son of a Bishop, who in establishment terms would have seemed beyond question. What kind of legacy are we talking of?

In practice it is only necessary to look at the debacle in Australia and the events leading up to the *Spycatcher* trial to find excellent examples. As we concluded, the legacy of Hollis's activity at this level is also the legacy of the political realities of the time. A retired MI5 officer who read the text of this book remarked, "In many instances Hollis's refusal to take action is as well explained by the political climate of the time as by any clandestine motive."

The political climate during the crucial period of the fifties, when Hollis was at the height of his influence, was set not so much by the Government as by the leaders of the opposition in Britain at the time, and most importantly the man who was to become Prime Minister in 1964, Harold Wilson. Wilson features in *Spycatcher*, and the allegations there were soon worked up into one of the great "scandals" that was stopping publication of the book—that it would reveal details of an MI5 plot to remove Wilson from office. The "plot" turned out to be the work of Peter Wright himself and a few of his associates, based on generalised suspicions which Wright expressed in simple terms in his book:

> It was inevitable that Wilson would come to the attention of MI5. Before he became Prime Minister he worked for an East-West trading organisation and paid many visits to Russia. MI5, well aware that the KGB will stop at nothing to entrap or frame visitors, were concerned that he should be well aware of the risks of being compromised by the Russians.

The worries about Wilson at this level are somewhat naïve in light of facts which have emerged over the writing of this book, but they were focussed dramatically in a book which appeared in 1988 purporting to be an exposure of Wright's iniquitous activity but actually giving a far fuller account of Wilson's Soviet connections than Wright had ever done. Called *The Wilson Plot*, it was written by David Leigh, a left-wing journalist with strong connections in the pro-Hollis camp who cited "impeccable" MI5 sources, unnamed, for many of his views. His purposes in writing the book are unclear, but he concentrated at one point on the main concern about Wilson's time in Russia and concluded that there was, in reality, nothing at all to worry about. But there is quite sufficient material in the Public Record Office about Wilson's activities, apparently unknown to both Leigh and Wright, to make close examination of them worthwhile here.

Wright believed that Wilson was a Soviet agent. The suggestion originally came from James Angleton of the CIA, but Wright could never find the fire which caused the smoke that wafted so temptingly across the Atlantic. The periods of most concern were those of Wilson's visits to Russia in 1953, 1954 and 1956. It was said that his movements were unknown. Leigh cites a statement by Wilson that Churchill gave his backing for the visits, actually quoting Churchill as saying "Certainly you go, my boy, you'll meet some of the top leaders." The truth was very different: Churchill had objected in the most bitter terms to Wilson's activities and caused a major row within the diplomatic services as a result.

Wilson's formal reason for going to Russia was the impeccably capitalist one of furthering the business interests of one of the main timber importing companies in Britain, the firm of Montague Meyer, for whom he had worked since leaving his post as Minister at the Board of Trade with the fall of the first postwar Labour government. Initially he did do some business but that was never his main purpose, as reports from successive British Ambassadors in Moscow reveal. Sir Alvary Gascoigne, ambassador on his first visit, remarked, "The ostensible purpose of his visit is to talk timber but I gather he is at least as much interested in getting a general view of the present position." Gascoigne's successor, Sir William Hayter, went further:

> It appears that his visit is mainly connected with timber but that he has no particular business to transact here and his visit is principally a holiday.

The first major row involving Churchill came about because Sir Alvary Gascoigne, in good faith, arranged introductions for Wilson with various Soviet leaders and himself went along to some of them. It must be remembered that Wilson was in the opposition at the time, not the Government. Churchill wrote a stinging rebuke to Gascoigne:

> I do not think we ought to go out of our way to add to the influence and apparent authority of ex-Ministers who are associated with the Bevanite faction. If any of the official leaders of the opposition, like Mr. Attlee or Mr. Herbert Morrison went to Moscow the Ambassador should certainly facilitate their contacts.

The Bevanite faction was, of course, that of the far left of the Labour Party. Although Churchill caused some ill-feeling by this attack, in retrospect he was quite right, both in detail and his apparent suspicion that something was not quite right. Wilson had absolutely no need for introductions to the Soviet leaders. He had gotten to know them very well indeed, particularly Anastas Mikoyan, during the negotiations in 1946–47 which had led to the notorious sale of Rolls-Royce jet engines to the Russians. The British Ambassador was being used to give the visit greater authority in international terms. Later communications from Gascoigne make it obvious that Wilson had learnt much about current Russian conditions and intentions and had seen far more of the country than had anyone at the Embassy who lived there all the time. Wilson did provide some briefings of his interviews with the most important leaders, but these only showed how close his connection was.

Despite the fuss caused by his visit, Wilson returned to Russia the following year to build on his connections, accompanied as always by his private secretary, Mrs. Elise Cannon. Churchill made the same objections about the visit but Anthony Eden effectively overruled them. For the most part, Gascoigne was involved only as a spectator to the many meetings Wilson crammed into his schedule. Wilson's meetings were so important that on his return, Col. Douglas Dodds-Parker, Conservative Minister at the Foreign Office, called on Wilson to get information about them. Wilson avoided the encounter but on 23 July 1954 Mrs. Cannon wrote to Dodds-Parker, sending him a copy of Wilson's notes on his discussion with Mr. Kabanov, the Soviet Minister of Foreign Trade. Intended no doubt as a conciliatory gesture, this in itself revealed that Wilson had been acting as a *de facto* Minister at an extraordinary level, despite being in the opposition. One sentence gives the tone:

> We had a discussion on the strategic list [the list of goods banned from Russia for security reasons] and I repeated arguments I had used in the House of Commons. Kabanov made one short reference in connection with the strategy that to his

feeling that "ruling circles in Britain were still dominated by fear of the Americans in this connection."

And this was not the only significant meeting. A Foreign Office official remarked, "If Wilson did in fact call on the Heads of all the Soviet Trading Organisations, he must have had a very special opportunity of sensing the drift of Soviet trade policy." At the height of the Cold War this was an understatement. Wilson's connection with the Russian leaders was so close, so direct, and so secret that it is hardly surprising that Russia saw him as their man, and many defectors to the West were convinced of it.

In 1956, perhaps encouraged by his success on his two previous visits, Wilson overstepped all bounds of diplomatic propriety and acted in a way which should indeed have raised eyebrows in every quarter. Rather than approach the British Ambassador in Moscow, at least out of courtesy as he had done before, he simply ignored him. Sir William Hayter's messages from Moscow record the facts with increasing desperation. After first remarking that Wilson was making all his own appointments and not informing the Embassy of what they were, from Khrushchev downwards, he finally had to admit: "Mr. Wilson was so tied up with business discussions [sic] while he was here that he did not have time to call on me . . ." Wilson did make a parting gesture, leaving the Embassy a copy of the notes made during his interview with Khrushchev before flying out. But this was simply a backhanded insult, for he gave the same notes to the London *Daily Mirror* as soon as he landed and they were printed there over the next three days.

More importantly, he also wrote an extensive article on his interviews with Mikoyan, which was published in the *Liverpool Daily Post*. Together they painted a picture of a man who was totally committed to the closest alliance with Moscow, and who regarded America as a foreign power. He remarked that it seemed to him that:

> . . . in the next generation Russia's industrial challenge may well dominate the world scene . . . Let no one think that we can halt this industrial revolution inside Russia by our footling

restrictions on exports from the Western world. I discussed the restrictions with Mikoyan who said, "They are not harming *us*, but they *are* harming the West."

In one aside Wilson remarked that it was Mikoyan's brother who had designed the MIG, the plane that had fought against the allies in Korea and whose engines he had sold to the Russians while at the Board of Trade—a piece of inside information that carried things just a stage too far in revealing how close he was to the Soviet machine when so few years before, many British and American lives had been lost through the actions of just those planes.

It can be seen that Wright and MI5's simple attempts to warn Wilson against entrapment while he was in Russia were naïve in the extreme. The attempt to see Wilson as an "agent," secret or otherwise, was a little beside the point. He was a self-appointed principal in the matter. But even in espionage terms Wilson had become so confident on his visits to Moscow that in 1954 he took one chance too many, providing evidence that even at that level was reported back to London in a ciphered confidential telegram which has fortunately escaped the "weeders" at the Public Record Office.

The incident involved a British subject living in Moscow. The fame of Burgess and Maclean has overshadowed the existence of other defectors who were then in Moscow. Two had recently been revealed to the world's press, much as Burgess and Maclean were later to be. These two were called Archibald Johnstone and a Major Richard Squires. Squires faded rapidly from view but Johnstone became quite well known among the expatriate community in Moscow and was recognisable at sight by most correspondents there. He was a veteran of World War I and the Spanish civil war. The ciphered report on his connection with Wilson, dated 30 June 1954, was included at the end of a rather full report on other aspects of Wilson's visit and hence must have been missed by the censor who scanned the report before releasing it. It was brief but quite clear:

> At 11:30 one night Wilson thought to call on Archie Johnstone whose address he had. He found him at home . . . and later

[the following day] lunched with him at his hotel . . . We may hear more about Johnstone as [name deleted for legal reasons] who is spending a month here for the *News Chronicle* knew him in Spain. He met him briefly with Wilson and has made an appointment to meet him again.

Although most of the report cites Wilson himself as the origin of the information in it, this section obviously emanates from someone else, probably the *News Chronicle* reporter who had recognised Johnstone on his visit to Wilson.

Wilson was given to acting entirely freely in Moscow as we have seen, with the use of a diplomatic car and chauffeur supplied by the Russians, but it is difficult to see any plausible explanation for this visit. Johnstone had defected in bitter circumstances which were well known, and had any other visitor to Moscow been discovered making clearly a clandestine meeting with him late at night, MI5 would have found it suspicious in the highest degree. Since this incident was reported to London by the Embassy in Moscow, MI5 must have been advised of it. Wright made it plain that MI5 were acutely interested in Wilson, and he himself pursued the case over many years, but he obviously knew nothing of this meeting, or of the general atmosphere surrounding Wilson on his Russian visits, expressed in Wilson's own words. Had he done so, then MI5 would have produced more than a warning to Wilson that he was in danger of compromising himself. In American terms one would have to think of the response from the FBI if a leading contender for the Democratic nomination for the Presidency was discovered to have been making midnight rendezvous in Moscow with, say, Alger Hiss, and keeping all his activities secret from the American Ambassador in Moscow.

It is needless to speculate whether Hollis, who had become Deputy Director General of MI5 in 1953, and Director General in 1956, intercepted this report on Wilson's activity in Moscow and no doubt others like it. What the entire episode does do is show precisely what the "political climate" was at the time. No matter what the American government or the CIA might urge on their opposite numbers in Britain, the scope for action was minimal when the leader of the opposition, indeed the next Prime Minister, did not stop short at clandestine midnight meetings with known defectors in Moscow, and had long private conversations with all the Russian leaders without even bothering to speak to the Ambassador on the spot. If Hollis did not vet reports coming in about Wilson, and their absence was due to a breakdown of communication of some kind, then it is still obvious that he did not educate the coming generation of MI5 officers on the "political climate" that made him act in the way that he did, any more than he divulged his friendship with Cockburn. Having lived through a time when Russia was Britain's ally against Nazi Germany, it may be that Hollis simply found that the gap between his generation and those who had grown up with Communism as the undoubted enemy was too large to bridge. If this was so, then the unresolved issues of political reality which directly gave rise to the chaos at the end of his term of office and after are no small part of his legacy.

When Harold Wilson became Prime Minister he soon found an opportunity to talk to Hollis. The meeting has been described indirectly on many occasions, and the main point raised, by all accounts, was Wilson's insistence that no Member of Parliament suffer the inconvenience of having his phone tapped legally or otherwise, and that no MP be used by MI5 in any of their operations. This thin account, if true, must be one of the most underplayed encounters in espionage political history. Leaving aside such delicate questions as whether Hollis divulged any information the service had on Wilson's times in Moscow, one wonders if Tom Driberg, to light on an obvious example, was discussed in the context of Labour MPs and MI5. Not only had he been involved with the Communist Party and MI5 since he and Hollis were at Oxford together, he had also recently performed valuable duties for Hollis in the course of writing his book on Burgess. More important, he was about to become Chairman of the Labour Party itself in 1957 and 1958, having been on the National Executive Committee of the Party since 1949, a position he held until 1972.

Those in the know in MI5 who heard of this anodyne meeting between the new Prime Minister and his security chief must have realised that the country was entering on a period of tolerance on questions of political extremism in Britain, to say the least. And this raises the next aspect of the spymaster's legacy, the possibility voiced by Wright that when Hollis retired, he might have left behind him others with similar ideas, if not actual agents. The retired MI5 officer referred to above made this comment:

> MI5's policy of showing its hand as little as possible and acting only when the security of the realm appeared to be directly threatened, was deeply in accord with Hollis's own temperament and indeed may well have been formed long before his appointment as Director General, partly under his influence.

The reference to MI5's having a policy is revealing. It amounts to what could be called a philosophy and it is clear that this officer shared it. The statement that it had been formed under Hollis's influence is explicit and shows that discussion of the spymaster's legacy in this sphere is not idle. If Hollis left behind such a philosophy, then this showed not only the power of his personality but also the great problems caused by a secret and autonomous organisation having its own standards operating within a free society. Lord Denning, outlining the responsibility of the Security Service in his report on the Profumo affair, attempted to determine why MI5 under Hollis had decided to do nothing about the information that came its way and whether it was right to do so. It was a fruitless task. The decision was Hollis's own and the results a direct consequence of his philosophy successfully grafted onto MI5's. Hollis's proper responsibility was to the elected Officers of the State, that is, the Prime Minister and the Home Secretary, and he should have reported what he knew exactly and in detail as soon as it crossed his desk. Had he done so it is arguable that the case would not have developed in the way that it did and many have even suggested that among the consequences of this neglect was the fall of the Macmillan government itself. The wider possibility that Hollis was behind the entire event is best left as it has been presented in the preceding chapter.

Other cases which seem to be covered by this philosophy, where Hollis took no action but simply accumulated information, must be

257

found among those seen in this book, since the officer who made the comment quoted read almost the identical text to that published here. Aside from the Cockburn issues this leaves, for example, Fuchs and Nunn May—presumably it was thought they were no danger to Britain as they were not actually going to bomb it with nuclear weapons themselves. It also leaves Blunt and Philby, both of whom were offered immunity deals arranged by Hollis. These examples alone show that the legacy, if that is what it is, is a dangerous one, and should have been known to be dangerous at the time. If we extend it to the failed operations which so worried the Fluency team, then it seems almost as though the philosophy could be used to justify sabotaging such operations, since all that was required was to watch and listen but not act. When matters came to a head with the possibility of action and someone's being arrested and imprisoned or deported, then the philosophy of not showing the hand and acting only when the security of the state was directly threatened would suggest that the operation be deflected in some way to allow those threatened to go free as Blunt and Philby did. To tell the operatives on the ground what was going on would, of course, be to tell them more than they had a "need to know" in the great game.

The most obvious danger of this line is that agents of a power that took a more serious view of politics, professional revolutionaries for example, might actually take advantage of such a philosophy when alerted to it. Just as nothing was done about the *Daily Worker* in World War II until the absolute final limit of tolerance had been reached—and even then only under direct instruction from superiors—so nothing was done about spies in Britain or political activists until some accident forced action.

The Fluency Committee came to the conclusion that Hollis was the most likely suspect for the mole in MI5. It is hard to believe, if Hollis's policy was responsible for all the failures, that Hollis did not realise the result of it as his work for all that. It could be said that espionage is just a "game" both sides play, and there is roughly equal exchange of information without any direct action being necessary on either side. But this is a Cold War concept that is not relevant to situations *within* a country, situations that may not have anything directly to do with, say, Soviet interests but might still be a danger to the state and its stable political systems. There has indeed been a classic example of this weakness in Hollis's spymaster legacy in recent years.

Harking back to Christopher Hollis's book on Lenin referred to earlier, the quotation on infiltration is worth repeating here:

> All the activities of the secret societies of Russia always seem to have been perfectly well known to the Police. That is why the secret societies almost always failed in their coups; when they succeeded, they succeeded not because they had escaped the notice of the Police but because the policemen whose duty it was to prevent them were themselves members of the secret society.

The Russian method was to have "moles" in all potentially dangerous movements. And this is a method that has been used by MI5 almost to the present time. The inestimable advantage of a mole over phone tapping and other means of surveillance was that the action could be controlled and even instigated by such a person. The public first heard of this kind of activity in recent times over the case of Harry Newton. In a television program an ex-MI5 officer revealed the workings of a department that had been responsible for monitoring fringe political activity, mostly by phone tapping. But it was also revealed that they had used the veteran Left activist Harry Newton as an infiltrator. Newton was dead but he left a wife and many colleagues who were deeply shocked to find that the man they had worked with for a quarter of a century or more had been betraying them. They felt the blow all the more acutely because it came in a program that promised to reveal MI5's secret activities, which they would have welcomed. In any event, the program itself, which must have been authorised, was MI5's final and most lethal attack, signalling, it was believed, the final end of the lenient "arm's-length" Hollis regime.

Newton had spent his life in fringe political groupings such as the Institute for Workers Control and CND, the Campaign for Nuclear Disarmament. The classic case of this kind involved an

entire political movement. What happened, seemingly by accident, illustrated precisely the situation envisaged as one of set
purpose in Christopher Hollis's study of Lenin: that those movements that succeeded did so because the policemen (that is, political police or MI5 in Britain) were involved in them and wished
them to succeed. In this case, however, the wish for their success
is shrouded in mystery and could range from a complete failure to
understand that they were creating the problem they were trying to
solve, to the presence of a far-Left faction in MI5 who consciously
backed the movement while pretending to their superiors to be
monitoring it.

The movement concerned worked within the Labour Party itself
and is still a great concern to it. At first it followed the usual pattern
of early enthusiasm followed by a plateau, and then a decline as
people left and new members joined a more recent movement.
However it then reversed this decline. Indeed, it became so prominent that it caused a split within the Labour Party, with the more
honest members shocked by the rapid drift to extremism and setting up a new party, the Social Democrats. The movement's main
stronghold was Liverpool, and witnesses have said that at its peak
of seven leading figures, no fewer than four were either MI5 infiltrators or under its direct control. It is always most difficult for
revolutionary movements to get full-time activists enrolled under
their banner, particularly in a stable democratic society where such
work precludes a normal life. Not the least difficulty is that of
finding adequate income. Infiltrating a movement on such a scale
should have been realised as almost certainly running the risk of
causing it to flourish. This would be particularly the case under
Hollis's philosophy for, whatever was found out about the movement, action would never be contemplated against it. This case,
centered on Wilson's old stamping grounds in Liverpool, does seem
to provide a textbook example of the kinds of results to be expected from a combination of the Hollis legacy and the political
climate of tolerance of revolutionary movements and revolutionaries, including those who had defected to Russia.

Unfortunately, despite the very active role played in modern
domestic politics in Britain by MI5 it is most unlikely that the truth

will ever be made public, even if the split in the Labour Party did turn out to have direct links to a typical MI5 operation of the period. Espionage may be the second oldest profession but it shares with the oldest a characteristic that has lasted through the ages: that of the possession of power without responsibility. Hollis's legacy is a plausible justification for that power, cloaked in the language of the British establishment as it has developed this century. We can only hope that it will not be a legacy carried forward to the new millennium.

Appendix 1:
The Conflict in China,
by Roger Hollis

A public lecture given to the Royal Central Asian Society on 20 October 1937, Mr. J. S. Scott in the chair, and later published in "Transactions of the Royal Central Asian Society," vol. xxv, 1938

Before taking my plunge into the situation in China, it may be as well to present my credentials—very slender ones, I am afraid, for addressing so distinguished a gathering. I have lived for nine years in China, first as a journalist in the south, and later I travelled fairly extensively through Central and North China on business, and have been resident at one time or another in most of the important cities of this part. I make no pretence to having the inner knowledge of a diplomat, or close personal acquaintance with Chinese leaders and officials. Consequently I shall not attempt to make any *ex cathedra* pronouncements upon the policy and secret aims of either side, though I shall in all humility advance my own suggestions of these aims, based on my reading of a situation which I have studied closely.

I do not propose to go back to the conquest of Manchuria, and the establishment of the East Hopei Autonomous Area and the Hopei-Chahar Political Council under General Sung Che Yuan. But it is necessary to look at some of the more immediate antecedents of the present outbreak.

During the last two years or so there has been an increased

feeling of confidence among Chinese bankers and industrialists, due in part at least to greater stability as a result of the Government's monetary policy. During this same time the Government has increased its control over the provincial authorities, and has reached some sort of working agreement with the Red armies which have been such a thorn in its side.

The confidence engendered by this had inspired a firmer attitude towards Japan, with successful results. Manchurian troops, backed and to some extent officered by Japanese, had invaded Suiyuan Province and had been defeated by the Chinese. The Nanking Government had got into closer touch with the Hopei-Chahar Political Council, and with General Sung Che Yuan playing the rôle of Cunctator with great skill, a number of Japanese demands had been shelved, and proposals for Sino-Japanese demands had been shelved, and proposals for Sino-Japanese economic cooperation had been firmly set aside. Briefly, China believed that she had called Japan's bluff.

Internal dissension among the political and military leaders in Japan made it highly unlikely that she would wish to enter into further commitments on the mainland. The army's North China policy had been found expensive and lacking in practical results, and was discredited.

But while the responsible people both in Nanking and Tokyo were firmly of opinion that peace would best suit them, the men on the spot felt differently. The Chinese troops and junior officers, fired with a ready enthusiasm, believed that the time had come to drive the Japanese into the sea. The Japanese army, sullen with the ill-success of its North China plans, and impatient of the controlling hand of the diplomats at home, was prepared to take the bit between its teeth.

Such was the position when the Japanese manoeuvres started near Liukouchiao at the beginning of July this year. I have seen Japanese manoeuvres in North China, and I can easily believe that they were carried out with a degree of *hubris* calculated to inflame the hatred of any Chinese sentry. Discipline is fairly lax in the Chinese army, and the sentry opened fire. There is no need to look for deep-laid schemes behind this. The incident—a very minor one—occurred quite spontaneously.

There was every indication that the settlement would be effected without friction. General Chiang Kai Shek stated on July 19 that his conditions were that there should be no infringement of China's territorial integrity or sovereign rights, nor the removal of officials through outside pressure. General Chiang felt himself strong enough not to be browbeaten, and the Tokyo authorities showed no desire to precipitate a crisis. On July 24 the Tokyo correspondent of *The Times* could report "The situation in North China is now entirely clear."

It is true that Chinese opinion was considerably inflamed, and that there was a popular demand for military action against the Japanese. The more optimistic believed that North China could be cleared of them, while the less sanguine felt that the granting of Japanese demands would only encourage them to ask for more, and that this was the best time to put a stop to it, whatever the risk. Nevertheless, left to himself General Chiang could have controlled national opinion, and prevented any major display of anti-Japanese feeling.

I do not propose to go into details of the sporadic fighting of the next few days. From a national, as opposed to a local, point of view, the next important move occurred on July 29, when General Sung Che Yuan retired to Paotingfu, leaving General Chang Tzu Chung in charge of Peking. On the same day General Chiang Kai Shek issued another clear warning to the Japanese, saying that peace negotiations were impossible and the traditional Japanese tactics to confront Nanking with a *fait accompli* were useless unless the Japanese Government recognized his minimum conditions. From now on local settlements would not be considered, as relations with Japan had now become a national affair.

By August 2, however, a new Peking Government had been set up with Japanese advisers, and three days later the headquarters of the East Hopei Government had been moved from Tungchow to Peking.

The Japanese had thus deliberately ignored General Chiang's minimum conditions.

This is a very significant point in the history of the conflict, and it seems to me to prove that the Japanese had decided in favour of war. There can have been no essential reason for so immediate and provocative an act, which was tantamount to daring the Chinese Government to come on and fight.

Meanwhile there was also considerable tension further south. In Shanghai a Japanese bluejacket disappeared, and the Japanese alleged that he had been abducted by the Chinese. The inhabitants of Chapei, scenting trouble, began to trek into the International Settlement, as they did in 1932. The Shanghai Chinese is far more excitable than the phlegmatic northerner, but there were in fact very few provocative incidents, in spite of the fact that national feeling was running high.

Let me briefly outline what seem to me significant points in the next few days.

On July 30 it was reported that none of the crack Nanking divisions or air squadrons had moved northwards, and to the best of my knowledge there was no indication of an intention to send them to the northern front during the next few days. This is open to various interpretations, but it is fair to say that the Government forces, as opposed to the 29th Army, avoided all provocative action in the north.

On August 3 a Japanese aircraft-carrier was reported off the estuary of the Yangtsze River. If Nanking troops had been moving north, which they were not, it might have been argued that air attack on them at entraining points was defensive action. As things were, however, the aircraft-carrier was definitely an offensive weapon, as planes would have been of little use for the protection of Japanese communities up the river.

On the same day a schedule fixing dates for the evacuation of Japanese civilians from points on the Yangtsze and elsewhere was published in the Japanese press.

On August 6 a Tokyo message stated that anti-Japanese activities along the Yangtsze River had been intensified. "As a result," it continued, "Japanese residents at Hankow since August 3 have been refused food supplies by the Chinese. The Japanese Concession in that city has been surrounded by about a division and a half of Chinese troops, and the situation is extremely grave. One thousand Japanese civilians, including men, are being evacuated."

Two days later, on August 8, another Tokyo message stated that all Japanese residents had been evacuated from Hankow, and Japanese marines and gunboats had been withdrawn.

This total withdrawal of all armed forces from the Japanese Concession at Hankow seems to me another significant fact.

The evacuation in times of stress of Japanese trading communities from points up country is a precautionary measure which has been taken several times in the past. But the Hankow Concession is more than a trading post. The position as regards concessions is somewhat anomalous, but during the period of tenure they are to all intents colonial possessions, in which the occupying Power has full rights of administration, police and defence. Without striking a single blow for their property, the Japanese yielded up to the Chinese their Hankow Concession, with its administrative offices, police headquarters, and barracks. I am unable to trace any precedent for such an evacuation of a concession by the Japanese.

During the Shanghai fighting of 1932 and the Manchurian crisis it was not thought necessary to evacuate the concession. At the beginning of August the Yangtsze is at its highest, and ocean-going cruisers of 10,000 tons can and do regularly visit Hankow. Japan therefore could have sent a force sufficient to ensure the safety of her property in any ordinary emergency. Under such circumstances the withdrawal seems to prove that Japan was already determined on a major war in some part of China, and did not wish to face the embarrassment of having to maintain isolated posts of no military value miles behind the fighting lines.

On August 9 a report from Shanghai stated that "At about six o'clock this evening a party of Japanese in a motor-car tried to enter the Hungjao aerodrome on the outskirts of Shanghai. They were challenged by the Chinese but refused to halt, and it is alleged that a Japanese officer drew his pistol. A Chinese sentry fired, killing the Japanese officer and mortally wounding another Japanese. One Chinese was also killed in the scuffle."

There seems little reason to doubt the general truth of the report. The Japanese have maintained that the officer did not open fire, that the dead Chinese was killed by machine-gun bullets and planted there for effect. But these are small matters. Knowing the acute state of tension which existed, what man in his senses would visit an important aerodrome and flout an armed sentry? If the Japanese had official business there, surely the natural thing would have been to get an official pass, or take a Chinese officer to sponsor them. If they had no official business there—and the Hungjao aerodrome is miles from the Japanese area—they should have kept away under the circumstances. The Japanese neglected these elementary precautions, and were deliberately provocative. They were asking for trouble, and it seems to me that the Chinese sentries would have failed in their duty if they had not given it to them.

The incident was thus an even less important one in itself than that at Liukouchiao in the north. A settlement could undoubtedly have been arranged if the Japanese had adopted a reasonable attitude. Instead of that, and without even waiting for an enquiry, fifteen vessels of the Japanese Third Fleet appeared in the Whangpoo River with decks cleared for action, and landed a force of 4,000 marines in the International Settlement, bringing their land forces in Shanghai to about 9,000. The Japanese admiral, alleging a breach of the 1932 Agreement, demanded the withdrawal of the Peace Preservation Corps and all other military effectives to a distance of not less than thirty miles from Shanghai, and the dismantling of all defences. The Chinese reply was to move up the 88th Division and take up a defensive position.

There has been considerable discussion on the origins of the Shanghai conflict, owing to belated attempts by the Japanese to present their side of the case. I think it is worth our while to make a further examination of this question.

Military arguments seem to me to prove that it was overwhelmingly to Japan's disadvantage to fight at Shanghai. Large scale operations here were bound to tie up numbers of troops which were urgently needed in the northern campaign. For the Chinese, on the other hand, major fighting in Shanghai was an advantage, once it was obvious that a major war in China was inevitable. Not only did it split the Japanese effort, but it allowed General Chiang Kai Shek to use his picked troops against a limited Japanese force near his own base, and in country so cut up by creeks and canals that the Japanese superiority in mechanized units was of little advantage. Added to this—and it is very important in the case of the Chinese—the 19th Army had put up a very gallant resistance on this ground in 1932. The memory of this would have an excellent effect on the morale of the troops.

Fighting in the Shanghai area was bound to bring the war before the eyes of the world in a way that no amount of battles in the north would do, and ensuing foreign complications were almost certain to embarrass Japan more than China. The presence of extensive foreign interests would either limit the wholesale nature of the Japanese attack or would involve her with other Powers. The presence of foreign observers would probably prevent the use of such refinements of warfare as gas. I mean this quite impartially: the Chinese have no more humanitarian instincts than the Japanese in warfare, but the Japanese have the equipment, and the Chinese have not. It would obviously be to the Chinese advantage to limit weapons to swords and spears if that were possible. It is important to realize that the Chinese leaders know that they cannot at present gain a final military victory over the Japanese. Their policy is to delay them until the Powers intervene, or until Japan finds the strain of the war so great that she becomes exhausted. Japan on the other hand can only gain anything from the Shanghai war if she is able to shatter the Chinese forces so comprehensively that they cease to exist. The Chinese forces facing her at Shanghai are the only ones which can compare with her own in training and equipment, and the annihilation of China's only modern army would remove the most serious potential threat to Japan's military security on the mainland. But the prospects of such a rapid and wholesale victory were remote at the outset, and I do not believe that Japan intended to make the attempt.

Let us assume, then, that China wanted to fight in Shanghai, and Japan did not. It was still necessary to find a *casus belli*. China is far too astute to alienate the world's goodwill by appearing as the aggressor. Japan with almost unbelievable obtuseness played into her hands. The situation at Shanghai on August 9 was not hopeless.

The only Chinese troops in the Shanghai area were the Peace Preservation Corps, which is a comparatively ineffective body in the military sense. If the Japanese had appealed immediately to the international Joint Committee which supervised the working of the 1932 Agreement the whole situation would have been immobilized. Instead of this the Japanese admiral made a definitely hostile naval demonstration, and demanded the immediate withdrawal of all military effectives from the Shanghai area. Could the Chinese reasonably be expected to acquiesce in face of this threat? They seized the opportunity to move up their regular troops, and when the Japanese did make a belated appeal to the Joint Committee, the Chinese were able to point out quite correctly that the Japanese had already violated the Agreement by stationing troops in the prohibited area and by their naval preparations.

Japan had forced a major war upon China, and I cannot see that China was in any way compelled to confine the fighting to ground of Japan's choosing. She was fully entitled to reap the advantage of her superior man-power by extending the war to as many fronts as she wished.

There is one other point. The Japanese Foreign Office spokesman has spoken of "a well-considered Chinese plan to attack and annihilate the Japanese in the Settlement, numbering 30,000. Their strategy," he continued, "was to overrun the Settlement before reinforcements arrived and force us, and, if possible, all other 'foreign devils,' out of Shanghai." The last part of this statement can be dismissed as a clumsy attempt to rank other nations with Japan as objects of China's anti-foreign feeling. For the rest, China would have gained nothing by the wholesale massacre of Japanese civilians, and would have set the world against her, as she would by an invasion of the International Settlement. Is it conceivable that she could have planned such an action at a time when she was so dependent upon the goodwill of the world?

The fighting in the north was caused by the Liukouchiao incident, and this was an accident. But though I do not believe that the Japanese had planned any aggressive action for that particular time, they were certainly not caught unprepared. Eighteen months ago the Japanese scheme of an autonomy movement in the five northern provinces was the common talk of China. This was shelved at the time, but there is no question that it was fully worked out, and it seems likely that it is now being put into effect in some form.

But Japanese interests in North China are twofold—military and commercial—and it is necessary to examine them separately. We will take the military objectives first, as they are fairly simple and have already been largely attained.

One of the main guides to all Japanese military policy in the north is fear of Russia. It has been with her for over forty years, and is likely to remain unless it is settled by war. Ever since the seizure of Manchuria, Japan has been strengthening her defences along the Soviet border. From Korea round to Chahar these defences are highly organized and equipped with wireless stations, landing grounds and adequate garrisons. West of this they have established a series of military missions and depots running along the Russian border as far as Chinese Turkistan, but these are of course more listening posts than defensive establishments. Behind these posts, serving the passes which run up to the high Inner Mongolian plateau, is the Peking-Suiyuan Railway. From a military viewpoint the provinces of Chahar, Suiyuan, and Northern Shansi with the Peking-Suiyuan Railway and the remaining part of the Peking-Mukden line south of the Great Wall—all this is of vital importance to the Japanese scheme of defence. The Liukouchiao incident gave them the opportunity, and they have appropriated, or are about to appropriate, all this. Incidentally, they have also obtained valuable coal mines near Tatung and much of the best sheep-grazing in China, but important though these are I think they were incidental to the military need.

With the capture of Chahar and Suiyuan and the Peking railway junction at Fengtai the military have practically all they want for their northern defences. But in order to cash in on the adventure they must go considerably further south.

Early prophets of Japan's mainland policy always spoke of the Great Wall as Japan's first step—which was obvious—and the Yellow River as the second. I do not set myself up as a prophet, but I am convinced that if the Japanese stop at the Yellow River, the pause will be only a temporary one to consolidate their gains. The Shantung peninsula, where Japan has already considerable railway and mining interests, lies south of the Yellow River. The large cotton areas of Honan—and all cotton-growing areas are of vital importance to Japan—lie south of the Yellow River. The Lunghai Railway, running from Haichow on the coast to Sianfu, is all south of the Yellow River, and from Kaifeng to Tungkuan runs close to its banks. It seems almost inevitable that the Japanese sphere of influence will ultimately extend to the hills which run along the Honan-Hupeh border and will stretch to the banks of the Huai River in Anhwei, finally running thorugh Kiangsu to the coast somewhere south of Haichow.

This is a vast, but not an insuperably vast, undertaking from a military point of view. Once the Suiyuan troops have been defeated, the territory along the Ping-Sui line can be held by Manchukuo-Mongolian levies, releasing the Japanese troops for the other front. In the Hopei plain the Japanese at first made slow progress, but this was largely due to the nature of the country over which they were operating. South of Peking and Tientsin it is very much cut up by a network of rivers and canals, while heavy rains, making the dirt roads impassable to wheeled traffic, must have hindered them badly. Further south the country is more rapid. Communications in the central plain are by no means bad. Shantung is particularly well supplied with roads, as is North Kiangsu, while in South Hopei and Honan cross-country communication is not difficult. Both the Peking-Hankow and the Tientsin-Pukow railways serve the fighting line, and these railways, running across the plain with few large bridges, cannot be seriously disabled. Later the Chiao-Tsi Railway from Tsingtao to Tsinan and the Lunghai line from the port of Haichow will be invaluable further feeders.

The hills east of Taishan, the holy mountain in South Shantung, will be a stumbling block to the Japanese advance, but it should be possible to isolate them and carry out mopping-up operations later. They have always been a home of bandits, but are too barren to support an army capable of putting up a sustained resistance.

The one real thorn in the side of any Japanese advance is Shansi

Province. This province is a lofty tableland, almost everywhere 3,000 feet high, and surrounded by mountains running up to 7,000 feet. On the northern side the only practicable pass is the Yenmenkuan, south of Tatung, through which runs a well-built motor-road. On the east also is only one accessible pass, the Niangtzekuan, through which the narrow gauge Chengtai Railway runs up to Taiyuanfu. Any entrance from the west necessitates the crossing of the turbulent Yellow River by boat, which is only possible in one or two places. Entry from the south-west across the Yellow River is comparatively simple.

Not only is the province a natural stronghold, but it adjoins the western province of Shensi and the wild lands beyond, and would afford a covered approach to the Japanese flank. It is essential to Japanese security in South Hopei that they should have control of Shansi Province.

The Japanese have made more rapid progress than one might have expected in the conquest of this province. After brisk fighting they penetrated two of the lesser passes in the north and so took in the rear the Yenmenkuan, a pass which no invader has ever before crossed. The capture of the central tableland of Shansi is now a matter of no outstanding difficulty though they are meeting with determined opposition. But the mountains along the Hopei-Shansi border are lofty and wild. It will be quite impossible for the Japanese to police them thoroughly, and though they are too barren to support anything like an army, they are an admirable base for guerilla raids on the Peking-Hankow Railway which runs at their feet. Already the Japanese have had to double their railway guards as a result of such raids. When one thinks that vast sums are still being spent on bandit suppression in Manchukuo after six years of Japanese rule, one can begin to realize the problem that the Japanese have undertaken here, in the heart of a patriotic China.

Even that is not the end of their difficulties. At the time of their attack, the weather in the Shansi mountains was at its best. Soon the bitter winter winds will bring the temperature down far below zero, and the Yenmenkuan, which is over 6,000 feet high, becomes almost impassable. The Chengtai Railway on the east is a highly picturesque line, which skirts precipices and spans chasms in a way which must thrill even the most unromantic traveller. It is thus highly vulnerable to guerilla raids, even if the Chinese do not wreck it comprehensively before they are driven out of the pass. Under such circumstances the problem of maintaining a garrison in Shansi during the winter by way of these wild passes is going to be a ticklish one.

That states briefly the Japanese military aims and the difficulties they are likely to encounter, as I see them. Before turning to the commercial outlook, it is necessary to mention one or two points where Japanese military policy may come into direct conflict with foreign rights and interests. The paralyzation of legitimate foreign trade, the destruction of foreign property and the danger to foreign lives as a result of Japanese military activity, is a subject too large to deal with here. Apparently this has now to be regarded as a necessary risk in trading with China. The blockade of Chinese ports, even though the blockade applies only to Chinese vessels, is a potential source of added difficulties and misunderstandings. Already a P. and O. liner of some 16,000 tons has been stopped by a Japanese patrol, though it is common knowledge to the Japanese and everyone else that the Chinese possess no vessel of anything approaching this size.

The Japanese navy has already seized the Pratas Shoals between Manila and Hongkong, and has established a seaplane base there. There have been reports that the Japanese are planning to take Hainan Island and turn it into a naval base. Such a base in the Western Pacific would be a direct threat to Hongkong and Singapore, the Philippines and French colonial interests, and it is to be hoped that Japan will not carry provocation so far as to attempt to put this plan into effect.

Let us now see what Japan hopes to gain on the commercial side as a result of this conflict.

She will get under her own control large cotton areas in Shantung, Hopei, Shansi, and Honan, and obtain a closer hold on the sheep producing lands of Inner Mongolia. These are important points, especially in Japanese eyes, for she is obsessed by the fear that supplies of essential raw materials may be cut off from her. Iron ore is another commodity of which she has insufficient supplies in Japan. With the capture of Manchuria she obtained 75 per cent of the iron ore resources of China, which are situated in Liaoning Province. The seizure of Chahar has given her approximately another 10 per cent. Most of the remainder—and these are the richest deposits—are situated in the Yangtsze Valley, and the Japanese hold large interests in these workings.

Another commodity of the greatest importance to Japan is coal, especially coking coal, of which her home supplies are very slender. China is fairly well off as regards coal, and Hopei, Shantung, Shansi, and Honan all yield coal of good quality, while half the reserves in China are situated in Shansi Province. This Shansi reserve, according to the figures of the Geological Survey of China in 1934, is about fifteen times as much as the total estimated reserves of Japan and Korea, and nearly thirty times greater than the reserves of Manchuria.

Other minerals of which Japan is short are either not found in China, or are mined in southern provinces outside the sphere of direct Japanese control.

The North China market is to a large extent undeveloped and unexploited, both as regards production and consumption. Under any normal circumstances it is obvious that Japan, being the greatest purchaser of China's raw materials and her closest neighbour, would also be the leading seller in this market. Everything was in her favour, for her prices were low, foreign trade—especially in consumption goods—was small, considering the size of the area, and Chinese industrial enterprises had hardly begun to develop. But Japan, by her policy towards China in the last six years, has built a barrier of ill-feeling that will limit her trade for years to come. She has complained of Kuomintang anti-Japanese propaganda, but the propaganda of her bombs, and even more the domineering attitude of her soldiers, has been far more effective in instilling a hatred of all things Japanese into all classes from the illiterate coolie upwards. Japan may beat China to her knees, but it will be a China united by hatred of Japan as nothing before has united her.

This dawning of a national consciousness is bound to create an added demand for national goods. When the time comes for Japan to administer her new territories, she will do well not to attempt to stifle this demand, not to put obstacles in the way of growing Chinese industries. She will only aggravate a hatred which it is her first duty to appease. Economically this competition with Japanese goods may hit her merchants hard at first, but the added prosperity which it will bring to North China will soon be reflected in a growing demand for goods which Japan, in her special position, will have to supply. Japan's one duty in North China will be to ensure peace and maintain a stable government, while effacing herself as much as possible. It is not a rôle for which she has shown much aptitude.

The outlook for foreign business in North China is not necessarily bad in the long run, though for the immediate future it is gloomy. As in Manchuria, Japan will no doubt declare that she abides by the policy of the Open Door, but that will be little encouragement to those who know the fate of many of the foreign firms operating in Manchuria. Under any Japanese-controlled régime I do not think that we can expect to maintain a trade in cheap consumption goods. Japan, for all her unpopularity, is in too good a position, and even though she may not capture the market with her own products, she will organize Sino-Japanese concerns which can supply the demand at prices impossible to foreign imported goods. Even foreign industries in China will be at a disadvantage, as they frequently are today, owing to the fact that Chinese goods are—at least in some cases—allowed reduced freight rates on the railways and in all probability other secret preferences. All this may be expected to continue and to increase under Japanese control.

A Japanese occupation of North China can be one of two things. Either it can be a ghastly fiasco, bringing in its train oppression and further bloodshed, or it can be the means of accelerating the development of North China. It depends upon the Japanese method of handling the situation. If the former case comes to pass, foreign trade will perish in the general chaos. But in the latter case, capital and capital goods will be needed in quantities far beyond the capacity of Japan alone, and increased purchasing power will create a demand for high-grade goods which only foreign manufacturers can supply. It may be a conclusion of little comfort to those who have seen their China trade dwindle to nothing, but it is in the broader sense an encouraging outlook. The industrialization of China was bound to come, and for years we have been fighting a losing battle in the market for cheap goods of general consumption.

The most ominous point in the whole situation is that Japan is living in an atmosphere of fear, and a frightened nation, like a frightened man, is apt to act rashly. On the sea she fears the naval power of the United States and ourselves. On land she fears Russia and the growing military efficiency of China, while she is haunted by the fear of being cut off from essential raw materials. She has tried to put herself in a position to defy the world, and as a result Japan has forced upon the United States her new naval programme. Japan has built up the powerful Soviet Far Eastern Army, and has driven China to modernize her military machine. She has compelled China to recognize present Japanese superiority, military and industrial.

But the Chinese are a proud race. They were prepared to admit the greater technical efficiency of the Western nations in some material things—it was a matter which did not affect them very closely. With Japan the case is different. Every Chinese not only believes, he knows, that China is the superior of Japan in culture, in size and in natural resources. Japan has taken pains to force upon China the realization of her present ineffectualness. A decadent nation might accept the proof, but China has taken up the challenge, and will never admit to permanent domination by her former pupil.

In my opinion the belligerent attitude of Japan since the capture of Manchuria has been a grave error in policy. The loss of Manchuria was a blow to China's *amour propre*, but it was a blow from which she would have recovered. Manchuria had for years retained a measure of independence of the Chinese Government. Japan should have realized that her seizure of Manchuria was bound to stir up popular resentment in China, and should have followed a policy of conciliation until this resentment had died down. Instead of that she has persistently inflamed it by provocative action in North China. Chinese pride very properly demands that she should be treated as an equal, and that her territorial integrity should be respected. If Japan had handled the situation with tact, I believe that she could have built up a vastly increased trade with North China by this time, and have earned the friendship and goodwill of the Chinese Government. Instead of that her military-inspired policy has brought her to a point from which there is no withdrawing. Evacuation or defeat in North China would be a blow from which the prestige of the Japanese army in Japan would never recover. The only remaining hope is that she should settle the Shanghai affair and achieve her objectives in the north as quickly as possible, and then abandon this suicidal policy of provocation. China is more ready than most nations to accept a *fait accompli*, if she is allowed to do it without loss of dignity.

This time there must be no autonomy movement, no emperor, no clumsy farce of a new state. The Nanking Government must be allowed a nominal authority over the area, even though in practice it will be self-governing as regards internal affairs. Chinese officials must administer it, backed by Japanese advisers. This is essential, not only to propitiate the Chinese, but because the Japanese have no trained body of civil servants sufficient to take over such an area. Above all, the Japanese army must be confined as far as possible to garrison and police work, and must not be allowed to take an active hand in the administration of the territory. These seem to me the necessary antecedents of peace in North China, and I feel that the chances of achieving them are slender.

Such conditions may appear a poor return for a war of conquest, but Japan has undertaken more than she can handle, and will be lucky to get out of it without ruining herself. China will never agree to become a subject nation to Japan, and Japan's one aim must be to prevent her becoming an implacable enemy. Japan must give up all hope of immediate gain from this conquest, and in true sincerity help the Chinese to develop the north. It will be a hard task to win back China's confidence, but if she can do it her reward, both in increased trade and increased security, will be enormous.

The temptation to look into the future is one which few can resist, and I confess to a belief that Japan is digging her own grave in the present war. China, even in the humiliation of a defeat by the neighbour she despises, has learned that the Japanese are not invincible, and Japan's bombs have sowed the seed of a new patriotism. What Japan has done China can do, both in the military and industrial field, and Japan cannot suppress a nation-wide determination in so vast a country. China will bide her time, but when her time comes she will return to the leadership of Asia. The world will be the better for so mighty an ally in the cause of peace.

Mr. C. Milnes-Gaskell: Is it likely that China will adopt a very strong anti-foreign and anti-European policy if she succeeds in throwing off the domination of Japan?

Hollis: For some time past China has been bringing her internal administration into line with Western standards, and I think it only right that she should abolish extra-territoriality within her own borders in the not too distant future. I am positive that she has no thought of expansion into other lands. She would, of course, like to get back control of Manchuria, but her only real aim is to be allowed to exercise her sovereign rights within her own territories.

A Member: How does the equipment of the Chinese army compare with that of the Japanese?

Hollis: The Government troops on the Shanghai front are said to possess equipment which is up to modern standards. Some of the troops in the north are supplied with up-to-date rifles, machine-guns, trench-mortars, etc., but they have very little artillery. Others are very poorly turned out, and are armed with ancient rifles, or sometimes only with large executioner's swords.

A Member: Is this Red Army the same as that of the Communists in Kiangsi who made that long march through Hunan and Szechuan up into Kansu?

Hollis: It is the same Red Army, and they are now in the Government fold. It is difficult to find out exactly what promises General Chiang Kai Shek had to make to get their adherence, and also to get his own liberty after the Sianfu revolt.

A Member: The Chinese have absorbed many invaders in the past, would you agree that they are prepared to look on the Japanese invasion with equanimity?

Hollis: The Chinese may be able to absorb invaders, but it is difficult to believe that they are prepared to accept the present invaders with equanimity. China is not prepared to face the indignity of serving her former pupil—a pupil whom she always despised, and who now has added the insult of discarding much of her teaching. This in particular rankles. Bad manners on the part of other foreigners the Chinese can forgive, they recognize that they cannot be expected to know how to behave; but they feel that the Japanese do know how they ought to behave, and therefore they cannot forgive them when they behave badly.

A Member: Would the lecturer tell us exactly what he means by "China" and what by "Japan"?

Hollis: By "Japan" I mean generally those responsible for the present policy towards China, which I believe has been inspired by the military. At present all Japan supports this policy, but when the war fever has died down the critics of this military domination will appear again. I think it is clear from the context when I have used "Japan" to refer to Japan as a trading nation. By "China" I mean the Chinese speaking people, whose loyalty is not to an emperor or a government, but to a civilization and a scheme of life which they have served for centuries.

The Chairman: It now only remains for me to thank Mr. Hollis on your behalf for his most interesting talk. But before I do so, there are two points which struck me in what he said. He expressed the view, with which I agree, that the main theatre of operations is in the north and the Shanghai fighting is merely a side show, which serves to tie up large numbers of Japanese troops effectively in the public eye and on ground that is familiar to them. I am no strategist, and I know the Chinese are deliberately and probably rightly spreading out the contest and engaging the Japanese at as many points as they can. But it seems to me that the Japanese are probably deriving as much advantage, from tying up China's *only* well-armed and trained troops on a local Shanghai conflict, as the Chinese are by holding only a small part of the Japanese army there.

Secondly, Mr. Hollis remarked on the blockade of the China coast. Actually, the Japanese blockade is only very partially effective, as it does not apply to foreign shipping. But the Chinese played to form and decided to go one better by blockading their own coast for themselves. They therefore seized all the Japanese ships within reach, and sank them to form barriers at the mouth of every river, which is making the transport of all kinds of goods into the interior of China a far more difficult matter than the Japanese blockade could ever do.

Appendix 2: Contemporary Documents

(i)

*Extract from security conference notes
prepared by UK representatives
concerning Tripartite talks on security standards
at Washington, June 19–21, 1950*

Mr. Perrin then suggested that U.K. delegates should review the Fuchs case and explain the action that was taken at the times when he joined the atomic energy project, when he was transferred to the U.S.A. and when he was given an established post at Harwell in 1946.

Mr. Hollis began by pointing out that he had not been briefed in detail for this discussion and was speaking "off the record," but he had, throughout, been concerned with all the security clearance aspects of the case and was confident that the facts as he would report them were substantially correct and represented all that was known at the times in question.

Fuchs came to England at the end of 1933 and took up university work in Bristol. In 1934 the German consul there reported, unofficially, that Fuchs was a Communist. This was based on a claim by the Gestapo, and similar accusations were being made about many anti-Nazi German refugees in England. The source was regarded as "tainted" and the claim was not considered to be of real significance when set against a British Police report that there was no evidence of Fuchs taking part in Communist activities while he was in Bristol.

In June 1940 Fuchs, with other enemy aliens, was interned. In the confusion then existing he was sent to a camp in Canada which was intended for active Nazis only. Also by mistake a well-known Communist was sent to the same camp and it was known that Fuchs associated with him there. This, however, was again judged to be of relatively little significance and a natural result of the presence of two anti-Nazis in a crowd of active sympathisers.

Fuchs was released from internment and came to Edinburgh University at the beginning of 1941 on the recommendation of his scientific colleagues with whom he continued non-secret academic work. There were no Police reports showing any political activity on his part during his stay there.

At the end of 1941 his potential use for the Tube Alloys project was recognised. Mr. Perrin explained that, at the time, competent theoretical physicists were nearly all engaged on important war work in other fields and the Department then responsible for the atomic energy project (D.S.I.R.) was very anxious to get the services of Fuchs. When his security clearance came up for consideration the Security Service reported the adverse information known to them, explained their reasons for doubting its validity and pointed out that they had no positive adverse information on his activities in the U.K. The Department took the decision to allow Fuchs to join the team at Birmingham University which was then working under a secret contract.

In 1942 Fuchs was naturalised. This step was taken, although normally not permissible during war time, on the strong recommendation of the Directorate of Tube Alloys in order to avoid the administrative difficulties involved in getting access for an enemy alien to "prohibited places" where T.A. work was in progress.

Naturalisation proceedings involve the active participation of the individual and an open investigation is carried out that is comparable with the F.B.I. security clearance procedure. This disclosed no adverse information and, on naturalisation, Fuchs took the Oath of Allegiance.

When Fuchs was transferred to the U.S.A. in December 1943 he was made a temporary Government official and taken off the payroll of Birmingham University. The M.E.D. authorities were informed that he had been through the security clearance procedure.

On his return to Harwell in 1946 Fuchs was given a post as an established civil servant. Because he was not British born of British parents his case was very specially considered and the Security Service maintained, for several months, a very careful secret check on his activities. This disclosed nothing derogatory and it has subsequently transpired that, during this particular period, he was not engaged in any espionage activities.

Mr. Hollis concluded by reminding the conference that it was in September 1949 that information was received indicating that someone had passed atomic energy information to the Russians. Between then and March 1950 the counter-intelligence organisation identified Fuchs as the individual, evidence against him was obtained and he was prosecuted and convicted.

In summing up it was pointed out that a serious mistake had undoubtedly been made but that a type of espionage was involved which necessitated positive action only during a few periods in a year each of which might not last more than half an hour. Three detailed Police reports, one thorough covert investigation by the Security Service and the Naturalisation proceedings investigation had disclosed nothing adverse and the evidence from the German consul in 1933 and from the internment camp contact in 1940 was, as a matter of considered judgment, discounted.

This account was sympathetically received and the U.S. representatives expressed their gratitude for having been given a firsthand explanation. Very few questions were asked. Mr. Sumner Pike brought out the point that security clearance questions must ultimately depend on personal judgments as it was impossible to conceive of any system which would ensure continuous coverage of the activities of every individual in the project.

Dr. Smyth asked whether the M.E.D. authorities were told of the adverse information about Fuchs and the British reasons for discounting it, and whether Fuchs' security clearance was reexamined immediately before his transfer to the U.S.A. or whether the original decision was reported. It was explained that it was never the practice to report from one country to another the details of a security investigation but that each Government must take responsibility for its own employees. Fuchs' security clearance was reviewed carefully with the Security Service before his transfer to the U.S.A.

As an illustration of the alternative method of attack on personal security status Wing Commander Arnold then gave a short account of his "psychological" approach to members of the A.E. Establishment at Harwell in his capacity of Security Officer there. He believed that this might have broken down the Fuchs case independently and would provide a valuable lead if other cases occurred.

(ii)

Report concerning the disappearance of two former Foreign Office officials. The full text of White Paper, Cmd. 9577, 23 September 1955

On the evening of Friday, 25th May 1951, Mr. Donald Duart Maclean, a Counsellor in the senior branch of the Foreign Service and at that time Head of the American Department in the Foreign Office, and Mr. Guy Francis de Moncy Burgess, a Second Secretary in the junior branch of the Foreign Service, left the United Kingdom from Southampton on the boat for St. Malo. The circumstances of their departure from England, for which they had not sought sanction, were such as to make it obvious that they had deliberately fled the country. Both officers were suspended from duty on 1st June 1951, and their appointments in the Foreign Office were terminated on 1st June 1952, with effect from 1st June 1951.

2. Maclean was the son of a former Cabinet Minister, Sir Donald Maclean. He was born in 1913 and was educated at Gresham's School, Holt, and Trinity College, Cambridge, where he had a distinguished academic record. He successfully competed for the Diplomatic Service in 1935 and was posted in the first instance to the Foreign Office. He served subsequently in Paris, at Washington and in Cairo. He was an officer of exceptional ability and was promoted to the rank of Counsellor at the early age of thirty-five.

He was married to an American lady and had two young sons. A third child was born shortly after his disappearance.

3. In May 1950 while serving at His Majesty's Embassy, Cairo, Maclean was guilty of serious misconduct and suffered a form of breakdown which was attributed to overwork and excessive drinking. Until the breakdown took place his work had remained eminently satisfactory and there was no ground whatsoever for doubting his loyalty. After recuperation and leave at home he was passed medically fit, and in October 1950 was appointed to be Head of the American Department of the Foreign Office which, since it does not deal with the major problems of Anglo-American relations, appeared to be within his capacity.

4. Since Maclean's disappearance a close examination of his background has revealed that during his student days at Cambridge from 1931 to 1934 he had expressed Communist sympathies, but there was no evidence that he had ever been a member of the Communist Party and indeed on leaving the University he had outwardly renounced his earlier Communist views.

5. Burgess was born in 1911 and was educated at the Royal Naval College, Dartmouth, at Eton and at Trinity College, Cambridge, where he had a brilliant academic record. After leaving Cambridge in 1935 he worked for a short time in London as a journalist and joined the BBC in 1936 where he remained until January 1939. From 1939 until 1941 he was employed in one of the war propaganda organisations. He rejoined the BBC in January 1941 and remained there until 1944 when he applied for and obtained a post as a temporary press officer in the News Department of the Foreign Office. He was not recruited into the Foreign Service through the open competitive examination but in 1947 took the opportunity open to temporary employees to present himself for establishment. He appeared before a Civil Service Commission Board and was recommended for the junior branch of the Foreign Service. His establishment took effect from 1st January 1947. He worked for a time in the office of the then Minister of State, Mr. Hector McNeil, and in the Far Eastern Department of the Foreign Office. In August 1950 he was transferred to Washington as a Second Secretary.

6. Early in 1950 the security authorities informed the Foreign Office that in late 1949 while on holiday abroad Burgess had been guilty of indiscreet talk about secret matters of which he had official knowledge. For this he was severely reprimanded. Apart from this lapse his service in the Foreign Office up to the time of his appointment to Washington was satisfactory and there seemed good reason to hope that he would make a useful career.

7. In Washington, however, his work and behaviour gave rise to complaint. The Ambassador reported that his work had been unsatisfactory in that he lacked thoroughness and balance in routine matters, that he had come to the unfavourable notice of the Department of State because of his reckless driving and that he had had to be reprimanded for carelessness in leaving confidential papers unattended. The Ambassador requested that Burgess be removed from Washington and this was approved. He was recalled to London in early May 1951 and was asked to resign from the Foreign Service. Consideration was being given to the steps that would be taken in the event of his refusing to do so. It was at this point that he disappeared.

8. Investigations into Burgess's past have since shown that he, like Maclean, went through a period of Communist leanings while at Cambridge and that he too on leaving the University outwardly renounced his views. No trace can be found in his subsequent career of direct participation in the activities of left-wing organisations; indeed he was known after leaving Cambridge to have had some contact with organisations such as the Anglo-German Club.

9. The question has been asked whether the association of these two officers with each other did not give rise to suspicion. The fact is that although we have since learned that Maclean and Burgess were acquainted during their undergraduate days at Cambridge, they gave no evidence during the course of their career in the Foreign Service of any association other than would be normal between two colleagues. When Burgess was appointed to the Foreign Office Maclean was in Washington and at the time Burgess himself was appointed to Washington Maclean was back in the United Kingdom awaiting assignment to the American Department of the Foreign Office. It is now clear that they were in communi-

cation with each other after the return of Burgess from Washington in 1951 and they may have been in such communications earlier. Their relations were, however, never such as to cause remark.

10. In January 1949 the security authorities received a report that certain Foreign Office information had leaked to the Soviet authorities some years earlier. The report amounted to little more than a hint and it was at the time impossible to attribute the leak to any particular individual. Highly secret but widespread and protracted enquiries were begun by the security authorities and the field of suspicion had been narrowed by mid-April 1951 to two or three persons. By the beginning of May Maclean had come to be regarded as the principal suspect. There was, however, even at that time, no legally admissible evidence to support a prosecution under the Official Secrets Acts. Arrangements were made to ensure that information of exceptional secrecy and importance should not come into his hands. In the meantime the security authorities arranged to investigate his activities and contacts in order to increase their background knowledge and if possible to obtain information which could be used as evidence in a prosecution. On 25th May the then Secretary of State, Mr. Herbert Morrison, sanctioned a proposal that the security authorities should question Maclean. In reaching this decision it had to be borne in mind that such questioning might produce no confession or voluntary statement from Maclean sufficient to support a prosecution but might serve only to alert him and to reveal the nature and the extent of the suspicion against him. In that event he would have been free to make arrangements to leave the country and the authorities would have had no legal power to stop him. Everything therefore depended on the interview and the security authorities were anxious to be as fully prepared as was humanly possible. They were also anxious that Maclean's house at Tatsfield, Kent, should be searched and this was an additional reason for delaying the proposed interview until mid-June when Mrs. Maclean who was then pregnant was expected to be away from home.

11. It is now clear that in spite of the precautions taken by the authorities Maclean must have become aware, at some time before his disappearance, that he was under investigation. One explana-

tion may be that he observed that he was no longer receiving certain types of secret papers. It is also possible that he detected that he was under observation. Or he may have been warned. Searching inquiries involving individual interrogations were made into this last possibility. Insufficient evidence was obtainable to form a definite conclusion or to warrant prosecution.

12. Maclean's absence did not become known to the authorities until the morning of Monday, 28th May. The Foreign Office is regularly open for normal business on Saturday mornings but officers can from time to time obtain leave to take a weekend off. In accordance with this practice Maclean applied for and obtained leave to be absent on the morning of Saturday, 26th May. His absence therefore caused no remark until the following Monday morning when he failed to appear at the Foreign Office. Burgess was on leave and under no obligation to report his movements.

13. Immediately the flight was known all possible action was taken in the United Kingdom and the French and other Continental security authorities were asked to trace the whereabouts of the fugitives and if possible to intercept them. All British Consulates in Western Europe were alerted and special efforts were made to 26th or 27th May. As a result of these and other inquiries it was established that Maclean and Burgess together left Tatsfield by car for Southampton at midnight, caught the SS *Falaise* for St. Malo and disembarked at that port at 11.45 the following morning, leaving suitcases and some of their clothing on board. They were not seen on the train from St. Malo to Paris and it has been reported that two men, believed to be Maclean and Burgess, took a taxi to Rennes and there got the 1.18 P.M. train to Paris. Nothing more was seen of them.

14. Since the disappearance various communications have been received from them by members of their families. On 7th June 1951, telegrams ostensibly from Maclean were received by his mother Lady Maclean, and his wife Mrs. Melinda Maclean, who were both at that time in the United Kingdom. The telegram to Lady Maclean was a short personal message, signed by a nick-name known only within the immediate family circle. It merely stated that all was well. That addressed to Mrs. Maclean was similar,

expressing regret for the unexpected departure and was signed "Donald." Both telegrams were dispatched in Paris on the evening of 6th June. Their receipt was at once reported to the security authorities, but it was impossible to identify the person or persons who had handed them in. The original telegraph forms showed, however, that the messages had been written in a hand which was clearly not Maclean's. The character of the handwriting, and some misspelling, suggested that both telegrams had been written by a foreigner.

15. On 7th June 1951, a telegram was received in London by Mrs. Bassett, Burgess's mother. It contained a short and affectionate personal message, together with a statement that the sender was embarking on a long Mediterranean holiday, and was ostensibly from Burgess himself. The telegram had been handed in at a Post Office in Rome earlier on the day of its receipt. As with the telegrams from Paris to Maclean's family, there was no possibility of identifying the person who had handed it in. The handwriting had the appearance of being foreign, and was certainly not that of Burgess.

16. According to information given to the Foreign Office in confidence by Mrs. Dunbar, Maclean's mother-in-law, who was then living with her daughter at Tatsfield, she received on 3rd August 1951, two registered letters posted in St. Gallen, Switzerland, on 1st August. One contained a draft on the Swiss Bank Corporation, London, for the sum of £1,000 payable to Mrs. Dunbar; the other, a draft payable to Mrs. Dunbar for the same sum, drawn by the Union Bank of Switzerland on the Midland Bank, 122 Old Broad Street, London. Both drafts were stated to have been remitted by order of a Mr. Robert Becker, whose address was given as the Hotel Central, Zurich. Exhaustive inquiries in collaboration with the Swiss authorities have not led to the identification of Mr. Becker and it is probable that the name given was false.

17. Shortly after the receipt of these bank drafts Mrs. Maclean received a letter in her husband's handwriting. It had been posted in Reigate, Surrey, on 5th August 1951, and was of an affectionate, personal nature as from husband to wife. It gave no clue as to Maclean's whereabouts or the reason for his disappearance but it

explained that the bank drafts, which for convenience had been sent to Mrs. Dunbar, were intended for Mrs. Maclean.

18. Lady Maclean received a further letter from her son on 15th August 1951. There is no doubt that it was in his own handwriting. It had been posted at Herne Hill on 11th August.

19. Mrs. Bassett, the mother of Burgess, received a letter in Burgess's handwriting on 22nd December 1953. The letter was personal and gave no information as to Burgess's whereabouts. It was simply dated "November" and had been posted in South-East London on 21st December. The last message received from either of the two men was a further letter from Burgess to his mother which was delivered in London on 25th December 1954. This letter was also personal and disclosed nothing of Burgess's whereabouts. It too was simply dated "November." It had been posted in Poplar, E. 14, on 23rd December.

20. On 11th September 1953, Mrs. Maclean, who was living in Geneva, left there by car with her three children. She had told her mother, who was staying with her, that she had unexpectedly come across an acquaintance whom she and her husband had previously known in Cairo and that he had invited her and the children to spend the weekend with him at Territet, near Montreux. She stated that she would return to Geneva on 13th September in time for the two elder children to attend school the following day. By 14th September her mother, alarmed at her failure to return, reported the matter to Her Majesty's Consul-General in Geneva and also by telephone to London. Security officers were at once dispatched to Geneva where they placed themselves at the disposal of the Swiss police who were already making intensive inquiries. On the afternoon of 16th September Mrs. Maclean's car was found in a garage in Lausanne. She had left it on the afternoon of the 11th saying she would return for it in a week. The garage hand who reported this added that Mrs. Maclean had then proceeded with her children to the Lausanne railway station. On the same day, 16th September, Mrs. Dunbar reported to the Geneva police the receipt of a telegram purporting to come from her daughter. The telegram explained that Mrs. Maclean had been delayed "owing to unforeseen circumstances" and asked Mrs. Dunbar to inform the

school authorities that the two elder children would be returned in a week. Mrs. Maclean's youngest child was referred to in this telegram by a name known only to Mrs. Maclean, her mother and other intimates. The telegram had been handed in at the Post Office in Territet at 10.58 that morning by a woman whose description did not agree with that of Mrs. Maclean. The handwriting on the telegram form was not Mrs. Maclean's and it showed foreign characteristics similar to those in the telegrams received in 1951 by Lady Maclean, Mrs. Maclean and Mrs. Bassett.

21. From information subsequently received from witnesses in Switzerland and Austria, it seems clear that the arrangements for Mrs. Maclean's departure from Geneva had been carefully planned, and that she proceeded by train from Lausanne on the evening of 11th September, passing the Swiss-Austrian frontier that night, and arriving at Schwarzach St. Veit in the American Zone of Austria at approximately 9.15 on the morning of 12th September. The independent evidence of a porter at Schwarzach St. Vein and of witnesses travelling on the train has established that she left the train at this point. Further evidence, believed to be reliable, shows that she was met at the station by an unknown man driving a car bearing Austrian number plates. The further movements of this car have not been traced. It is probable that it took Mrs. Maclean and the children from Schwarzach St. Veit to a neighbouring territory in Russian occupation whence she proceeded on her journey to join her husband.

22. There was no question of preventing Mrs. Maclean from leaving the United Kingdom to go to live in Switzerland. Although she was under no obligation to report her movements, she had been regularly in touch with the security authorities, and had informed them that she wished to make her home in Switzerland. She gave two good reasons, firstly that she wished to avoid the personal embarrassment to which she had been subjected by the Press in the United Kingdom, and secondly, that she wished to educate her children in the International School in Geneva. It will be remembered that Mrs. Maclean was an American citizen and in view of the publicity caused by her husband's flight it was only natural that she would wish to bring up her children in new surroundings.

Before she left for Geneva the security authorities made arrangements with her whereby she was to keep in touch with the British authorities in Berne and Geneva in case she should receive any further news from her husband or require advice or assistance. Mrs. Maclean was a free agent. The authorities had no legal means of detaining her in the United Kingdom. Any form of surveillance abroad would have been unwarranted.

23. In view of the suspicion held against Maclean and of the conspiratorial manner of his flight, it was assumed, though it could not be proved, that his destination and that of his companion must have been the Soviet Union or some other territory behind the Iron Curtain. Now Vladimir Petrov, the former Third Secretary of the Soviet Embassy in Canberra who sought political asylum on 3rd April 1954, has provided confirmation of this. Petrov himself was not directly concerned in the case and his information was obtained from conversation with one of his colleagues in Soviet service in Australia. Petrov states that both Maclean and Burgess were recruited as spies for the Soviet Government while students at the University, with the intention that they should carry out their espionage tasks in the Foreign Office, and that in 1951, by means unknown to him, one or other of the two men became aware that their activities were under investigation. This was reported by them to the Soviet Intelligence Service who then organised their escape and removal to the Soviet Union. Petrov has the impression that the escape route included Czechoslovakia and that it involved an aeroplane flight into that country. Upon their arrival in Russia, Maclean and Burgess lived near Moscow. They were used as advisers to the Ministry of Foreign Affairs and other Soviet agencies. Petrov adds that one of the men (Maclean) has since been joined by his wife.

24. Two points call for comment: first, how Maclean and Burgess remained in the Foreign Service for so long and second, why they were able to get away.

25. When these two men were given their appointments nothing was on record about either to show that he was unsuitable for the public service. It is true that their subsequent personal behaviour was unsatisfactory, and this led to action in each case. As

already stated Maclean was recalled from Cairo in 1950 and was not re-employed until he was declared medically fit. Burgess was recalled from Washington in 1951 and was asked to resign. It was only shortly before Maclean disappeared that serious suspicion of his reliability was aroused and active inquiries were set on foot.

26. The second question is how Maclean and Burgess made good their escape from this country when the security authorities were on their track. The watch on Maclean was made difficult by the need to ensure that he did not become aware that he was under observation. This watch was primarily aimed at collecting, if possible, further information and not at preventing an escape. In imposing it a calculated risk had to be taken that he might become aware of it and might take flight. It was inadvisable to increase this risk by extending the surveillance to his home in an isolated part of the country and he was therefore watched in London only. Both men were free to go abroad at any time. In some countries no doubt Maclean would have been arrested first and questioned afterwards. In this country no arrest can be made without adequate evidence. At the time there was insufficient evidence. It was for these reasons necessary for the security authorities to embark upon the difficult and delicate investigation of Maclean, taking into full account the risk that he would be alerted. In the event he was alerted and fled the country together with Burgess.

27. As a result of this case, in July 1951 the then Secretary of State, Mr. Herbert Morrison, set up a Committee of Inquiry to consider the security checks applied to members of the Foreign Service; the existing regulations and practices of the Foreign Service in regard to any matters having a bearing on security; and to report whether any alterations were called for. The Committee reported in November 1951. It recommended, among other things, a more extensive security check on Foreign Service officers than had until then been the practice. This was immediately put into effect and since 1952 searching inquiries have been made into the antecedents and associates of all those occupying or applying for positions in the Foreign Office involving highly secret information. The purpose of these inquiries is to ensure that no one is appointed to or continues to occupy any such post unless he or she is fit to be

entrusted with the secrets to which the post gives access. The Foreign Secretary of the day approved the action required.

28. A great deal of criticism has been directed towards the reticence of Ministerial replies on these matters; an attitude which it was alleged would not have been changed had it not been for the Petrov revelations. Espionage is carried out in secret. Counter-espionage equally depends for its success upon the maximum secrecy of its methods. Nor is it desirable at any moment to let the other side know how much has been discovered or guess at what means have been used to discover it. Nor should they be allowed to know all the steps that have been taken to improve security. These considerations still apply and must be the basic criterion for judging what should or should not be published.

(iii)

The full text of the statement issued in Moscow on Saturday 11 February 1956 by Guy Burgess and Donald Maclean, describing themselves as "former members of the British Foreign Office"

It seems to us that doubts as to our whereabouts and speculation about our past actions may be a small but contributory factor that has been and may again be exploited by the opponents of Anglo-Soviet understanding.

Accordingly we have thought it best to issue the following statement:

We both of us came to the Soviet Union to work for the aim of better understanding between the Soviet Union and the West, having both of us become convinced from official knowledge in our possession that neither the British nor, still more, the American Government was at that time seriously working for this aim.

We had in the positions we occupied every reason to believe that such an understanding was essential if peace was to be safe. We had every reason to conclude that such an understanding was the aim of Soviet policy.

We had had every opportunity to know and grounds for fearing the plans and outlook of the few but powerful people who opposed this understanding.

At Cambridge we had both been Communists.

We abandoned our political activities not because we in any way disagreed with the Marxist analysis of the situation in which we still both find ourselves, but because we thought, wrongly it is now clear to us, that in the public service we could do more to put these ideas into practical effect than elsewhere.

It was probably our action in necessarily giving up political activities by entering the public service that, falsely analysed, led the Foreign Office to say through its spokesman it "believed" we had been Soviet agents at Cambridge.

The Foreign Office can, of course, "believe" anything it wishes. The important point, however, is that on this question we know, and it does not.

We neither of us have ever been Communist agents. So far the ground was common for us both.

Details of our subsequent careers were completely different and had, therefore, better be dealt with separately.

As regards Maclean, he worked in London and in Paris, Washington and Cairo as a regular member of the Foreign Service from 1935 to 1951, and as such was part of the machine which, with the exception of the war period, carried out a policy unacceptable not only to him but to many others.

He was by no means alone inside the Foreign Service in objecting to British foreign policy before the war, particularly as regards Abyssinia, the Spanish Civil War and Munich. But he was increasingly isolated in doing so after the war.

It became more and more difficult to find anyone willing to think or speak of anything but the "menace of Communism" or to understand the folly and danger of American policy in the Far East and Europe.

Further work in the Foreign Service was becoming impossible. In May 1951 there were clear signs that whatever future course he might work out for himself, the Foreign Office and security authorities had plans of their own.

His telephones in his office and private houses were used as microphones. Plain-clothes policemen followed him wherever he went, and one of his colleagues was put up to act as provocateur.

Maclean therefore decided to come to the Soviet Union to do whatever he could to further understanding between East and West from there.

The difficulty of leaving the country while being tailed by the police was solved by a meeting with Burgess shortly after the latter's return from the Washington Embassy to London. The latter not only agreed to make arrangements for the journey but to come too.

The risks of such a journey would have been too great for Mrs. Maclean, who was shortly expecting a child. She and the children came to the Soviet Union in 1953.

As regards Burgess, when he decided to leave Cambridge, he joined the BBC (British Broadcasting Corporation). Subsequently, positions were offered to him which he accepted, first in a department of the Secret Service and secondly in the Foreign Office.

Throughout he sympathized with Soviet policy and became increasingly alarmed by the postwar trend of Anglo-American policy.

Most alarming of all was its failure first to reach, and later even to seek to reach, a *modus vivendi* between East and West.

Neither in the BBC nor in the Foreign Office, nor during the period that he was associated with the Secret Service and also M15 itself, did he make any secret from his friends or colleagues either of his views or the fact that he had been a Communist.

His attitude in these positions was completely incompatible with the allegation that he was a Soviet agent.

This statement of Burgess's position is necessary to understand the situation which arose a week or so after his return to London from Washington in 1951.

He went to see Maclean as head of the American Department of the Foreign Office. They found that their information and opinions about the political situation and the danger of war were in agreement.

What now happened was determined by the following facts. Burgess, who some months previously had himself initiated arrangements to obtain a new job with a view to leaving the Foreign Office, was faced with the fact that the Foreign Office had independently and subsequently decided that they would no longer employ him.

It is, of course, obvious that no agent would take the initiative in arranging to leave the Foreign Office.

However, when the break came, Burgess was doubtful whether he wanted or could conscientiously do the new job he had been arranging.

Therefore when Maclean told Burgess that he himself had decided that he could no longer work for the Foreign Office and its policies and suggested that they should both go to the USSR, Burgess had no difficulty in agreeing.

There alone there appeared to both to be some chance of putting into practice in some form the convictions they had always held.

As the result of living in the USSR we both of us are convinced that we were right in doing what we did.

(iv)

Statement by Margaret Thatcher about Anthony Blunt, Hansard, 15 November 1979, col. 679ff

Mr. Leadbitter asked the Prime Minister if she will make a statement on recent evidence concerning the actions of an individual, whose name has been supplied to her, in relation to the security of the United Kingdom.

The Prime Minister: The name which the hon. Member for Hartlepool (Mr. Leadbitter) has given me is that of Sir Anthony Blunt.

In April 1964 Sir Anthony Blunt admitted to the security authorities that he had been recruited by and had acted as a talent-spotter for Russian intelligence before the war, when he was a don at Cambridge, and had passed information regularly to the Russians while he was a member of the Security Service between 1940 and 1945. He made this admission after being given an undertaking that he would not be prosecuted if he confessed.

Inquiries were of course made before Blunt joined the Security Service in 1940, and he was judged a fit person. He was known to have held Marxist views at Cambridge, but the security authorities had no reason either in 1940 or at any time during his service to doubt his loyalty to his country.

On leaving the Security Service in 1945 Blunt reverted to his profession as an art historian. He held a number of academic appointments. He was also appointed as Surveyor of The King's Pictures in 1945, and as Surveyor of The Queen's Pictures in 1952. He was given a KCVO in 1956. On his retirement as Surveyor, he was appointed as an Adviser for The Queen's Pictures and Drawings in 1972, and he retired from his appointment in 1978.

He first came under suspicion in the course of the inquiries which followed the defection of Burgess and Maclean in 1951, when the Security Service was told that Burgess had said in 1937 that he was working for a secret branch of the Comintern and that Blunt was one of his sources. There was no supporting evidence for this. When confronted with it, Blunt denied it. Nevertheless the Security Service remained suspicious of him, and began an intensive and prolonged investigation of his activities. During the course of this investigation he was interviewed on 11 occasions. He persisted in his denial, and no evidence against him was obtained.

The inquiries which preceded the exposure and defection of Philby in January 1963 produced nothing which implicated Blunt. Early in 1964 new information was received which directly implicated Blunt. It did not, however, provide a basis on which charges could be brought. The then Attorney-General decided in April 1964, after consultation with the Director of Public Prosecutions, that the public interest lay in trying to secure a confession from Blunt not only to arrive at a definite conclusion on his own involvement but also to obtain information from him about any others who might still be a danger. It was considered important to gain his co-operation in the continuing investigations by the security authorities, following the defections of Burgess, Maclean and Philby, into Soviet penetration of the security and intelligence services and other public services during and after the war. Accordingly the Attorney-General authorized the offer of immunity from prosecution to Blunt if he confessed. Blunt then admitted to the security authorities that, like his friends Burgess, Maclean and Philby, he had become an agent of Russian intelligence and talent-spotted for them at Cambridge during the 1930s; that he had regularly passed information to the Russians while he was a member of the Security

Service; and that, although after 1945 he was no longer in a position to supply the Russians with classified information, in 1951 he used his old contact with the Russian Intelligence Service to assist in the arrangements for the defection of Burgess and Maclean. Both at the time of his confession and subsequently Blunt provided useful information about Russian intelligence activities and about his association with Burgess, Maclean and Philby.

The Queen's Private Secretary was informed in April 1964 both of Blunt's confession and of the immunity from prosecution on the basis of which it had been made. Blunt was not required to resign his appointment in the Royal Household which was unpaid. It carried with it no access to classified information and no risk to security, and the security authorities thought it desirable not to put at risk his co-operation in their continuing investigations.

The decision to offer immunity from prosecution was taken because intensive investigation from 1951 to 1964 had produced no evidence to support charges. Successive Attorneys-General in 1972, in June 1974 and in June 1979 have agreed that, having regard to the immunity granted in order to obtain the confession which has always been and still is the only firm evidence against Blunt, there are no grounds on which criminal proceedings could be instituted.

(v)

Statement by Margaret Thatcher about "Their Trade is Treachery," Hansard, 26 March 1981, col. 1079ff

The Prime Minister: With permission, Mr. Speaker, I will make a statement about the security implications of the book published today that purports to give a detailed account of the investigations into the penetration of the Security Service and other parts of the public service that were undertaken following the defection of Burgess and Maclean in 1951.

The events into which those investigations were inquiring began well over 40 years ago. Many of those named or implicated in this book as having been the subject of investigation have died. Others have long since retired. None of them is still in the public service.

The extent of penetration was thoroughly investigated after the defection of Burgess and Maclean, as indeed, the author of this book makes clear. The book contains no information of security significance that is new to the security authorities, and some of the material is inaccurate or distorted. All the cases and individuals referred to have been the subject of long and thorough investigation.

The investigations into the possibilities of past penetration have inevitably extended widely. They have covered not only those suspected of being guilty but all those who could conceivably fit the often inconclusive leads available. The fact that somebody has been the subject of investigation does not necessarily, or even generally, mean that he has been positively suspected. Many people have had to be investigated simply in order to eliminate them from the inquiry.

The results of the investigations into Philby and Blunt are now well known. There were good reasons for suspecting a few others, but as it was not possible to secure evidence on which charges could be founded they were required to resign or were moved to work where they had no access to classified information. Many others were eliminated from suspicion.

Apart from the main allegation, to which I will come, I do not propose to comment on the allegations and insinuations in this book. Nor can I say which allegations are unsubstantiated or untrue—as some certainly are—since by doing so I should be implicitly indicating those that were suspected of having a degree of substance.

I must, however, comment upon the grave allegation that constitutes the main theme of the book—that the late Sir Roger Hollis, Director General of the Security Service from 1956 to 1965, was an agent of the Russian intelligence service.

The case for investigating Sir Roger Hollis was based on certain leads that suggested, but did not prove, that there had been a Russian intelligence service agent at a relatively senior level in British counter-intelligence in the last years of the war. None of these leads identified Sir Roger Hollis, or pointed specifically or solely in his direction. Each of them could also be taken as pointing to Philby or Blunt. But Sir Roger Hollis was among those that fitted some of them, and he was therefore investigated.

The investigation took place after Sir Roger Hollis's retirement from the Security Service. It did not conclusively prove his innocence. Indeed, it is very often impossible to prove innocence. That is why, in our law, the burden of proof is placed upon those who seek to establish guilt and not on those who defend innocence. But no evidence was found that incriminated him, and the conclusion reached at the end of the investigation was that he had not been an agent of the Russian intelligence service.

This view was challenged, however, by a very few of those concerned, and in July 1974, Lord Trend, the former Secretary of the Cabinet, was asked to review in detail the investigations that had taken place into the case of Sir Roger Hollis and to say whether they had been done in a proper and thorough manner, and whether in his view the conclusions reached were justified. Lord Trend examined the files and records and he discussed the case with many of those concerned, including two people who considerd that the investigation should be reopened.

Mr. Pincher's account of Lord Trend's conclusions is wrong. The book asserts that Lord Trend "concluded that there was a strong prima facie case that MI5 had been deeply penetrated over many years by someone who was not Blunt," and that he "named Hollis as the likeliest suspect." Lord Trend said neither of those things, and nothing resembling them. He reviewed the investigations of the case and found that they had been carried out exhaustively and objectively. He was satisfied that nothing had been covered up. He agreed that none of the relevant leads identified Sir Roger Hollis as an agent of the Russian intelligence service, and that each of them could be explained by reference to Philby or Blunt. Lord Trend did not refer, as the book says he did, to "the possibility that Hollis might have recruited unidentified Soviet agents in MI5." Again, he said no such thing.

Lord Trend, with whom I have discussed the matter, agreed with those who, although it was impossible to prove the negative, concluded that Sir Roger Hollis had not been an agent of the Russian intelligence service.

I turn next to the arrangements for guarding against penetration now and in the future.

All Departments and agencies of the Government, especially those concerned with foreign and defence policy and with national security, are targets for penetration by hostile intelligence services. The Security Service, with its responsibilities for countering espionage and subversion, is a particularly attractive target. Recent security successes, such as the expulsion of members of the Russian intelligence service from this country in 1971, would hardly have been achieved if the Security Service had been penetrated.

The Security Service exercises constant vigilance not only against the risk of current penetration but against the possibility of hitherto undetected past penetration, which might have continuing implications. But, however great our confidence in the integrity and dedication of those now serving in the Security Service, we need to make sure that the arrangements for guarding against penetration are as good as they possibly can be, both in this area and throughout the public service.

Existing security procedures were introduced during the years following the Second World War. Burgess, Maclean, Philby and Blunt were all recruited by the Russian intelligence service before the Second World War and came into the public service either before or during the war, well before existing security procedures were introduced.

It was in 1948 that the then Prime Minister announced the Government's intention to bar Communists and Fascists and their associates from employment in the public service in connection with work the nature of which was vital to the security of the state. This led to the introduction of what came to be known as the "purge procedure."

In 1952, the positive vetting procedure was instituted, with the object of establishing the integrity of civil servants employed on exceptionally secret work. In 1956, it was publicly declared that character defects, as distinct from Communist or Fascist sympathies or associations, might affect a civil servant's posting or promotion. In 1961, security procedures and practices in the public service were reviewed by an independent committee under the chairmanship of the late Lord Radcliffe.

The committee's report, published in 1962, contained an account of those procedures, and made various recommendations for modifying them, which the Government accepted. These procedures, as modified in 1962, are still in operation.

These arrangements have over the years substantially reduced the vulnerability of the public service to the threat of penetration and have served the interests of national security well. But it is 20 years since they were last subject to independent review. In that time the techniques of penetration and the nature of the risks may have changed. We need to make sure that our protective security procedures have developed to take account of those changes. I have therefore decided, after consultation with the Right Hon. Gentleman the Leader of the Opposition, to ask the Security Commission: "To review the security procedures and practices currently followed in the public service and to consider what, if any changes are required."

These terms of reference will enable the Security Commission to review, and to make recommendations as appropriate, on the arrangements and procedures used in all parts of the public service for the purposes of safeguarding information and activities involving national security against penetration by hostile intelligence services, and of excluding from appointments that give access to highly classified information both those with allegiances that they put above loyalty to their country and those who may for whatever reason be vulnerable to attempts to undermine their loyalty and to extort information by pressure or blackmail.

There are difficult balances to be struck here between the need to protect national security, the nature and cost of the measures required to do so effectively, the need for efficiency and economy in the public service, and the individual rights of members of the public service to personal freedom and privacy. The Security Commission will be able to consider how these balances ought to be struck in the circumstances of the present time, as it conducts its review and prepares its recommendations. It will be my intention to make its findings known to the House in due course, to the extent that it is consistent with national security to do so.

In conclusion, Mr. Speaker, I should like to emphasise once again that this statement arises out of a book that deals with investigations of matters and events that occurred many years ago. My concern is with the present and with the future. That is why I am asking the Security Commission to undertake the review that I have described.

Sources and References

The following list gives the location of all passages cited in the text, together with a few notes to elucidate passages with supplementary information. To avoid encumbering the text I have not noted the source of every single fact related. Wherever it is not self-evident from the text it may be assumed that the passage is based on a printed or archival source. No fact, as I have said, stems from any employee or ex-employee of the security services or from anyone who has a lifelong duty of confidentiality to the Government. The sources are given by page; when more than one quotation occurs on a page the first is numbered (i), the second (ii), and so on.

page

26   Christopher Hollis, *Along the Road to Frome* (1958) 13.
27   Ibid., 13.
28   Ibid., 15.
29   Michael Davie (ed.), *The Diaries of Evelyn Waugh* (1976) 158.
30i.   Ibid., 189.
  ii.   Ibid., 250.
32   Hollis, op. cit., 65. Note, however, that Evelyn Waugh did not leave Oxford without a degree but took a Third.
34   Evelyn Waugh, *A Little Learning* (1964) 192.

38   Harold Acton's remark about Hollis was made to Chapman Pincher and is cited in *Too Secret Too Long* (1987 ed.) 20.

40   Hollis's letter was originally published in *The Times* on 3 April 1982 and was republished by Anthony Glees in *Secrets of the Service* (1987) 384.

41i.   PRO F3274/2956/10 in FO index for A. Rose memorandum.

ii.   Passage from F. C. Jones, *Manchuria Since 1931*, cited in Edward Behr, *The Last Emperor* (1987) 201.

iii.   Hollis quotation: see Appendix 1.

41/2 iv.   The astute observer was Ann Trotter, and the text is from her *Britain and East Asia 1933–1937* (1975) 54–5. The information about the Leith-Ross mission is also from her, or from PRO sources cited by her.

43   Allegations against H. V. Tieckcken are in PRO FO index F981/981/10.

43   Memoranda cited are from the file on the incident: PRO FO371.20240; F4137/90/10.

44   Ibid. The memorandum was by S. Harcourt-Smith.

45i.   Chapman Pincher's remark: op. cit., 46.

ii.   Hollis quotation: Glees, op. cit., 386.

iii.   Chapman Pincher quotation: op. cit., 36.

46–7   Information about Agnes Smedley and her time in China obtained from the Edgar Snow file in the FBI Archives.

48i.   Chapman Pincher, op. cit., 30–1. It is instructive to compare Pincher's account of this interview, obtained from Wright at an early stage, with the account of it published in *Spycatcher:* "Tony Stables was a brusque, old-fashioned military officer, and he remembered Hollis well. He said he never knew his political opinions, but always assumed that they were left-wing becuase he mixed with people like Agnes Smedley, a left-wing journalist and Comintern talent spotter, as well as another man called Arthur Ewert, whom Stables described as an International Socialist." The shaping of the material is absolutely clear.

ii.   Glees, op. cit., 383.

50   Ibid., 385.

50–1   John Costello, *Mask of Treachery* (1988) 292.

53   PRO FO371.20258; F5974/335/10.

56   Peter Wright interview: Granada TV, 16 July 1984.

57   *Waugh Diary*, op. cit., 419. There is a further brief entry in Waugh's diary which reads: "22 January 1937. . . . Dined with [Christopher] Hollis, Woodruff's etc. Odious brother of Chris. Very expensive and sad evening." It is not clear which brother is referred to. In later life Waugh always spoke warmly of Roger Hollis, so it would seem likely that it was another brother. (Private communication Auberon Waugh.)

61i.   See Appendix 1.

  ii.   Ibid., p. 195.

 iii.   Glees, op. cit., 392.

63i.   Chapman Pincher, op. cit., 53, citing Stephen Knight, *The Brotherhood* (1984).

  ii.   The references to freemasonry in MI5 are in Peter Wright, *Spycatcher* (1987) 30 and 187.

66   Kingsley Martin, *Editor* (1968) 301.

69   Philip Knightley, *Philby* (1988) 1.

71i.   PRO FO395.563.

  ii.   Ibid. Andrew Boyle mentions Philby's connection with Smollett (to whom he refers by his pre-naturalisation name "Smolka") in *The Climate of Treason* (1979) 138. He suggests that their connection was a Viennese one, and says that the agency they were involved in was London Continental News Ltd. which acted as a feed for the Exchange Telegraph Company. However, Boyle was unaware of the latter connection, which is established here for the first time.

72   Canadian National Archives RG25 vol. 2705; file 44-GK-40.

73   American National Archives 841.00B/197 for a report from A. J. Drexel Biddle Jr. citing the shop stewards committee manifesto.

74   Hansard, July 1940, vol. 362 coll. 1358–9.

76   PRO HO144/21540. The suggestion that Hollis might have been using Cockburn as an agent is referred to subsequently.

77   American National Archives 841.00B/207 for the report on Cockburn and others in the CPGB.

81   Hansard, 28 June 1940.

82   D. N. Pritt, *A Call to the People* (1940) 16.

85i.   The original rumour was published in *The Week*, no. 385, 25 September 1940.

  ii.   *The Week*, no. 390, 29 October 1940.

86   The account of the student delegation to the Proctors is from *Student News*, no. 10, 7 February 1941.

87i. *Tribune*, 8 November 1940, 23.

 ii. *The Week*, no. 397, 17 December 1940.

88i. *Tribune*, 22 November 1940.

 ii. Ibid., 11 October 1940.

89   *Daily Worker*, 18 January 1941, 4.

90i. PRO HO144/21540.

 ii. Patricia Cockburn, *The Years of the Week* (1968) 276.

92i. Claud Cockburn, *Crossing the Line* (1959 ed.) 72.

 ii. *The People Speak: The Official Report of the People's Convention* (1941) 51.

93   The account of Pritt's approach to Eden through Sir Walter Monckton, whose pupil he had been, is in PRO FO371.29465; N2565/3/38.

97   PRO INF.I.676.

99–101 BBC Written Archive Centre (BBC.WAC) MOI file, cited in W. J. West (ed.), *Orwell: The War Commentaries* (1985) 20ff.

102–104 BBC.WAC R51/520/1 15 July 1941, cited in W. J. West, *Truth Betrayed* (1987) 59f.

105i. Files on political bias allegations cited are BBC.WAC Political Broadcasts (General): Leftwing bias files.

 ii. Ibid.

106 BBC.WAC: Soviet affairs.

111 Wolfgang zu Putlitz, *The Putlitz Dossier* (1957) 247.

 ii. BBC.WAC: Memorandum on proposed series "Parliament."

 iii. Ibid.

112 Ibid.

116 BBC.WAC: Programme files: "Can I help you?"

119 BBC.WAC: Contributors file for John Hilton. The letter from the War Office has the reference A.M.I/152.

120 BBC.WAC: ibid.

122 Ibid.

124 Ibid.

127 PRO FO371/36185; Z8024/36/39.

128 Rumbold quotation; ibid., as are all background papers on this question.

130 Frank Pitcairn [pseud. Claud Cockburn], *Where France Begins* (1943) 11.

134i.   As quoted in contemporary press. Origin of translation unknown.

  ii.   *The Times*, 24 May 1943.

137   The "Darlanism" and related material may be found in PRO FO371.34416.

140   Siegbert Kahn, *The National Committee "Free Germany"* (1943) 1.

142   Giffard Martel, *The Russian Outlook* (1947) 122.

144   Winston S. Churchill, *The Second World War*, Vol. V, Appendix.

152   *Daily Express*, 7 June 1951, and as cited in Geoffrey Hoare, *The Missing Macleans* (1955).

153   John Fisher, *Burgess and Maclean* (1978 ed.) 181.

155   BBC.WAC: Programme Files: War Commentary, Foreign Affairs.

156   Tom Driberg, *Guy Burgess: Portrait with Background* (1956) 62.

157   Ibid., 70.

162   Christopher Mayhew, *Time to Explain* (1987) 109.

165–7   PRO FO371.75749;F5503/1015/10.

169i.   Tom Driberg, op. cit., 81.

  ii.   Peter Lowe, *The Origins of the Korean War* (1986).

170   Tom Driberg, op. cit., 80.

176   Chapman Pincher, op. cit., 4–5.

180   Headline cited from a press cutting from the *Washington News* 28/9/55 in the FBI Archives, Burgess and Maclean Files.

182   Tom Driberg, op. cit., 2.

184i.   Philip Knightley, op. cit., 8.

  ii.   John Whitwell [pseud. Leslie Nicholson], *British Agent* (1966) half title.

187   Barrie Penrose & Simon Freeman, *Conspiracy of Silence* (1986) 482.

188   Andrew Boyle, *Climate of Treason* (1979) 419.

189   Letter cited by Chapman Pincher, *The Spycatcher Affair* (revised US ed. 1988) Appendix A. 263.

190   Malcolm Turnbull, *The Spycatcher Trial* (1988) 17.

192   Michael Bialoguski, *The Petrov Story* (1955) xv.

198   Anthony Glees, private communication by telephone.

199   Glees, op. cit., 323.

200	Ibid., 325.
202	See the full text of this report in Appendix 2(i). Glees's selective version of this appears in Glees, op. cit., 350–1.
203	Glees, op. cit., 366. The fuller version of this statement and other related quotations may be found in Margaret Gowing, *Britain and Atomic Energy (1939–45)* (1964) 350 and 358–9.
206	Glees, op. cit., 327.
208i.	Ibid., 327.
ii.	Glees's version is not merely selective but involves the substitution of phrases: for example, "the Foreign Office" for "Mr. Allen and I." The correct text, or rather the text on which Glees's text is based, however loosely, may be found in PRO FO371.34416c 13941. Glees had earlier used this same quotation in a slightly more accurate though still erroneous form in his *Exile Politics during the Second World War* (1982) 193, though he cites this in his note 23 from a completely irrelevant file: FO 371.39919c 1370.
iii.	PRO FO371.34416c 13941.
209	Chapman Pincher, *Too Secret Too Long* (1987 ed.).
210	Ibid., 202.
212	Glees, op. cit., 344.
215	Knightley, op. cit., 133–4.
218i.	BBC.WAC: scripts microfilm for Anthony Blunt. For further information about Blunt's broadcasts see W. J. West, *Truth Betrayed* (1987) 51f.
ii.	*Manifesto of the Catholic Crusade* (place and date of publication unknown) cited in Kenneth Brill (ed.), *John Grosser: East London Priest* (1971) 15.
221	Christopher Hollis, *Lenin: Portrait of a Professional Revolutionary* (1938) 130.
225i.	Glees, op. cit., 352.
ii.	John Bulloch, *M15* (1963 Corgi ed.) 11.
227	Chapman Pincher, op. cit., 293f.
229i.	Wolfgang zu Putlitz, op. cit., 250.
ii.	Cited in Barrie & Penrose, op. cit., 394.
233	Peter Wright, *Spycatcher* (1987) 199.
234	Ibid., 290. At this point Hollis made a possibly revealing remark. When asked if he read the reports of the Fluency Committee he said: "They made fascinating reading. All

that history. Always good to blow a few cobwebs off the pipes." In view of Hollis's wide knowledge of matters which he never divulged to Wright or the others, he may have been suggesting that he wasn't bothering because it was just "history."

Bibliography

This is a list of books and other sources that have been referred to in the text, with the page numbers after each entry referring to the pages of this book where the work is cited. Page numbers in **bold** type indicate where passages from the work in question are quoted.

Harold Acton, *Ponies and Peonies* (1941), 38

American National Archives, 841.00B/197, **73**; 841.00B/207, **77**

BBC Written Archive Centre files, **99–106, 111–2, 116, 119–121, 155, 218**

Edward Behr, *The Last Emperor* (1987), 38

Michael Bialoguski, *The Petrov Story* (1955), 180; **192**

Andrew Boyle, *The Climate of Treason* (1979), 188; **69**

Kenneth Brill (ed.), *John Grosser: East London Priest* (1971), **218**

John Bulloch, *MI5* (1963), 225, 230–1; **225**

———, *Spy Ring* (1961), 230–1

Canadian National Archives, RG 25, Vol. 2705, file 44-GK-40, **72**

Claud Cockburn, *Crossing the Line* (1959), **92**

Patricia Cockburn, *The Years of the Week* (1968), 90; **90**

E. H. Cookridge, *The Third Man* (1968), 186.

John Costello, *Mask of Treachery* (1988), 117, 217; **51–2**

Bibliography

Michael Davie (ed.) *The Diaries of Evelyn Waugh* (1976), **29–30, 57**

Richard Deacon, *The British Connection* (not published), 188

Tom Driberg, *Guy Burgess: Portrait with Background* (1956), **156–7, 169–170, 182**

John Fisher, *Burgess and Maclean: A New Look at the Foreign Office Spies* (1978 ed.), 187; **153–4**

Peter Fleming, *News from Tartary* (1936), 57

Simon Freeman and Barrie Penrose, *Conspiracy of Silence* (1986), 217; **187, 229**

Anthony Glees, *The Secrets of the Service* (1987), 132, 197; **40, 45, 48–50, 61, 199–208, 212, 225**

———, *Exile Politics during the Second World War: The German Social Democrats in Britain* (1982), 196; **208**

Margaret Gowing, *Britain and Atomic Energy (1939–45)* (1964), **203**

Graham Greene, *The Third Man* (1950), 216

Geoffrey Hoare, *The Missing Macleans* (1955), 180; **152**

Christopher Hollis, *Along the Road to Frome* (1985), **26–8, 32**

———, *Lenin: Portrait of a Professional Revolutionary* (1938), **221**

Siegbert Kahn, *The National Committee "Free Germany"* (1943), 140; **140**

Stephen Knight, *The Brotherhood* (1984), **63**

Philip Knightley, *Philby: The Life and Views of a KGB Masterspy* (1988), 69; **69, 184–215**

Giffard Martel, *The Russian Outlook* (1947), **142**

Kingsley Martin, *Editor* (1968), **66**

Christopher Mayhew, *Time to Explain* (1987), **162**

George Orwell, *Nineteen Eighty-four* (1949), 56

———, *Animal Farm* (1945), 81, 148

Bruce Page, David Leitch and Philip Knightley, *Philby: The Spy who Betrayed a Generation* (1968), 183

The People Speak: The Official Report of the People's Convention (1941), **92**

Eleanor Philby, *The Spy I Loved* (1968), 185

Kim Philby, *My Silent War* (1968), 185, 216

Chapman Pincher, *The Spycatcher Affair* (1988), **189**

———, *Their Trade Is Treachery* (1981), 190, 194

———, *Too Secret Too Long* (1984), 37, 194, 197, 199, 206; **45, 48, 176, 209, 227**

Frank Pitcairn [Claud Cockburn], *Where France Begins* (1943), 130; **130**

D. N. Pritt, *A Call to the People* (1940), 81; **82**

———, *Another Lie Nailed: The Pritt-Attlee Letters* (1940), 83

315

PRO F981/981/10 [FO Index], **44**

PRO F3274/2956/10 [FO Index], 41

PRO FO371.20240; F4137/90/10, **44**

PRO FO371.20258; F5974/335/10, **53**

PRO FO371.29465; N2565/3/38, 93

PRO FO371.34416, **137, 208**

PRO FO371.36185; Z8024/36/39, **127–8**

PRO FO371.75749; F5503/1015/10, **165–8**

PRO FO395.563, **71**

PRO HO144/21540, **76, 90**

PRO INF.I.676, **97**

Anthony Purdy and Douglas Sutherland, *Burgess and Maclean* (1963), 183

Wolfgang zu Putlitz, *The Putlitz Dossier* (1957), 229; **110, 229**

Goronwy Rees, *A Bundle of Sensations* (1960), 186

Patrick Seale and Maureen McConville, *The Long Road to Moscow* (1973), 187

H. P. Smolka [Peter Smollett], *Forty Thousand Against the Arctic: Russia's Polar Empire* (1937), 70, 200

Ann Trotter, *Britain and East Asia (1930–1937)* (1975), **42**

Malcolm Turnbull, *The Spycatcher Trial* (1988), **190**

Evelyn Waugh, *A Little Learning* (1964), **34**

———, *Waugh in Abyssinia* (1936), 57

W. J. West (ed.), *Orwell: The War Commentaries* (1985), **99–102**

———, *Truth Betrayed: Radio and Politics between the Wars* (1987), 15, 58, 187; **102–4**

John Whitwell [Leslie Nicholson], *British Agent* (1966), 184–5, 190; **184**

Peter Wright, *Spycatcher* (1987), 11, 12, 13, 15, 37, 47, 54, 63, 185, 190–2, 227, 233–4; **48, 63, 233, 234**

Index

Index

Profumo Affair, 219, 226, 231, 234–5, 237, ch. 14 *passim*
Provisional Committee of the Aircraft and Engineering Shop Stewards National Council, 73
Pryce-Jones, Alan, 32
Purdy, Anthony, 183
Putlitz, Wolfgang zu, 67–8, 72–3, 110, 141, 149, 160, 224, 227
Pu Yi, Emperor (Deposed), 38, 40

Radcliffe, Lord, 304
Radcliffe, Major R.A.C., 119
"radishes," 49
Rees, Goronwy, 61, 182, 186
Reilly, Sir Patrick, 212
Rent Restriction Act, 114
Reuters, 133, 181
Ribentrop, J. von, 142
Ridsdale, Sir William, 155–6, 159
Robson-Scott, Mr, 208–9
Rose, Archibald, 41
Rothschilds, 70
Royal Central Asian Society, 54, 59
    Hollis talk given to, 263–281
Royal National Lifeboat Institution, 181
Rumbold, Sir Anthony, 127–9
Russia, USSR, Soviet Union, 40–4, 49–52, 60, 62, 67, 74–5, 79–80, 92–4, ch. 6 *passim*, 124, ch. 9 *passim*, 179, 183, 200, 210, 215–7, 221, 233
    alleged Japanese fear of, 271, 277

St Malo, 285, 289
St Thomas of Canterbury, 219
Salisbury, Lord, 163
Sandforth, Thomas, 38
Sandys, Duncan, 179
Sargent, Orme, 94
Sayle, Murray, 185
Scarlett, Sir Peter, 169
Schmidt, Professor O.Y., 70
Seale, Patrick, 187
Security Executive, 74–6, 81, 89, 98–9
Shanghai, 196, 220
Shaw, George Bernard, 38
Sherfield, Lord, Oliver Makins, 126–7
Siberia, 70
Simon, Sir Ernest, 103
Sistine Chapel, 217
Sitwell, Osbert, 38
Smedley, Agnes, 46–7, 49, 51, 67, 220
Smollett, Peter (also known as H.P. Smolka) 69–71, 95–191, 106, 134, 147, 162, 200, 216
Snow, Edgar, 39, 60
Solomon, Flora, 61
Sorge Ring (of Comintern agents), 45
Soviet Information Bureau, London, 106
Spain, 42, 58, 62, 68–9, 138, 217–8
Spanish civil war, 58, 62, 68–9, 138, 216, 218, 296
Sparrow, John, 121–2
Spender, Sir Stephen, 221, 229
Springhall, D.F., 143, 145, 210
Spycatcher Affair, 32, 47, 54, 185, 190–2, 233–4, 236, 240, 249–50
Squance, W.J.R., 82
Stables, Tony, 46, 48, 220
Stalin, Joseph, 49, 70, 79, 93–4, 99, 101–2, 123, 132–4, 156, 165, 203, 223
Stalingrad, 137
"Stanley," 215
Starrett, Vincent, 39
Stephensen, P.R., 32
Strachey, John, 80, 158, 179
Straight, Michael, 186, 232
Strasser, Otto, 71–2
Summerfields Preparatory School, 27
Sunday Times, 183–4, 187
Sutherland, Douglas, 183
Swinton, Lord, 74

Switzerland, 192

Tasmania, 190–1
Tedder, Air Marshal, 124
Thatcher, Margaret, Prime Minister, I, 189, 193, 195, 298–300
"Third Man," 152, 153, 172, 180, 186, 216
Thirty Year Rule, 178
Thomson, Professor George, 204
Thwaites, Mr. MOI official, 208
Times, 37, 39, 44–5, 58–9, 70, 77, 97–8, 134, 147, 149, 177, 181, 188, 195, 211
Times Literary Supplement, 58
Tisdall, Sarah, 191
Tito, Josip Broz, Marshal, 131, 173
Torr, Dona, 219
Torr, Rev. William, 219
Trans-Siberian Railway, 40, 49–50
Treasury, 121
Trend, Sir Burke, 193, 302
    Trend Report, the, 195
Tribune, 80, 87–8
Tripartite Conference on Security Standards 1950, 201, 282–5
Tube Alloys, *see* atmoic bomb
Turkey, 93
Turnbull, Malcolm, 190–1

Ulbricht, Walter, 138
United States of America, 40, 53, 67–8, 77, 84, 90, 101, 115, 118, 142–3, 161, 165, 171–3, 177–80, 204–6, 224–8
Uren, Captain Ormond L., 143, 210
Ustinov, Klop, 68

Vansittart, Lord, 72
Vassal Tribunal, 230
Vatican, 85
"Venona," 198–9, 226
Vienna, 216
Vivian, Valentine, 144–5, 154, 212
Vlasov, General, 211
Volkov, Konstantin, 184–5, 198

Ward, Stephen, 220, ch. 14 *passim*
Warner, Sir Frederick, 142, 156, 159
Watson, Alister, 218
Waugh, Evelyn, 29–34, 57–8, 214
Weardale Iron and Coal Company, 27
Webb, Maurice, 150, 153–4, 179, 181–2, 226
Week, The, 47, 68, 75, 77, 84, 87, 90–1, 142, 223, 237–8
"Week in Westminster," 153
Weizman Institute, 232
Wells Cathedral, 26, 59
West, Nigel (pseudonym of Rupert Allason M.P.), 234
Westminster Confidential, 246–7
Whitwell, John (pseudonym), *see* Leslie Nicholson
Wigg, George, 246
Williams, Francis, 148–9, 159
Williams, Raymond, 86
Willoughby, C.A., 164
Wilson, Harold, 82, 158, 248, ch. 15 *passim*
Winant, John G., 126–7
Windsor, Duke of, 117
Wong, Anna May, 39
Wootton, Barbara, 103
"Workers Challenge," 82, 88, 107
Workers Educational Association, 220
Wright, Peter, 54, 56, 63, 76, 184–5, 190–2, 195–7, 199, 214–5, 233–4

Yalta, 147
Younghusband, Sir Francis, 36, 57
Yugoslavia, 131

Zeitgeist Bookstore, 47
Zinoviev letter, 179